1970

A COMPANION TO BEETHOVEN'S PIANOFORTE SONATAS

(Bar-to-bar Analysis)

DONALD FRANCIS TOVEY

Published by

THE ASSOCIATED BOARD OF THE
ROYAL SCHOOLS OF MUSIC

Royal Academy of Music   Royal College of Music
Royal Manchester College of Music   Royal Scottish Academy of Music

14 Bedford Square, London, W.C.1

PREFACE

THE methodical analysis of musical masterpieces is an exercise that concerns both players and composers. First let us consider the player.

Players should understand what they play. In the case of conductors, who play upon the whole orchestra, this is never disputed; nor is much doubt raised in regard to chamber-music. The solo player and his critics are often more sceptical as to the good effects of the analytical insight upon performance. But current ideas on this subject seem confused. It is usually supposed that an " analytical " performance will chop the music up into small sections with gaping joints. Anyone who tries to follow the contents of the present volume will soon discover that the only possible bad effect that an analytical view could have on the performance of Beethoven would be to hasten its tempo and to make it pour out the music in one breathless stream. Almost the first impression that a correct analysis will give is that of " AB closing into CD closing into EFG closing into . . . XYZ." It is not clear what is commonly meant by " analytical playing "; but the expression is probably inspired by the kind of playing that emphasizes accidental details. Such is the playing that in the G minor episode of the first movement of Beethoven's Violin Concerto turns the solo part into an adagio, through which the horns cannot make any recognizable sense of the main rhythmic figure. Such is the playing that in the first movement of the Sonata Appassionata puts hard accents on the quintoles of bars 81-90 and so chops into 2-bar snippets a sequence which is divided between two parts ranging over 5 octaves with 8-bar limbs. Such is the playing that brings out the subject of a fugue as if on trumpets and trombones, while displaying a crass ignorance of all counter-subjects and counterpoints. In all these cases the effect of a correct analysis can only be to inculcate a broader view; and if genuinely analytical performance can have a fault, that fault can only be a tendency to present the music with too little care for euphony and too much of the technical per-functoriness that composers are apt to show in their own playing.

iii

The main lesson of the analysis of great music is a lesson of organic unity. And in the last resort it should investigate euphony also.

For students of composition the use of analysis depends on practice. The contents of the present volume will be useful to the young composer in proportion as he attempts his own analysis before consulting a printed one. Some great teachers have made their pupils write a complete musical paraphrase of a classical work. There are grave objections to this discipline. At great cost of labour it inculcates a view of form as a mould into which matter can be shovelled. And even on this fallacious basis only a small number of different forms can be taught during the years of studentship. If any truth about form can be learnt by paraphrasing, this should be done extempore at the pianoforte, where mistakes can be repaired at once, and half a dozen complete attempts made in an hour. For the composer the real lesson of the classical forms is their infinite variety and their immense rhetorical and dramatic force. This lesson can be learnt only through a large number of examples. The present volume may serve the student of composition, first as an example of Sir Hubert Parry's method of musical précis-writing, and secondly as a work of reference by which to correct his own efforts at analysing Beethoven's pianoforte sonatas, and as a stimulus to the study of other musical classics.

PUBLISHER'S NOTE

THE system adopted in numbering the bars in each movement is as follows:

1. The numbering commences at the first *complete* bar.

2. Repeat bars, 1st and 2nd time, are numbered " a " and " b " respectively.

Bar-numbers corresponding with the Analyses are given in each fifth bar in the Associated Board's edition of Beethoven's Sonatas.

Professor Tovey's Commentaries printed with the text in the Associated Board's edition are of the greatest importance. They should always be consulted by users of this book. (See page 286.)

CONTENTS

Allegro

2. SONATA IN A MAJOR, OP. 2, No. 2 - - - - 17
   Dedicated to Joseph Haydn.
   Allegro vivace.—Largo appassionato.—Scherzo and
   Trio.—Rondo.

Allegro vivace

3. SONATA IN C MAJOR, OP. 2, No. 3 - - - - 24
   Dedicated to Joseph Haydn.
   Allegro con brio.—Adagio.—Scherzo and Trio.—
   Allegro assai.

Allegro con brio

4. SONATA IN E FLAT MAJOR, OP. 7 - - - - 35
   Dedicated to the Countess Babette von Keglevics.
   Allegro molto e con brio.—Largo, con gran espres-
   sione.—Allegro.—Rondo.

Allegro molto e con brio

CONTENTS

Andante

Adagio sostenuto

sempre pp e senza sordino

Allegro

Allegro vivace

CONTENTS

CONTENTS

Allegro con brio

Tempo di Menuetto

Allegro assai

Adagio cantabile

CONTENTS

LUDWIG van BEETHOVEN

INTRODUCTION

(A) FORM.

1. THE TIME-DIMENSION.

THE first condition for a correct analysis of any piece of music is that the composition must be regarded as a process in time. There is no such thing as a simultaneous musical *coup d'œil* ; not even though Mozart is believed to have said that he imagined his music in that way. Some students begin their analysis of a sonata by glancing through it to see " where the Second Subject comes " and where other less unfortunately named sections begin. This is evidently not the way to read a story. The listener has no business even to know that there is such a thing as a " Second Subject " until he hears it. Similarly, the listener has no business to know that the Ninth Symphony begins on the dominant of D minor. What he hears is a sustained vibration on a bare fifth. If he has absolute pitch he may notice that its bass is A; and if he has sense he will not notice that he has noticed such a jejune fact, unless he has to mention it for the purpose of drawing up an analysis.

2. TERMINOLOGY.

Besides the defect that it leaves the printed page in a spatial category instead of putting its information into the time category, musical analysis suffers from a terminology that is bad in all countries and made worse in England by mistranslation. Instead of trying to correct that terminology here we shall avoid it altogether. Instead of " First Subject and Second Subject " we shall say " First Group and Second Group," thereby leaving Haydn free to build both groups out of the same theme, and Spohr free to turn out his standard scheme of a noble first theme, some well-drafted semiquaver passages to lead to the dominant, a cantabile second theme and a *quantum suff.* of brilliant passages with a purple modulation where the painter puts his brown tree, and a neat cadence-theme derived from the opening.

As to the terms " binary and ternary," there is at present no remedy. A " binary " tune consists of two strains, of which the first does not end on the tonic and the second does. A " ternary " tune has a first strain ending on the tonic. This produces a sense of completeness which gives rise to the expectation that anything that follows will be a middle strain, and will lead to a *da capo* of the first strain. This expectation is so often realized that the resulting form, A, B, A, is called " ternary " because it obviously divides into three. But the real difference between the " ternary " and " binary " types has nothing to do with this divisibility. The so-called " ternary " impression is irrevocably made as soon as the first strain has completed itself by its tonic close. What follows is often no longer than the first strain ; and the only rule we can find for it is that in some way, whether by crowd of detail (theme of slow movement of Op. 57) or by wider range of harmony (Arietta of Op. 111), it will seem to cover more ground, whatever its length. The Arietta of Op. 111 shows a subtle swing between the two types. Both its strains are repeated in the usual way; but the first strain closes in a manner which is biassed to the dominant the first time, and just poises itself on the tonic the second time. This subtlety is faithfully reproduced in the variations.

The vital distinction between " binary " and " ternary " is that between an aggregate whose members are inseparable and an aggregate containing one or more things already complete. The so-called " binary " type develops, by enormous expansion, into the higher sonata forms. The so-called " ternary " type develops in two ways—by expansion and by multiplication. Besides this, it is imitated on a large scale by the mere alternation of two complete melodic forms, in the Menuet and Trio. In this case organic unity is altogether disclaimed, for in the resulting A, B, A we have a B as complete as A. Nor does the organization become much higher when Beethoven in his greatest scherzos multiplies this into A, B, A, B, A. There is a definite place in æsthetics for the abstention from organic devices; in fact, there is an organic reason for it. We must not forget, then, that the Menuet-Trio group represents something different from an A, B, A organism. When the A, B, A organism develops by expansion, all its members become enlarged, and the return to A may be a dramatic affair. When the organism develops by multiplication we have the Rondo forms, in which A remains of the dimensions of one or two melodic strains and returns after each episode B, C, etc.

The ways in which these larger forms are related to each other will appear in the analysis of individual works. One word more is needed as to the two types of melody. In both types it is a frequent and natural phenomenon that the divided parts are repeated. The " binary " form is so called because it falls into two repeatable portions. Now take the most complete ternary melody you can find—say, the theme of the variations in the

Kreutzer Sonata. Will it fall into three repeatable parts ? The experiment of so arranging the repeats is worth trying, in order to see how utterly impossible it is to regard the form as based on ternary division. The form shows conclusively that it is not A:B: A, but A:B+A. This is not theory but immediate æsthetic experience. You will find one case in Beethoven where the phenomenon A A:B B:A A appears, and it is in one of the most highly organized Rondos ever written, the Rondo of Op. 90. Here B simply behaves like another theme, which it is. This ostentatiously inorganic structure is the backbone of the whole movement. Let us not vex our souls with attempts to classify what the composer invented as a special creation. I deeply feel the need of single terms to distinguish " form-with-an-incomplete-first-member" from "form-with-a-complete-first-member"; and I should be grateful if such terms could be coined either from Latin or from Greek, but not from both, and not more than eight syllables long. But I do not feel the need of a term that shall describe the theme of the Rondo of Op. 28 or of that of Op. 90.

3. METHOD OF ANALYSIS.

The student will be well advised to attempt musical analysis on his own initiative after the method of the present commentary. He may take Beethoven's Sonatas and use the present analyses afterwards as a means of correcting his work, or he may apply the method to other classics. It is of the utmost importance that he should never set down anything that his ear has not recognized apart from the appearance of the printed page. The ear will never learn to recognize subtleties if the power of judgment has been debilitated by *a priori* fancies. Such fancies abound in the minds of those writers who believe that the " logical " development of a composition consists in the way in which one theme can be derived from another. Such derivations are interesting as a feature of style. They come and go as the composer deals at one time with material that is more familiar to him, and at another time enters upon pioneer work. The student who fails to recognize them misses a certain amount of witty detail, and this is bad for his chances of revealing the style in his playing; though, even so, the faithful reporter of a witty thing may raise a smile, he knows not why. But the student who, thinking that sonatas are built by thematic wit, begins by imputing it wherever he can see that there is a " b " in " both," will never understand anything at all.

Many, if not most, students will find that some things in the analyses given in the present volume are by no means obvious, though the main bulk of the information may seem trite. But the most obvious and the least obvious things are all facts. The

method proceeds from point to point as the music pursues its
course, and where several facts overlap they are stated in the order
of their function in the design. Thus, when a whole section is in a
certain key, the key is mentioned at the head of the paragraph;
and, if it is not the tonic, its relation thereto is mentioned, unless
(as in the course of a long development) that point is immaterial.
Then the music is taken phrase by phrase. The first point is the
length of the phrase, and, together therewith the way in which it is
subdivided:—*e.g.*, the opening of Op. 28 is a 10-bar phrase (6+4).
Much may be learnt from this point alone. A favourite way of
increasing the sense of movement is to cut off smaller and smaller
figures in what may be called tapering rhythm. Modern criticism
is beginning to take notice of such things. But it is apt at first to
mistake them for mannerisms, or even to discover the fundamental hypothesis of an art-form and call it a fatal defect. Electri-
city owes its name to a mannerism in the behaviour of amber:
but it turns out to be a fundamental property of the universe.
Similarly, the Neapolitan mannerism of echoing the ends of
phrases merges into an essential dramatic property of the sonata
style.

In analysis the parts of themes that become detached and
recombined in various ways of development may be quoted and
identified by letters. When the student is making his own analysis
he need not trouble to put such letters in any order except that of
his own identification; but in the present edition advantage is
taken of previous knowledge.

Pupils of Parry will find the whole method familiar.

The principle of treating music as a time-process would, if
strictly applied, forbid us to specify the sections of any composition until we had finished its analysis. But in view of the shortness
of life we may allow ourselves to assume that the first full-sized
quick movement of a sonata will be in first-movement form
(especially if we notice a double-bar and repeat-mark about a
third of the way through it), and that if Beethoven calls a movement " Rondo " it will be in Rondo form. (Even this is not always
the case with Mozart !)

4. HARMONIC ANALYSIS.

The treatment of keys and key-relations is one of the most
important things in musical æsthetics. Space is not available for
arguing in defence of the theory adopted here and summarized in
the table of key-relations given below. Details of harmony are
not dwelt upon except where they illustrate an important principle.
Students ought to know that the second group in the first movement of Op. 2, No. 2 contains a series of remote enharmonic

modulations; but the student who most rejoices in identifying the roots of the diminished sevenths concerned therein will be very likely to miss the enormously more important point that the bass is steadily rising. Indeed, students have been known to fail to recognize any change when roots have been substituted for that rising bass. It is better to know no " theory " at all than to drift into such a deafness to all dramatic expression in music. Harmonic analysis is useful only when it illustrates the composer's rhetorical power. For this reason a steady rise or fall in the bass is enormously more important than the chords above it. If they are ordinary, it dramatizes them; if they are astonishing, it makes them more so by making them inevitable; and this without attracting attention to itself.

(B) TONALITY.

Classical key-relations do not depend on the ease with which one key may be reached from another. Modulation is a device which has never submitted to restriction. Key-relation is a fact with definite properties not to be confused with other facts.

The scheme here tabulated will be found to represent Beethoven's practice accurately. The underlying theory is explained in the article " Harmony " in the fourteenth edition of the *Encyclopædia Britannica*. Whether the student does or does not concern himself with the theory, he will find that what is set down here is plain fact. When we postulate the known history of scales, of harmony, and of the key-system of major and minor modes transposable to any pitch that can be named, the following fundamental principles are seen to govern all classical key-relations:—

1. Keys are related only as between two tonics; never through the medium of a third tonic. (It is thus fundamentally wrong to say that D minor " is related to C because it is the relative minor of the subdominant F.")

2. Each major key is, for purposes of relation, identifiable with the minor key on the same tonic.

3. Two keys are directly related when the tonic chord of one is among the common chords of the other. Thus, D minor is directly related to C major, because it is its supertonic triad. When the tonic is minor, the key-relation cannot always be found by looking for common chords in the unstable minor scale, but we can always look to the second key and reverse the relation. Thus, D minor being the supertonic of C major, we see that C major is the flat 7th of D minor.

4. *In* THE DOMINANT AND *On* THE DOMINANT.—As the chord on the dominant is penultimate in every full close, the persistent

emphasis on any dominant chord is strong evidence of the intention to establish the key of which that chord is dominant. Such emphasis is heightened by decorating that dominant chord with detail (such as a " leading note ") in a dominant relation to it. Hence the dominant of the dominant (the supertonic major, as D major from C) seldom, if ever, means a key in its own right. It is almost always a mere enhanced dominant. Until the student clearly understands the difference between being *on* the dominant and *in* the dominant the further study of key-relations should be postponed. The matter is not difficult to test. Such a passage as bars 19-24 in the Sonata in G, Op. 14, No. 2 should never be described as in A major. Such a mistake is far more than a matter of terminology; if the student is not trained betimes to recognize the effect of the context on such passages his musical sense will be seriously warped. Fortunately a simple demonstration is possible. Translate the whole passage from bar 9, or even from bar 1, into the minor mode. If the original goes into A major the translation will go into A minor. This is obviously wrong; it may be tolerable in itself, but nobody with an ear for music will accept it as a translation of the original. But now let us make it the dominant of D minor, a rather tiresome task involving diplomatic handling of accidentals and other details—

and, with all its awkwardness, the result is evidently a correct translation.

5. INDIRECT RELATIONS.—In consequence of the identity of major and minor keys on the same tonic, Beethoven (following a line initiated by Haydn and capriciously anticipated by D. Scarlatti) greatly extends the range of key-relations by changing the modes on either side, or even on both. The supertonic does not admit of this change, since the result usually appears as a merely enhanced dominant; and its converse, the flat seventh as between two major keys, fails for the same reason, making the tonic appear like a mere dominant of the subdominant, and being itself often used as an enhanced subdominant, as at the beginning of the Sonatas, Op. 31, No. 1, and Op. 53.

6. NEAPOLITAN RELATIONS.—The flat supertonic, seen in the " Neapolitan sixth," is, for purposes of key-relation, an integral part of the minor mode. (The whole system of major and minor

keys is itself the work of Neapolitan masters.) From this flat supertonic a series of "Neapolitan" relations, direct and indirect, may arise. A common form of opening in major movements announces a tonic phrase, and repeats it a step higher on the supertonic. (Beethoven: First Symphony, Quartet, Op. 59, No. 3; Quintet, Op. 29, etc.) Translate such an opening into the minor mode, and the only possible upward step will be to the flat supertonic. (Sonata, Op. 57; Quartet, Op. 59, No. 2; Quartet, Op. 95.)

7. Key-relationship is expressed only by immediate contrast of the keys concerned. " Dominant preparation "—i.e., preliminary emphasis of the intensified dominant of the new key—serves to establish a directly related key as a region in which the music settles so firmly that the original tonic has sunk beyond the horizon. With remoter keys even dominant preparation ceases to be necessary, and any more discursive preliminary modulation destroys the effect of relation.

8. Classical composers do not expect even the tonic to be recognized without the collateral evidence of a return to themes heard or expected to be heard in the tonic.

Tonality is inseparable from form, and key-relations are felt as such only in relation to the symmetries of the whole design. Thus they concern chiefly the relation between " first group " and " second group," between whole movements, between main sections and middle sections of *da capo* movements, and between main theme and episodes of Rondos. Each section has its own local effect of relation, and nothing of the kind is to be expected of discursive modulations.

(C) ORGANIC UNITY.

The Hummel-Spohr convention itself is, in the finest examples, too good to be treated as an abstraction. The archetype for all such abstractions is Humpty-Dumpty's complaint that Alice's features are arranged like all other people's, so that he cannot reasonably be expected to recognize her if he should meet her again.

What becomes of Beethoven's revolutionary tendencies when we treat his works as individuals and his forms as arising from the inner nature of his materials instead of being imposed from without ? Obviously, on such a view the strictest form is not that which is most like some average deduced from many classical examples, but that which, when adequately described, will account most nearly for every note in the work. A chorale-prelude (such as Bach's organ settings of *Aus tiefer Noth*) may use the chorale as a slow canto fermo and accompany it with fugue-texture on its own phrases in quicker notes. This definition describes the melodic function of most of the notes in the whole piece; harmonic grammar settles the rest—leaving Bach's consummate rhetoric to work its own miracles as if the form were perfectly free ! It is a merely practical accident that the free rhetoric did not produce the strict form instead of *vice versa;* in fact, as far as the chorale-tune was concerned, it did.

Seen in this light, Beethoven will be found to have attained his strictest form in his latest works; the very ones in which the form is popularly supposed to be broken down. We know nothing of form until we begin to study proportions and details. In the light of that study Beethoven's phrasing turns out to be far less intricate than Mozart's, and his form in its larger aspects far more symmetrical than Haydn's. The archetype of Beethoven's greatest codas is to be found in the perorations which Haydn substitutes for recapitulations in his ripest works. But the recapitulatory element in Beethoven's form is always as strong as in Mozart's, and it reaches its utmost importance in the latest works. Throughout Beethoven's career he strives for polyphony in spite of an almost physical difficulty in achieving smooth counterpoint. He did not always fail in that accomplishment, and he did not scruple to take the risk of failure. At the outset of his " third period " he enthusiastically rediscovered Bach and Handel. Bach's fugues revealed to him the power of a rule of form which causes things (like Kingsley's Mother Carey) to make themselves, while Handel's rhetoric was akin to his own. Hence Beethoven's last works can for pages together be construed by their polyphony, in spite of its harshness of style. A recapitulation does not become easier to recognize by being inverted in double counterpoint; but the original statement must be very exact to be capable of such treatment. Of course, you need not expect to extract the form of Beethoven's last quartets from the first violin part.

There are worse fallacies than a first-violin view of Beethoven's last quartets. Nothing, for instance, can be worse for a musician's mental health than the pursuit of fantastic derivations that are not verifiable by ear and by their own context. Against all such fallacies the student will be repeatedly warned in each analysis in the present volume. He or she is welcome—nay, invited—to suspend belief in any analytical statement so long as it fails to convince when compared with the sound of the music.

(D) TABLE OF KEY-RELATIONS.

The student should become familiar with the names and sounds of the cardinal points of a key—viz., I., the Tonic; II., the Supertonic; III., the Mediant; IV., the Subdominant; V., the Dominant; and VI., the Submediant. While the Supertonic is so named as being the note above the Tonic, the Subdominant should not be regarded as the note below the Dominant, but as an Anti-Dominant as far below the Tonic as the Dominant is above it. Thus we learn to know the polar opposition between the two, and thus we realize that the Submediant is rightly named as being a Mediant between the Tonic and Subdominant.

If the degrees of the scale are thus represented by Roman figures we can express all key-relations by using capital figures for major keys and small figures for minor. Raised degrees may be expressed by sharps and lowered degrees by flats, always in relation to the tonic in question. Thus, if the tonic be major, the directly related Mediant is iii. and the flat Mediant ♭III. But from a minor tonic the Mediant is normally flat and will be represented by III., while if the Mediant of the major tonic is annexed it will be represented by ♯iii.

The terms " relative major " and " relative minor " should be abandoned. The keys they represent are no more closely related than the other direct relations.

The following Tables represent only the keys that are brought into relation in classical tonality from Alessandro Scarlatti to Wagner. There is nothing to prevent a composer, classical or modern, from bringing other keys into contact. Relation can be revealed only by contact or by collateral evidence of design; but contact will reveal the lack of relation as surely as it will display relation. The term " natural modulation " used to be applied to modulation within the limits of direct relations. All others were indiscriminately called " extraneous." It would be a good thing if we could use the term " natural " for modulations so designed as to demonstrate key-relation whether it be direct or remote; as when Beethoven changes one triad into another, note by note. The term " dominant modulation " could be used for processes that establish the second key through its dominant. There is little merit in the term " extraneous " modulation, or in any terms based on the notion of " distance." The words " drifting " and " discursive " describe essential facts. An enharmonic modulation, if genuine, deliberately destroys all impression of key-relation. Mere changes of notation as when the key of G♭ is written as that of F♯, are not in themselves matters of modulation at all. But a sequence of normal modulations may include such a change and may take advantage of it to identify the key of, say, C major with what is strictly speaking that of B♯. In such *enharmonic circles* only the collateral evidence of design can re-establish the tonic.

Keys outside these Tables will produce certain effects in juxtaposition; but these will not be effects of key-relations. If the context can persuade you that II. is not a mere enhanced dominant the effect will be startling, as in the recapitulation of the first movement of the Eroica Symphony. The key-distances ♯IV., ♯iv., lie on the kink in harmonic space and are indistinguishable from their antipodes ♭V. and ♭v.

TABLE OF KEY RELATIONS

TABLE A. FROM A MAJOR TONIC.

Direct Relations:
ii. iii. IV. V. vi.

Indirect Relations through the Tonic Minor[1]:
♭III. iv. v. ♭VI.

Indirect Relations through changed mode of the Second Keys of Direct Relations[2]:
III. iv. v. VI.

Doubly Indirect Relations by change of both modes:
♭iii. ♭vi.

Neapolitan Relations[3]:
♭II. ♯VII. ♯vii.

Indirect Neapolitan Relation:
♭ii.

TABLE B. FROM A MINOR TONIC.

Direct Relations:
III. iv. v. VI. ♭VII.

Indirect Relations through the Tonic Major[1]:
♯iii. IV. V. ♮vi.

Indirect Relations through changed mode of the Second Keys of Direct Relations[2]:
iii. IV. V. ♭vi.

Double Indirect Relations by change of both modes:
♯III. ♯VI.

Neapolitan Relation[3]:
♭II.

Indirect Neapolitan Relations:
♭ii. ♯VII. ♯vii.

[1] The Supertonic and Flat 7th cannot establish themselves as new tonics when the modes are changed.

[2] The changed Dominant and Subdominant are thus reached from both sides of the relation.

[3] The Flat Supertonic is equally related to the major and the minor tonic, just as the Flat 6th impinges on a major dominant chord.

1

SONATA IN F MINOR, Op. 2, No. 1.

Allegro: F minor.

First Group.

Bars ½/1–8. — Eight-bar theme (A); 2+2 in sequence, followed by 1+1 in sequence, rising to 2-bar half-close on dominant. Pause. The theme contains two figures—

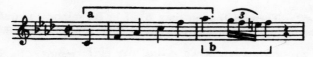

and from its 4th bar the bass rises up the scale from E♮ to C.

Transition.

⁸/9–19.—Bass enters with (a+b) in the unexpected key of dominant minor, as if beginning a counter-statement. At 3ʳd bar upper parts intervene, working (b) for four bars in a chain of suspensions towards dominant of. A♭ (III.), on which a 2-bar half-close, insisted upon twice, makes preparation for Second Group. There is no reason to suspect other than regular 4-bar periods in the twelve that have passed since bar 8; but the development of (b) lies midway across the 2nd and 3rd groups, and the *forte* in bar 18 tends to displace the rhythm. Hence there is a suspicion of overlap at bar 18, which we may, in the retrospect, carry back to bar 16. The ear must decide, and it cannot decide until Beethoven helps it with a *sforzando*.

Second Group: A♭ (III.).

20–40.—New theme (B) rhythmically allied to (a)+(b), on dominant of A♭ (with minor 9th), thrice repeating a 2-bar group across the period begun in bar 20. At the 3rd repetition a 2-bar quaver-figure in rising sequence intervenes, cutting short the preceding figure. Reaching the dominant, it repeats its cadence there, and repeats it twice again in an enhanced form over a tonic position, thence rising for another two bars, culminating in the next period. However successfully the *sforzandos* in theme (B)

11

may have placed it athwart the rhythm, the quaver figure, falling as it does into 2+3+2, has produced an irregularity. In the retrospect none of the accents, not even the *sforzandos*, have entirely destroyed a latent 4-bar momentum from the very beginning; and after all these cross-currents we are now at bar 32, which closes into a plain 4-bar group, closing into modified self-repetition, closing into

41–48.—Cadence theme, a new 2-bar phrase with touches of minor harmony, interlocking thrice in self-repetition, and the third time augmenting its last notes to two full bars. Exposition repeated.

Development.

⁴⁸/49–54.—Two 3-bar groups of (a) with (b) twice; starting in A♭ and proceeding (by descent of bass) towards dominant of B♭ minor.

55–62.—Theme (B) as in bars 20–27 in B♭ minor, the quaver-figure moving, over steady descent of bass, towards dominant of C minor.

63–80.—Continuation of theme (B) in C minor. Its third 2-bar group is taken over by bass as the beginning of a sequence falling by tones. The treble assents in cadential notes. The third step having reached dominant of A♭, the sequence continues without the theme, the bass making a syncopated outline, while the cadential notes of the treble become answering minims. In three more steps this outlined sequence passes into F minor, and in two more bars (completing a period) closes into its dominant—viz., the home dominant.

81–92.—Twelve bars dominant preparation, four interlocking with self-repetition, closing into twice two of the same kind; the whole continuing to avoid allusion to definite themes.

93–100.—The bare dominant remaining for two bars, a chain of suspensions drives the bass down in sequential steps, while (b) appears above (beginning with ♭II.), alternately low and high. The 8th bar of this period closes into the

Recapitulation.

First Group.

101–108 = 1–8 *forte*, with new *sforzandos* and a stiffened bass in last 4 bars.

109–118.—The continuation is now in the tonic; the intervention of (b) in upper parts involves ♭II. and iv. With an 8th bar the home dominant is reached and insisted on only once, closing into the

Second Group.
119–145 = 20–46 translated into unmixed minor.

Coda.
146–152.—The last chords of cadence-theme unexpectedly diverted to iv.; repeated a step lower in III.; thence carried in crotchets down two rapid steps with a cross accent to final close.

Adagio: F major (I.) Sonata Form without Development.

First Group.
½/1–8.—Eight-bar melody; 4 (twice two) with half-close, answered by 4 (unbroken) with full close.
⁸/9–16.—Second strain; twice 2 bars dominant to tonic, self-repeating with variation, and closing into 4 bars of first melody, substituting IV. for V. at second bar.

Transition.
¹⁶/17–22.—New theme beginning with 4 bars in D minor (vi.); passing in 2 more bars towards C (V.).

Second Group in Dominant.
23–26.—Four-bar phrase (1+1) self-repeating,+2 closing into next period
27–30.—Two-bar phrase in dialogue between treble and bass, closing into varied self-repetition, closing into
31.—Extra bar on home dominant, the bass figure having risen to treble and closing into

Recapitulation.

First Group.
32–47 = 1–16 with additional ornaments. A melodic link connects last bar with

Second Group.
48–55 = 23–30 in tonic, with additional ornaments, closing into

Coda.
56–61.—Third repetition of previous couplet. The close is repeated and expanded by an extra bar. An echo of this completes the period.

Menuetto: Allegretto.   F minor: with Trio in Tonic Major.
If we imagine the first accent to fall on bar 2, the whole Minuet

and Trio will be in 4-bar and 2-bar groups with all the cadences closing on to strong bars; until we reach the last 8 bars of the Trio, where we shall find that the melody has changed step though the total amount remains even. Meanwhile, there are so many cross-currents, and Beethoven's *sforzandos* in bars 31 and 33 (*not* in bar 32, where the *sforzando* of some editions is spurious) are so explicit, to say nothing of the positions of his sudden *fortes* and *fortissimos*, that out interpretation of bar 1 as preliminary will survive only for listeners who conscientiously support it with sniffs. After all, what sort of abstraction can an accent be if it is *never* the loudest note of a passage ? There is, then, no sufficient evidence that Beethoven is not conceiving this music in the sense which will reach the naïve listener who apprehends that it begins at the beginning. A *sforzando* on the third beat is a mere cross-accent; but the *sforzandos* on the first beat once in two bars will keep us in step. Meanwhile, what does it matter that the cadences are weak ? The long penultimate note in bars 39–40 almost suffices to suggest a weak cadence. A short chord in its place would have been much less amenable. You can shift your step if you like; but then, whichever way you take the Trio it will turn round upon you at the end. It seems simpler to suppose that the ear is right in accepting an irregularity than to suppose that Beethoven is addressing himself to Prout and Riemann as the only worthy recipients of his message.

First Strain.

⅓/1–14.—Four-bar phrase (1+1+2) in F minor containing a figure (a) in bar 1; repeated in A♭ (III.), and its second couple insisted on, completed by full close, with a figure (b). The full close is repeated, enhanced. Repeat.

Second Strain.

¹⁴/15–28.—Figure (a) rises in two 2-bar steps (with bass in contrary motion) from A♭ (with minor 6th) to B♭ minor (iv.), where the close with (b) plus its enhanced repetition completes an 8-bar period. Figure (b) twice insisted on (note contrast between short grace-note and full-sized quaver) and then carried over 4 bars in a continuous run reaching the home dominant.

Third Strain.

²⁸/30–40.—Theme (a) starting in lower parts, answered by treble and worked into an 8-bar phrase with the cadence (b) in tonic. The enhanced repetition of the cadence is in a lower octave and is followed by a plain full close in a third octave. Repeat.

Trio in Tonic major.

[40]/41–50.—Four-bar theme in 2-part counterpoint, quavers over crotchets; answered by 6 bars (4+2) with crotchets over quavers, closing in dominant.   Repeat.

[50]/51–65.—Four bars on dominant, the quaver-figure rising over three inner whole-bar notes in descending semitones.   Answer, with the whole-note semitones above, and the quavers in bass.   A middle part joins them during 3rd bar; and the rising sequence continues, a treble joining during 5th bar.   The climax is reached at 7th bar, from which the quavers run down through an 8th bar to the three whole-note semitones which (without completing a period, no matter how we scan the whole movement) glide into

66–73.—The 4-bar free double counterpoint, answered by four with exchanged parts closing in tonic.   The discrepant B♮ in bar 67 is not a misprint.   Repeat *Menuet Da Capo.*

Prestissimo: F minor.   Sonata Form with long Episode in Development.

First Group: F minor.

1–4.—Theme (A) of two bars (1+1) self-repeating, containing rhythmic figure (a) in the crotchets of *R.H.* and closing into

5–12.—Theme (B), a 4-bar melody (1+1+2) arising out of rhythm (a), starting (at half bar) in A♭ and closing into home dominant, thence repeated in tonic with new turn towards dominant of C minor (v.).

13–21.—Nine bars of dominant preparation of C minor, on figure (a), 2+2+2, +extra bar+2 of scale descending to

Second Group in Dominant Minor.

22–33.—New 8-bar theme in C minor (v.), four times 1 bar, in two posi.ions, answered by 4 of sequential fall from a higher position to a close into repetition of these 4 bars in a lower position, closing into next period.

34–49.—Another 8-bar theme in three 2-bar steps of a new figure with a 2-bar close into repetition of the whole 8 bars, closing into

50–56.—Cadence-group on theme (A), twice 2 bars, plus extra bar, plus two of final tonic chords, of which the last bar leads, at the first time, through home dominant 7th to the repeat of the exposition.   On the second time the last bar contains only the single final chord.

Development.

57–58.—The final chords echoed on dominant of A♭ (B♭ in bass).

Episode in Ab (III.)

59–68.—New 10-bar melody in Ab (in interlocking 2-bar groups) closing in (present) tonic.

69–78.—Repetition thereof in higher octave slightly varied.

78/79–94.—Second strain, a new 4-bar phrase repeated with variation and followed by the former melody reduced to 8 bars by omission of the 3rd and 4th bars.

95–108.—Repetition of second strain with slight variation. The cadence is cut off by the overlapping of the penultimate bar into the resumed development of the main theme.

109–126.—Figure (a) returns, built into 4-bar steps (1+1+2) with a new 2-bar figure (x) in bars 111-112. The steps move down from Ab through G (as part of dominant of F minor) into F minor, where a change of harmony in bass swerves to Db. The 2nd bar of x is insistent, making a climax in the 4 bars that now lead to the home dominant.

127–137.—Preparation on home dominant, with (a). Twice 2 bars; then 3 bars, a *sforzando* in the 2nd and 3rd bars showing that one of the 3 is extra; then 4, closing into

Recapitulation.
First Group.

138–146 = 1–9, the first 4 bars all *forte*.

147–160.—The continuation of theme (B) in the tonic repeats its figure in bass, instead of in the same part, adding a counterpoint which is used as a lead to the 9 bars of preparation on home dominant, corresponding to bars 13-21.

Second Group.

161–192 = 22–53, with change in positions of the first 12 bars and with the cadence-group giving the triplet quavers to *R.H.* and the chords of (a) to *L.H.* Instead of the irregular bars 54-56, the movement ends with a normal 4-bar group, 193-196. We have no reason to suppose that a bar was omitted between 54 or 56, though this is not impossible. But Beethoven does not believe in regularity, except for as special a purpose as any stroke of genius; and he positively dislikes uniformity. In some early editions a repeat of the second part is indicated. On principle this is (for patient listeners in private) generally good when the development is episodic. But Beethoven can hardly have imagined the effect of it here. To resume the episode without any connecting link sounds very crude, and the chords of bars 57-58 are not in the right position for that purpose after the close in F minor.

2
SONATA IN A MAJOR, Op. 2, No. 2.

Allegro Vivace: A major.

First Group :

Bars 1–8.—Eight-bar theme (2+2+4), closing on dominant and containing figures (a^1), (b), and (aa).

9–20.—New theme, 4 bars continued imitatively by another 4 closing into 4 of dominant (1+1+2); containing figures (c^1), (c^2).

²⁰/21–31.—Figures (a, b); followed by (c), starting in bass and imitated for 8 bars, leading to close into

32–41.—New imitative theme containing figures (d), (e),

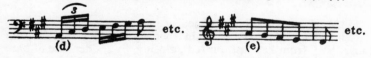

and moving in two 4-bar steps to dominant of dominant, which is reached in two more bars of the descent of figure (e). [As all the three themes so far contain scales, ascending and descending, a misplaced ingenuity might allege a " logical connexion " between them. But such ingenuity always goes with a marked failure to see the wood for trees.]

42–57.—Sixteen bars of dominant preparation for the key of E. In the first 4 an inner part continues to develop (e), after which a single part (arising from the bass and divided between the two hands) moves with three 2-bar steps of a new figure, passing into E minor and gathering harmony in 4 more bars, closing into *Second Group :* E minor and major (v. and V.).

17

58–75.—New theme in 4-bar steps of rising sequence. Each step makes an enharmonic modulation and rises a minor 3rd, thus carrying the passage from E minor through G major and the extremely remote key of B♭. Thence the sequence rises by tones in three 2-bar steps. All this process (epoch-making in the history of sonata-expositions) is founded on the systematic rising of the bass through a scale passing through these keys in sequence, at first with 2-bar steps, then chromatically bar by bar until F♯ is reached as bass of a dominant chord of E minor. Here a halt is called.

76–91.—Over this F♯ figures (b) and (a¹) put their question for 8 bars (2+2+1+1+1 and rest). It is answered by a new 4-bar cadence in E major (2+2), completing the steps of the bass up to the dominant (G♯, A♯, B) and closing into its varied repetition, which closes into

92–103.—Theme (d+e), with upper voice leading the first imitation, followed (as if by a 3rd voice) in the bass, answered in treble and continued in 5 bars additional downward scale of (e), reminiscent of bars 39–41, closing into

104–117.—Cadence theme on tonic pedal, 4 bars, consisting of imitative dialogue between two inner parts on rising scale suggestive of inverted (e) with a *canto fermo* in treble; closing into self-repetition and followed by 6 bars of tonic chord. The rests before the repeat show positively that in the main theme the 1st bar has the chief accent. This is important not only in itself but in connexion with the Development.

Development.

118*–122.—Last chords echoed in minor.
123–130.—Eight bars of main theme *forte* in C (♭III. from tonic; ♭VI. from key just quitted), closing, by sudden rise of bare dominant, into A♭.

131–161.—The theme (ab+aa) is displaced a bar forward, and proceeds thus for three 6-bar steps (ab) in bass, (aa) in treble, starting with A♭ as tonic, then its dominant (7th), and then dominant of F; from which point (aa) is separated, proceeding further in two 4-bar steps on dominant of F minor, closing into 5 (2+3 and pause) on its dominant chord. (The pause might be taken as completing an 8-bar period; but this would be too long and, if exact, too mechanical. It is better to regard it as representing only 2 bars and to prolong it a little beyond that. Pauses should never be exact multiples of the standard rhythm, unless the bars are very short. Then odd multiples will do.)

---

* Reckoning a one-bar rest, not a 2-bar, at 117.

[161]/162–170.—Theme (c) in F major for 7 bars, after which it breaks off into a new 2-bar limb, closing into

[170]/171–181.—Theme (c) led by bass, passing after 6th bar into D minor, and after 3 more bars there closed by the new limb into

[181]/182–202.—Figure (c) developed in close 3-part imitation. Four 2-bar steps in pairs (at 4ths and 5ths) passing from D minor to F. Then 3 bars new combination of (a^1) with fragment of (c), returning to D minor, closing with one limb of the 3-part imitation of (c) followed by the new 3 bars of (a^1+e), leading to A minor, where these 5 bars are repeated, closing on to the home dominant.

203–225.—Preparations on the home dominant for return. Four bars (2+2) of (c) on dominant of minor, divided in a new way between bass and upper parts; repeated with a difference; then three new rising 2-bar steps in major; then 4 of dialogue on (c^2), descending as well as rising; then 4 cadential chords, closing with pause, into

Recapitulation.

First Group.

226–243 = 1–18 unchanged except for *forte* throughout first 5½ bars.

244–251.—The dominant close (without its last chords) is repeated in subdominant, and then *fortissimo* in tonic, closing into the transition theme, and so omitting the counter-statement bars 21–31.

252–275.—Theme (d)+(e) repeats itself on tonic, instead of rising, and so is able to treat its 4th (or 8th) bar as a transposition of bar 39—following to tonic. Hence all the dominant preparation follows, leading to

Second Group.

276–335 = 58–117 in tonic, unaltered except for details forced on Beethoven by the limits of a 5-octave pianoforte. This saved Beethoven the trouble of introducing " discrepancies " for their own sake.

There is no coda; but it is worth while, in private, trying the effect of Beethoven's indication of a repeat from bar 123. The experiment will convey nothing to those who regard music and poetry as merely representing so much information. But those who can appreciate the artistic handling of the time-dimension, and the relation between tonality and form, will find that Beethoven meant something very definite by the effect of plunging again into ♭III. and the subsequent remote keys after his quiet close in his tonic. The result may not be convincing, and is certainly not addressed to the general public; but it is neither conventional nor accidental. In public performance, on the other hand, the movement is more impressive and dramatic without repeats at all.

Largo appassionato: D major (IV.), Rondo form.

Main Theme.

1–8.—Symmetrical 8-bar strain, with half-close at bar 4 answered by full close at bar 8.

8/9–19.—Four bars of dominant (dialogue between treble and bass) leading to expansion of opening 4 bars to 7; the 2nd bar being developed in rising sequence, passing through ii. and IV., whereon bass descends over more than an octave, and melody rises to climax and cadence.

First Episode : B minor (vi.) and modulations.

19/20–23.—Four bars (1+1+2) of new theme (a single figure twice varied) beginning in vi. and closing into iii.

23/24–31.—The new theme in inner part, in F♯ minor (iii.). At its 3rd bar the treble intervenes in the ♭II. of that key (G major), imitating a new 2-bar phrase, which is repeated with variation and change of harmony, upon which a 3rd bar (30) leads to the home dominant (31) so to

First Return.

32–49 = 1–18.—The treble and bass exchange parts in bars 9-12 and the final cadence loses its appoggiatura in order that the theme may overlap with

Second Episode.

50–57.—Starting in the tonic, as if to make a coda, this episode begins with a 4-bar phrase in 3-part imitation of a new figure, closing into repetition with variation. (The resemblance of the new figure to the accompaniment of bars 9-12 should be disregarded; the harm of missing subtle resemblances is far less dangerous than that of making false points.) The repetition closes into

58–63.—Outburst of main theme *fortissimo* in tonic minor, passing after 2nd bar into ♭VI. and continuing there, as to its rhythm, while bass rises in two octaves of scale. The 6th bar impinges on the home dominant.

64–67.—Four bars (1 + 1 + 2) dominant preparation with new figure, closing into

Second Return, modified and compressed.

68–71 = 1–4, an octave higher, with semiquaver movement in inner part.

72–74.—New continuation, closing with overlap into

Coda.

75–80.—Two-bar tonic-and-dominant group (new figures) in dialogue between right and left hand, closing into varied repetition, which closes into 2 bars of tonic chord. (The $\frac{6}{4}$ in the bass at the beginning of bar 79 anticipates a feature of Beethoven's latest style.)

SCHERZO AND TRIO: ALLEGRETTO. A major.

$\frac{3}{4}$/1–8.—Symmetrical strain; 4 bars closing on dominant answered by 4 closing in tonic, containing figure (a)—

 Repeated.

9–18.—Two 4-bar steps of sequence, with (a) in bass modulating to F$\sharp$ minor (vi.) and thence to G$\sharp$ minor; in which remote key two more bars (broken off from the rhythm of the previous bar) close into

19–32.—New cantabile in G$\sharp$ minor; 4 bars closing into repetition. This diverges after 2nd bar, and treats the new rhythmic figure imitatively for 6 bars, which drift back by 7ths through V., I., and IV. to home dominant. Two bars pause.

^{32}/33–39 = 1–8.

^{39}/40–43.—Four bars coda with (a) in bass. Repeat from bar 9.

TRIO: A minor (i.).

44–51.—Eight-bar phrase (2+2, +4) on an imitative scale figure with bass in contrary motion, modulating to dominant minor. Repeat.

^{51}/52–59.—Similar 8 bars, starting in III., and passing through iv. back to i., closing into

60–67.—First strain resumed, remaining in tonic, with stationary dominant bass added below the original moving bass and giving way at close. Repeat from bar 52.

Scherzo Da Capo.

Rondo: Grazioso. A major.

Main Theme.

1–8.—Symmetrical strain; 4 bars ending with half-close,

answered by 4 closing in dominant; containing figures (a), (b). Figure (a) is the arpeggio and top notes of bars 1-2; (b) is the *portamento* in bar 2.

8/9–16.—Second strain; consisting of four imitative bars (2+2), with a new figure, on dominant pedal, leading back to 4 bars of a, b, with new tonic full close.

Transition.

16/17–25.—New 4-bar theme (1+1+2), beginning on dominant and closing on tonic into self-repetition an octave higher, diverted at third bar into key of dominant and insisting thereon in an extra pair of bars overlapping into

First Episode in dominant.

26–40.—New cantabile beginning with a 2-bar phrase, with two variations arising from higher and higher top notes; continued with a descending sequence in two 2-bar steps (the bass falling a whole octave in the process). These lead to the subdominant of the present key; and the subdominant character becomes overbalanced by the sense of return to the main tonic, so that the five bars following the sequence (2+1+2) are of the nature of dominant preparation for the return. The whole passage is ambiguously poised as to which of each pair of bars has the main accent. In such a slow tempo the distinction between strong and weak bars is seldom appreciable. Mozart hardly ever gets through a common-time movement at this pace without finding himself half a bar out somewhere; nor does this worry him. But here Beethoven undoubtedly produces an overlap at bar 26, where the tonic chord of E must represent the beginning of a phrase. Yet so delicate is the balance that in the parallel passage, bar 122, the mere fact that the E major chord is felt as dominant, and not as tonic, suffices to bring the cantabile on to the first instead of the second bar of the phrasing. In both passages overlaps occur somewhere, but no human ear is interested in determining their exact places.

First Return.

41–56 = 1–16 with some new ornaments.

Second Episode in tonic minor.

56/57–66.—First strain of a new theme on a figure of chromatic staccato triplets above rhythmic chords for 4 bars (1+1+2); closing into continuation with triplets in bass and rhythmic chords above for 6 bars (1+1+4), closing in C (bIII.). **Repeat.**

67–79.—Second strain begins with imitative 2-bar sequence on chromatic figure, rising from C through D minor to E minor (v.), where a third step expands to a 4-bar close on to an E major chord, which, being major, is dominant of A minor; hence closing into resumption of first strain, finished off abruptly in tonic as a 5-bar phrase.

80–90.—Repetition of bars 67-77, the first 7 bars *pp legato*, the rest *ff*.

91–99.—The repetition diverges here, impinging with a sudden *pp* upon 8 bars of dominant preparation for return.

Second Return.
100–115 = 1–16 with new ornaments in both strains, (a) becoming a scale.

Tonic Recapitulation of Transition and First Episode.
¹¹⁵/116–123.—The transition-theme, by losing its insistent extra pair of bars, fails to produce more than a dominant effect with its 8th bar (123), and accordingly leads straight to
124–134 = 27–37 freely recapitulated and rounded off in tonic with cadence closing into

Third Return and Coda.
135–139 = 1–5 with other new ornaments.

140–147.—Here the theme digresses into F♮ (♭VI.) with enharmonic change (C♯ = D♭), and hovers there for 5 bars (2+2+1, counting from bar 140 as overlap); returning by the reverse enharmonic change (plus that from B♭ to A♯) to a cadence in tonic, closing into

148–155.—Eight-bar phrase developed from (a) in dialogue between bass and treble (2+2+4); at first in tonic-and-dominant swing, then through IV., closing into

156–160.—Repetition of last 4 bars diverted at 3rd bar by enharmonic change of D♯ (augmented 6th) to E♭, thus leading to B♭ (♭II.) with 2 bars (1+1) cadential insistence, closing into

161–172.—Allusion to Second Episode; 4 bars starting on bass F♮ in ♭II. and moving at 4th bar towards home dominant, upon which 8 bars of preparation (4 with the rhythmic bass, the remainder unaccompanied) lead to

173–179.—Final appearance of main theme with elaborate new ornament and a fresh turn to its 6th bar, after which a new 7th bar closes into

180–187.—Final tonic-and-dominant swing, 2+2+4.

3

SONATA IN C MAJOR, Op. 2. No. 3.

Allegro con brio: C major.

First Group.

Bars 1–12.—Eight-bar theme: 2+2 with reciprocal tonic and dominant, followed by 4 (1+1+2), closing medially in tonic. These last 4 bars are then repeated in bass, broadening the last two so as to close into the next period. The theme contains two figures, (a) and (b)—

Of these (a) is often detached from the initial minim, as ('a). In bars 5–8, (b) is hardly recognizable, lying, as it does, athwart the metrical feet; but it develops independently into an extended legato figure; and the syncopations in bars 11–12 anticipate important later incidents.

13–26.—New 4-bar theme (C) (1+1+2), with semiquaver motion, arpeggios followed by broken octaves, closing into self-repetition, diverted so as to close into passage on dominant consisting of 2 bars closing into enhanced self-repetition, closing into final run down. Notice that, in spite of the F♯, all this is only the home dominant, not the key of G. Such passages can be tested by translating their antecedents into the tonic minor, when the *key* of the dominant will at once be seen to be out of the question. It is particularly easy here to translate bar 13 foll. into C minor.

Second Group (*or Transition and Second Group*) in Dominant.

27–38.—The preceding home dominant is nevertheless treated as a real key. A new 6-bar theme (2+2+2) starts in G minor (v.), leading to repetition in D minor, closing into A minor in next period. These modulations are controlled by the steady descent of the bass from G to G♯, with only one backward step at the joint.

The device of following up the home dominant as the real key of a Second Group was already becoming archaic when this sonata was written. Followed by this remarkable modulating theme, it still makes its point; far less timidly, for instance, than in the first movement of Beethoven's First Symphony. He used it for the last time with a certain truculence in his *Namensfeier* Overture, Op. 115, and Brahms was able to revive it in a new light in the finale of his Horn Trio. Historically the most remarkable fact about the present passage is that these modulating themes and that of the slow movement of Op. 2, No. 1, belong to a quartet written by Beethoven at the age of 15.

39–46.—New sequence in 2-bar steps from A minor to G minor, theme diverted towards dominant of G; whereon we have 4 bars dominant preparation, twice 1 on the new figure and 2 of a melodic link.

47–60.—The key of the dominant being now re-established in an orthodox way, a new 8-bar melody begins: 2 tonic and 2 dominant with imitative middle voice, followed by 4 closing in dominant. A counterstatement, with the lower voice leading, moves in its 5th and 6th bars towards the present subdominant.

61–76.—Theme (C) interrupts, starting on subdominant and moving back to our present tonic in three 2-bar steps, the 3rd step continued with 4 self-repeating half-bars (the broken octaves of bars 15–16). After this the semiquavers stop and the bass descends more than two octaves (syncopated crochets) in 4 bars, leading to a new 4-bar cadence closing into next period.

Cadence Group.

77–90.—Taking its time from bar 77, a new 2-bar theme (D) closes into self-repetition with higher close into a 3rd step, which crowds its main figure four times into 2 bars, making, with final chords, a 4-bar cadence, closing into a 4-bar phrase in broken octaves (reminiscent of theme C), closing into 2 bars of final chords.

Exposition repeated.

Development.

90–96.—Theme (D), starting a note higher, moves into C minor, thence to F minor, and then rises with its compressed main figure up the dominant 7th of E♭.

97–108.—Rise of bass by semitones in 2-bar steps from B♭ to D♭, written as C♯, and dwelt on for three times 2 bars, with chords finally closing into D major. There is no theme in the semiquaver arpeggios of *R.H.*, nor is their figure derived from theme (C). There is no enharmonic modulation at bar 102. If the whole passage were raised a semitone it would start on the dominant of E, and bar 102 would become simply the dominant of G. But there is, in the outcome, an enharmonic circle in the whole development. The key here written as D major is " really " E♭♭, on which showing the recapitulation will be in D♭♭ instead of C. The difference of pitch in just intonation would be very slight; and when we hear our opening theme at so nearly the same pitch, with no means of measuring the difference, we shall certainly think ourselves in the same key. It is a fundamental mistake to imagine that this depends upon the tempered scale. The fact is that, after even one change of key confirmed beyond the limits of a lyric melody, the original tonic is recognized only by collateral evidence. There was, for instance, not the slightest feeling of a return to the tonic when the subdominant of G was so emphatically asserted in bars 60-62. At the present moment we have been travelling round the harmonic world, and it makes not the slightest difference whether we call the key here reached E♭♭ or D; we are interested only to know that it is very remote.

[The *diminuendo* required at bar 107 is very sudden. *Calando* implies a fainting away, with slackened pace while it lasts.]

109–112 = Bars 1–4 of the main theme in E♭♭ or D major. Call it D major.

113–128.—Figures (a) and (b) developed in 4-bar steps, 2 of (a) and 'a answered by 2 developing (b) in imitation at the upper 9th. The steps are down the dominants from G minor through C minor to F minor. At the 3rd step (b) is carried downward for 4 bars (amounting to descent of bass down an octave); and the 8-bar period (from 121) is finished by compressing (b) in 4 half-bars, landing (in the next period) on the home dominant.

129–138.—Ten bars dominant preparation for return; (a, b) in an inner part over dominant pedal in 2-bar groups repeated thrice, imitated (with (b) more clearly expressed) in rising positions in treble; then 4 bars descent of (a) and ('a) in treble, closing into the Recapitulation.

Recapitulation.

First Group.

139–146 = 1–8, with slight change in lower parts at bars 5-6.

147–154.—New development of (b), repeating bars 7-8 (145-146) in bass with new syncopated counterpoint; repeated in subdominant; then taken up by treble, with the counterpoint in bass, moving rapidly from D minor (ii.) in 4 bars (2+twice 1 as regards bass) to close into home dominant.

155–160 = 21–26.—The home dominant now has its proper function of preparing for the tonic. In fact, the object and result of the old device is that its orthodox use in the Recapitulation atones for the unfair advantage taken of it in the Exposition. Beethoven extracts a new point from it in the *Namensfeier* Overture by substituting tonic chords in the Recapitulation.

Second Group.

161–217 = 27–83 transposed to tonic.

Coda.

218–231.—The close of theme (D) is interrupted by a chord of A♭ (♭VI.), which first fills 4 bars with themeless quavers. Then the bass starts from A♭ and rises up the scale, first in three 2-bar steps, then in 4 single bars, the quavers becoming triplets and the harmony (all diminished 7ths) veering towards C.

232.—A $^6_4$ chord in C being reached, an unbarred cadenza, after a preliminary upward passage, develops (a) and ('a), passing as if through (vi.) to (ii.). Insistence upon (ii.) arouses the suspicion that this is only a part of the dominant chord, a suspicion which grows as ('a) becomes more and more like a trill. The trill, with its full dominant chord, arrives and leads to a chromatic scale, descending to the main theme in the next period.

237–251.—New development of (b) on lines suggested by bars 115-116. Here the upper part leads; the harmonies are at first tonic and dominant. Four bars (twice 1+2 initiating a rise) followed by another 4 moving down nearly two octaves (2 bars in syncopated steps, the other 2 in crotchet steps, with (b) diminished as falling quavers). Then 4 cadential bars of (b) in wide skips, but in its original rhythm (as in bar 2), with interrupted cadence and silent 4th bar. Then 3 answering bars, led *ff* by *L.H.*, answered at half-bar by *R.H.*, closing into

252-257 = 85–90.—Haydn is very fond of closing a movement thus, with the exact end of the Exposition, after something much more like a big Beethoven Coda than a Recapitulation.

Adagio: E major (III.).— Special Rondo Form, with one Recapitulated Episode containing two subordinate Groups.

Main Theme.

Bars 1–10.—Eight-bar theme with 2-bar modified echo; the whole built up in single bars, which remain abrupt until a syncopated sequence of half-bars at bar 7 leads into a medial cadence in bar 8. The echo of these 2 bars puts the syncopated figure into the lower parts and defers the cadence so that it closes into the next period. As to harmony, the first 4 bars deliberately test how often the dominant chord can end a figure without tautology, relying merely on the top note of the melody to save the integrity of bar 4. Bars 5-6, in (ii.), are a sequential repetition of 1-2; and the remaining bars, as already stated, complete the structure in a new rhythm, closing into

EPISODE.
First Group : Tonic minor (i.).

11–18.—New theme (B) in 3-bar phrases, 2 of slow rising sequence in bass, answered by 1 with semiquaver figure in treble; the *R.H.* maintaining a demisemiquaver accompaniment throughout both groups of the whole episode. The first 3 bars, modulating from (i.) to its III. (G major) are carried further in that key, the answering figure being continued for another bar, followed by a close into the next period. As a result the bass has risen nearly an octave since bar 11; one step each bar, stopping on G for 2 bars, and having now reached D.

Second Group : (♭III.).

19–25.—New theme (C) making 3-bar phrases on a syncopated half-bar figure. The 3 bars close into slightly varied self-repetition, closing into an extra bar, returning to minor tonic in next period.

Recapitulation of First Group.

26–36.—Return of theme (B). There are now 3 of the 3-bar steps, passing up to A minor (iv.), thence to a position in B minor (v.), back to E minor, and ending with 2 bars further dialogue on the semiquaver figure (answered in bass), closing on to home dominant in next period. During bars 26-36 the bass has steadily risen up a 9th.

Preparation for Return.

37–42.—Figure of theme (C) in 2-bar phrases on home dominant. The second pair is a modification of the first; the third pair is in the bass, descending and ascending the dominant chord.

First Return of Main Theme.

43–52 = 1–10, closing into

Recapitulation of Episode.

53–54 = 1–2, bursting out suddenly *ff* in C major (♭VI.).

55–58.—Theme (B), without the semiquaver treble, moving in 4 bars from ♭VI. to close into tonic.

59–66.—Recapitulation of theme (C), transposing bars 19–24 to the tonic, and adding a 2-bar full close containing an enhanced echo of the previous bar.

Second Return of Main Theme.

67–70 = 1–4 varied and an octave higher.

71–76 = 5–10, diverting bars 5-6 to (vi.) instead of (ii.), substituting an interrupted cadence for the medial close of bar 8, and smoothing out the rhythm of bar 10, closing into

Coda.

77–82.—Two bars tonic and dominant, with figure of main theme in bass shifted to second half of bar, answered by 4 declamatory bars of final close, melody in treble, with pause on subdominant before the penultimate dominant.

In some ways the form of this movement was anticipated by Beethoven in the Rondo of the earlier Sonata in G minor, published as Op. 49, No. 1.

Scherzo: Allegro. C major; with Trio, A minor (vi.).

However you pair the bars in the movement, you will find yourself out of step in the middle of the Scherzo, and again at the end of the Trio; unless you consent to listen naïvely and allow Beethoven's *sforzandos* and changes of pitch to push and pull you wherever he chooses. You will get into mere confusion if you try to make the cadences in the first strain fall on to strong bars by taking your time from bar 2, for you can maintain this only by supposing that the sudden *fortes* fall on weak bars; and if you can retain an " accentuation " so violently against the actual sounds, you will not be able to perceive any irregularity of rhythm that can prevent the theme from returning at bar 39/40 on the basis of weak cadences. On the other hand, this reversal cannot be supposed to be an intentional subtlety, so long as rhythm concerns the human ear at all. The plain facts that reach the ear are that none of the cadences in the scherzo is strong, and that the rhythm is sometimes displaced. The ear will probably take bars 33/34-36 as a 3-bar group echoed by bars 36/37-39. And the Coda is intelligible only when bars 60/61-64 are taken as a 4-bar clause entry on the 4th bar. The Trio begins on a main bar, but changes its step by the *sforzandos* in its second strain—an admirable illustration of Beethoven's way of appealing to human ears.

SCHERZO: *First Strain.*

$\frac{3}{8}$/1–8.—Three voices enter at 2-bar intervals, building a theme

(ab) into an 8-bar clause ending in half-close. Figures (a) and (b) overlap thus:

⁸/9-16.—Answering clause in G minor (v.) led by middle voice, while (a¹) rises in treble, the bass entering with (b) alone at 3rd bar, followed (at 5th bar) by octaves *forte* by way of final entry. Full close in dominant major. Repeat.

Middle Strain.

¹⁶/17-28.—Two steps of 2-bar sequence of (a¹) over (b) descending by tones through C minor, B♭ minor; followed by three steps with (b) over (a¹), through B♭ minor and A♭ to dominant of C minor, the home dominant. On this two more bars complete the period.

²⁸/29-39.—Dominant preparation for return; thrice 2 bars on (a¹) answered in higher octave by (a²) in various nuances of the dominant of C minor, with *sforzandos* on 3rd crotchet. The last of these 6 bars is given thrice and echoed by single treble voice, transforming (a²) into (a¹) in another 3 bars, merging into

Third Strain.

³⁹/40-47 = 1-8, substituting tonic full close for half-close.
⁴⁷/48-55.—Answering clause beginning in subdominant minor (iv.), followed by tonic minor and reproducing bars 13-16 *piano* in tonic.

Codetta.

⁵⁵/56-64.—Bars **²⁸/29-36** substantially reproduced in tonic, producing an emphatic flattened supertonic note. The sequel of the repeat, the Trio and the final Coda, all show that bar 60/61 initiates a 4-bar group, bringing the two last notes (x)

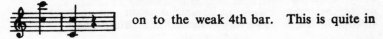 on to the weak 4th bar. This is quite in

conformity with the feeling of 3-bar groups aroused by bars 33/34-39. Repeat from bar 16/17.

TRIO: A minor (vi.).

65–72.—Eight-bar strain (thrice 2, +cadence; in effect 2+2+4) in A minor closing in its dominant minor. Repeated with crotchet up-beat.

73–88.—Continuation in two 4-bar steps (2+cadence); rising tequentially from C (♭III. of present key) through D minor (iv.) so dominant of present key. *Sforzandos* in the joints at bars 73/74 and 77/78 displace the rhythm, so that the cadences now end on strong bars. Eight bars in A minor, still emphasizing the change of step, complete the Trio. But the repeat from bar 72/73 is written out in full, because at the bar corresponding to 86 (the 3rd of the last 8-bar period as dated from the *sforzando*) the harmony is diverted so as to lead to an arpeggio on dominant of C. This makes, with the subsequent rests, a 4-bar dominant preparation for the Da Capo.

Coda.

106–109.—The Da Capo is followed by 4 bars, taking the close (x) down two steps of 3rds, closing into dominant in next period. This is intelligible only when the periods are dated from bar 60/61 of the Scherzo, a matter in which the ear finds no difficulty.

109/110–127.—Eight bars of sustained cadential melody over (a) and (a²) on dominant with flat 6th, closing into 8 similar bars on tonic with flat 2nd, closing into 3 final bars, the 4th represented by a pause. The conventional notation, omitting the anacrusis of bar 1, should really not be applied to bar 128 but to a 129th incomplete bar, as this Coda cannot possibly be construed with weak cadences.

Allegro assai: Rondo.   C major.

Main Theme.

1–8.—Eight-bar theme (A), 4 leading to threshold of dominant, answered by 4 returning to full close in tonic, containing figures (a), (b).

8/9–18.—New semiquaver theme (B) in complete contrast, producing effect of a middle strain. Three 2-bar steps lead into dominant, there closing into twice 1 bar, followed by 2 returning to tonic, closing into

Transition.

19–28.—Theme (A) resumed, diverted towards E minor (iii.);
figure (b) carried a step towards dominant of G (*not* D major)
and thence turned into a 4-bar descending scale, closing into that
dominant in next period.

First Episode in Dominant.

29–38.—Dating from 29, a new theme places a 2-bar figure
twice athwart the bar-accents (as usual Beethoven helps the ear
with *sforzandos*), the third time passing into an answering 4-bar
figure (1+1+2), closing into

39–54.—Repetition of above theme (note that bar 39 belongs
to the period) passing into minor, and carrying the answering
figure in 2-bar steps of sequence falling by tones, the third step
being carried downwards for 6 bars, finally closing into home
dominant. (The figure is itself sequential in half-bars descending
by 3rds. Hence its capacity for descending 3 octaves in 6 bars.)

55–68.—Dominant preparation for return; 4 times 2 bars in
dialogue between treble and bass, rising 3 octaves, and suggested
by previous figure (a kind of inversion); closing into thrice 2 bars
of (a) in dialogue, closing into

First Return.

69–76 = 1–8.

Transition to Second Episode.

⁷⁶/77–96.—Beginning like a counter-statement of theme (A),
the bass gives out a+b *fortissimo*, the harmony moving to (ii.).
This proves to be the first 4-bar step of a new sequence passing
from (ii.) to (iii.), where the 3rd step merges into a new process.
Vaguely suggested by (b) grouped with a scale-figure which,
whether upward or downward, cannot fail to remind us of (a), a
new sequence (quaver 3rds in contrary motion) passes down the
dominants (E minor, A minor, D minor) for three 2-bar steps,
followed by three 1-bar steps, closing, plus a new 4th bar, into A
minor (vi.).

97–102.—The new 4th bar gives rise to a further 4-bar cadence
into A minor, closing into 2 extra bars, closing into F in next
period. Beethoven might, with a larger pianoforte, have wished
to continue his bass figure in the lower octave at bar 100, but he
would certainly change it to the dotted crotchets at bar 101.

Second Episode, in Subdominant.

First Strain.

103–118.—New 8-bar melody (C) 4+4 (or 4 times 2), in F

major with dominant close, answered by 8 bars with melody in bass and tonic close.

Second Strain.

119–134.—New theme (D) on dominant, 4 times 2 bars with a figure given alternately with an upward and a downward direction, closing into 8 bars of first strain in soprano, closing in tonic.

135–166.—Repetition of Second Strain; but theme (C) diverges after 4th bar, being carried forward by bass in two 4-bar steps, F minor and A♭; thence continued by treble in C minor, the last 2 bars being detached in a further progression of 2-bar steps towards the home dominant, making 12 bars from the treble entry.

167–180.—Dominant preparation for return; 8 bars of theme (D) (2+2 with upward turn, 2+2 with downward, building up chord of 9th) and 4+2 of (a), closing into

Second Return.

181–188 = 1–8.

188/189–196.—The bass, entering with (a+b) as at bar 76/77, now achieves a complete repetition of the theme, the harmonies remaining entirely within the key.

196/197–206 = 8/9–18.

207–216.—Theme (A) is now prevented from modulating; figure (b) developing as in bars 23–26, but entirely within tonic key, closing into

Recapitulation of First Episode.

217–231 = 29–43 transposed to tonic.

232–244.—The theme rises from C minor to an additional step in E♭ (♭III.). The following 2-bar sequences now rise, instead of falling as in bars 45–49. Consequently, the 3rd step, when carried on in downward sequence for 6 bars, arrives punctually at the same home dominant as did the sequence of bars 49–54, with the less trouble since it does not need to shorten its stride in the last bar.

245–258 = 55–68.—The positions of (a) modified to suit new position of forthcoming return.

Coda.

259–268.—Theme (A) enters in lower parts below a trill, avoiding foreign harmony in 4th bar. *R.H.* takes up (b) (with trill below), using non-modulating chromatic detail.

269–297.—Rapid chromatic descent suggested by (b), 4 bars

with 3 steps a bar, followed by 6 rising bars (2 steps a bar), and the period completed by 2 bars with 2 chords leading to cadential $\frac{6}{4}$. This, after 4 bars of unaccompanied treble with rising scale like (a), resolves on to dominant represented by trill above and answering scale in bass. After 8 bars the trill, having become doubled and trebled, continues singly for 4 more, rising to D♯ as if to close into a melody beginning on E as 3rd of C.   Pause.

298–305.—The E arrives, but proves to be 5th of chord of A major (VI.), in which key the theme (a, b) enters in bass, faintly (*calando*).   Pause.

Again the theme is attempted in A minor (*rallentando*; not the same thing as *calando*), diverted towards home dominant.

306–312.—*Tempo primo*. Figure (a) on dominant in bass, closing into tonic, and answered by downward scale in treble, leading to final chords.

4

SONATA IN E FLAT MAJOR, Op. 7

Allegro molto e con brio. E♭ major.

First Group.

Bars 1–4.—Four-bar clause on tonic chord consisting of figure (a) in two positions.

5–16.—New 8-bar phrase (2+2+4) distributing a new 2-bar figure among three voices and closing into free repetition of last 4 bars in bass, closing into the next period. (Do not try to derive the three themes of the First Group from each other—*e.g.*, by alleging that the *L.H.* in bars 5–10 is developing (a) by filling out its steps and inverting it. The " logical development " of the sonata style depends on what sort of kaleidoscope pattern can be made of all its materials, and not upon their origins, whether single or multiple.)

17–24.—New 4-bar theme (B) in imitative scales, closing into repetition, led by treble instead of by bass, and leading to

Transition.

25–34.—Figure (a) on dominant of IV. (D♭ in bass) answered by new figure resolving the chord. These 4 bars again a step higher (B♭ minor v.). Figure (a) a third time on G♭ (augmented 6th), resolving in next clause on to dominant of V.

35–40.—Six bars of dominant preparation; twice 2 self-repeating, and 2 in quaver motion.

Second Group in Dominant.

41–50.—New 8-bar theme (twice 2 self-repeating, then 1+1+2) in double counterpoint, closing into 2 extra bars on tonic, leading to

51–58.—Variation of 41–48 with the parts interchanged in the manner of double counterpoint, though both parts are otherwise altered. This closes into

59–66.—New melody (C), built sequentially from new

figure (c)  with bass in contrary

35

motion, 2+2+4, closing into dominant.

67–80.—Bars 59–65 repeated with (c) varied thus:

 etc.

and after 6th bar expanding into a development of ć descending the scale on dominant pedal for 6 more bars, after which the bass suddenly rises to F♯ with a diminished 7th maintained for 2 bars.

81–92.—Resolution of the diminished 7th into C major. This is not an enhanced dominant but an intrusive key violently opposed to the present B♭. Self-repeating 2-bar figure in this key (with its dominant as bass); these 4 bars repeated with a new counterpoint in quaver scales, closing into 4 bars which, as if nothing had happened, calmly return to B♭, closing into

93–110.—New 8-bar theme (4 times 1, +4) closing into repetition in broken octaves, expanded by 2 extra bars closing into

111–126.—Slow-moving 8-bar tremolo theme on tonic pedal coloured by minor 9th, closing into repetition in lower position, closing into

127–138.—Cadence theme (d)

in three 2-bar tonic and dominant groups, the dominant in successively higher positions, closing into 4 bars (2+2) of tonic chord.

Exposition repeated.

Development.

137–140.—Four bars of (a) on dominant of C minor, closing into

141–152.—Theme (B), starting in C minor and passing in three 4-bar steps through A♭ to F minor, closing into

153–164.—Development of (d), starting with two pairs of bars in F minor. A third pair rises into G minor; a fourth pair confirms G minor; a fifth pair gets at its dominant from above and is endorsed by a sixth pair, which closes into

165–168.—Four bars continuing the syncopated rhythm *piano*, while the bass rises through D♯, leading to

169–188.—Figure (a) in A minor (dominant bass), alternating in 4-bar groups with a new cantabile figure (twice 2 self-repeating bars), closing into the same 8 bars in D minor, closing into (a) on D minor triad (2 bars), of which triad the fifth rises in *L.H.* to B♮ and falls in *R.H.*, as part of (a), to A♮. Thus from the remotest possible keys we have suddenly reached the home dominant, which immediately closes into the

Recapitulation.

First Group.
189–200 = 1–12, with *fortissimo* in first 4 bars.
201–214.—Bars 13 foll. are diverted towards subdominant, into which the first 4-bar group closes. A 4-bar descending scale-theme follows, suggestive of theme (B), and closing into self-repetition, which leads through 2 extra bars to the home dominant. (It is difficult to believe that the omission of a flat to the G in bar 214 is not an oversight, but there is no authority for G♭.)
215–220 = 35–40 on home dominant.

Second Group.
221–312 = 41–132 in tonic. Apart from changes induced by the limits of a 5-octave pianoforte (which cut both ways—*e.g.*, as between bars 66 and 245), the only alteration is in the upper counterpoint of bars 41–46.
The cadence-theme (d) after its 6th bar breaks into the

Coda.
313–322.—The bass rising unexpectedly to B, the melody makes figure (d) transform itself dramatically into (a). This initiates a new 8-bar group at bar 315, passing from (vi.) through (ii.) to home dominant chord, down which it drops in half-bars, closing into
323–338.—Resumed development of theme (c) and (c'); 4 bars of (c), repeated as 4 of (c') in inner part, and followed by carrying (c') down two octaves of scale in bass; arriving, after 8 bars, at dominant.
339–350.—Figure (d) developed on dominant implied as bass for the whole of these 12 bars, including the 4 of chromatic descent that lead to 2-bar close into
351–362.—Final appearance of (a), with its bar-accents reversed and with continuation in crotchets (by " diminution " rising up for 4 double-quick steps, completing its 8-bar period and closing into final chords—(4 bars, 2+1+⌢).

(Do not attempt to regard (a) as similarly displaced elsewhere. The whole point of its final appearance is that it has never before been shifted off the first bar of its period.)

Largo con gran espressione : C major (VI.).
A, B, A; with elements of recapitulation in an elaborate coda.

Main Theme.

1-8.—First strain, an 8-bar melody (2+2+4) closing in tonic and containing figure (a) in second bar, as answer to simpler

initial figure

9-14.—Second strain; a 2-bar clause in dominant, repeated with higher top-note and repeated again with descent of bass from A through Ab to G and dominant 7th at climax of melody, returning to

15-24.—Third strain, resuming the first melody and diverging after 2nd bar into rising sequences. These originate in (a), and proceed over a bass, that rises chromatically for 2 bars up to A. Sudden subsidence into full close, which is interrupted by diminished 7th in D minor (ii.). Here 2 bars in broken rhythm rise in sequence with a dramatic *fortissimo*, leading to F (IV.). A third bar, *pp* and *legato* in the same rhythm, leads back to the full close attempted at bar 19. This is no longer interrupted. It closes into bar 24, which thereupon modulates to Ab (bVI.).

Middle Episode Ab (bVI.) and allied keys.

25-36.—New melody moving in 4-bar clauses. First clause begins and ends in Ab. Second clause in F minor. The bass then leads to Db, where third clause begins and proceeds on rising bass, reaching Ab with augmented sixth, and so impinging upon home dominant in next clause.

37-41.—Twice 2 bars on and below home dominant, without definite theme, and with no harmony but octaves. Suddenly in a 5th bar the bass, treating its F# as Gb, resolves on to dominant of Bb, closing into

42-50.—Entry of main theme in Bb (bVII.), a key as repugnant to the tonic C major as the opposite modulation was to Bb in bars 81-89 of the first movement. After 2nd bar, figure (a) is repeated a step higher, thus reaching home tonic minor. Then it is developed by imitation for 2 bars, leading to a diminished 7th, which, lasting for 3 bars, drifts into a 4th bar of cadential

harmonies, closing into

Return of Main Theme.

51–72 = 1–22 with a few new ornaments in second and third strains.

73.—Instead of the resumed close at bars 23–24 there is a new and more melodious cadence into the

Coda.

74–78.—During the above cadence an inner part drifts into the theme of the Middle Episode transposed to the home tonic. In its 2nd bar it diverges into a sequence, rising through (ii.) and (IV.) (on a rising bass) until its 4th bar impinges upon the home dominant, on which we wait for another bar.

79–83.—Four tonic-dominant bars (twice 2) developing (a) in contrary motion, and followed by a 5th bar (bare octaves), closing into

84–86.—New cadence-theme, twice 1 bar with an added close.

86/87–90.—Over a chromatically descending bass the main theme is rounded off in a final 4 bars.

Allegro: Eb major.   Scherzo and Trio.

The scherzo is developed on a scale that, as in some of Mozart's largest menuets, gives its melodic form a suggestion of sonata-form with differentiated themes: the trio is a purely lyric melody.

First Strain.

1–16.—Eight-bar clause (4, +1+1+2) coming to half-close; containing figure (a) in bars 1–2 and detaching figure (b) from its 4th bar.

The next clause begins to repeat, but the bass diverts it to C minor at 4th bar. After a bar's rest, (b¹) is repeated a step lower, closing into Bb (the dominant). After another bar's rest the whole figure (minus the first note) is taken up in Bb. The pauses have made the ear unready to recognize that the music is still moving in regular 4-bar groups. Bar 16 is thus at the end of its period and preliminary to

17–24.—(Bb V.) Two more bars of (b²), closing into a running cadence-figure, 2 bars closing into repetition in lower octave, closing into 2 of tonic chord of Bb. Repeat from bar 1.

Middle Strain.

25–42.—Figure (a) arises in 2-part imitation (led by bass) on dominant (diminished 7th) of F minor (ii.). After 6 bars (thrice 2), the upper part carries (a) forward into a new phrase, 2+2 in (ii.), repeated with new grace-note, and then carried downwards in 4 bars on home dominant, closing into

Third Strain.

43–50 = 1–8 with slight change in bass.

51–57.—Theme (a, b) continued in tonic minor, moving to C♭ (♭VI.). Here the pause proves to be an extra bar, for the next two echoing fragments of (b²) must be counted from bar 56 so as to close into

58–69.—Two ruminating 4-bar phrases in ♭VI.; the first closing into self-repetition, in which the bass diverts the harmony at the 4th bar by continuing to rise; leading to another 4, rising above the home dominant, with pause.

70–79.—After 2 bars of home dominant, figure (b) in a new form slightly differing from that of bars 16 foll. is developed for 8 bars (2 repeated; and 2 in higher position, repeated). This passage closes into

80–85 = 19–22 expanded by a 3rd step in a lower octave, closing into

Codetta.

86–95.—Four-bar cadence-phrase on tonic pedal in double counterpoint, closing into repetition with parts interchanged, closing into 2 bars of final tonic in the shape of bars 23–24.

Minore (Trio in tonic minor).

96–111.—First strain of lyric melody outlined in thick arpeggios, and consisting of 16 bars ending in half-close on dominant; 4 answered by self-repetition, reharmonized so as to close into ♭III., thence proceeding to home dominant in 8 bars.

112–123.—Second strain beginning in key of minor dominant and, as in first strain, diverging at 7th bar, whence it impinges on home dominant, leading in a third 4-bar group to

124–139.—Third strain, resuming first strain and diverging at 7th bar to subdominant, whence another 8 bars close in tonic, overlapping the following Codetta by 2 bars.

138–149.—Codetta; new 4-bar cadence-theme (in plain notes, the arpeggio figure being confined to bass) on tonic pedal, closing into self-repetition, closing into bare 5th, from which arise the unaccompanied notes of the major triad, leading back to *Da Capo*. (Note the mark *ppp*, rare in Beethoven, but authentic here.)

Rondo: Poco allegretto e grazioso.   E♭ major.

Main Theme.

½/1–8.—Strain A of lyric melody; 4 bars poised on dominant, answered by varied self-repetition, closing into tonic. The figure of the 3rd bar becomes detached in a later development.

⁸/9–16.—Strain B; 4 bars (2 self-repeating) containing a new·

figure (b)   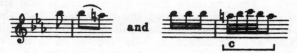   and closing on

bare dominant with pause.   Four more bars conclude recapitulating bars 3/4–8 an octave higher.

Transition.

¹⁶/17–26.—Figure (b) taken up by bass in 2-bar steps in dialogue with treble which echoes with (b²).   The 2nd step leads to C minor, and is followed by a dialogue in B♭ (V.) on (b²) for twice 2 bars.   The figure (b²), having gone through the following stages,

is now quite unrecognizable, and its last turn fairly deserves a new name (c).

27–35.—Four bars (2+2) tonic-and-dominant dialogue in B♭ (V.) between bass and treble, on a derivative of (c); leading to 5 cadential bars, 3 on (c)+2, closing into

First Episode B♭ (V.).

(There would be no harm in dating the whole Episode from bar 27, but this is the first really new paragraph.)

36–50.—New theme; best regarded as dating from bar 36, though the melody begins on the second half of that bar. In a 4-bar phrase (1+1+2), the first 2 bars, with melody in bass, descend sequentially from (ii.) to tonic, and are answered by 2 bars in treble closing on to dominant and into counterstatement. This has an imitative treble, and expands the second pair of bars in tonic, insisting on them twice; finally closing on to 3 bars of tonic which proves to be the home dominant, the 3rd bar merging into the initial half-bar of the main theme.

First Return.

[50]/51–62 = $\frac{1}{2}$/1–12 with slight variation in bar 11. The bare dominant is held for a whole measured bar instead of the pause.

63.—The dominant rises to B♮, closing into

Second Episode : C minor (vi.).

64–71.—First strain of a symmetrical theme (D) with repeats. Eight bars (twice 2+4), starting in C minor and modulating to its ♭III. (Notice that the ear does not perceive this as a return to the tonic. The sense of tonality depends on the sense of form.) In the first 4 bars the bass has a demisemiquaver figure which we may call (d), and the treble has a rhythmic figure (e). In the second 4 bars (d) is in treble, and (e) has been disintegrated except for the syncopated *sforzandos* in the *L.H.* which compress the rhythm. First strain repeated.

72–80.—Second strain. Four bars of (e) over (d) passing through subdominant to dominant of our present C minor, on which 4 bars (twice 2) of preparation plus 1 extra bar close into

81–87a.—Third strain, resuming first strain in 2 bars of (e) over (d) answered by 2 of (d) over (e); passing to subdominant and concluded by 4-bar cadence with (d) in both hands, the *L.H.* followed by the *R.* Repeat from bar 72.

87b–93. The repetition closes (with overlap) into six more bars of (d), the *R.H.* imitating the *L.* After 2 bars the *L.H.* ceases on the B♮ as bass of a diminished 7th, the *R.H.* reiterating (d). After another 2 bars the bass resolves on to B♭ as home dominant, thus proving that the previous B♮ has changed enharmonically to C♭. The treble glides into the

Second Return of Main Theme.

[93]/94–109 = $\frac{1}{2}$/1–16.

Recapitulation of Transition and First Episode, in Tonic.

[109]/110–119.—The transition diverges into (ii.), instead of (vi.) at its 4th bar, thus bringing the sequel into the tonic. Two bars longer, however, are spent in (ii.), where figure (c) appears before continuing in the tonic, which it reaches by a new downward step at bar 118.

120–139 = 27–46.

140–142.—The last close is diverted on to the home dominant, 2 bars on which lead to

Final Return of Main Theme.

142/143–154 = ½/1–12 with higher octave and new variation in strain A.

Coda.

155–156.—The home dominant (having paused as well as being held for the full bar) once more rises to B♮, but *pianissimo* and as dominant (C♭) of ♭II. (written as E♮ major).

156/157–165.—On the second bar of this remote dominant the main theme enters. Its 3rd bar, figure (a), is repeated, and followed by a sudden shift back to the home dominant. This is not an enharmonic modulation, but, like the E major itself, a mere change of notation. Such passages can be tested by transposing a semitone up or down, when the enharmonic notation will become impracticable unless the change is really enharmonic. Here, for instance, if the modulation were from F to E, no enharmonic change can be suspected; the bass of bars 160–161 will become simply

This abrupt return is followed by 4 bars in tonic, developing figure (a) into a cadence-phrase, closing into

166–183.—Epilogue on theme of Second Episode transformed into a calm lyric melody. Figure (d) is softened into a formula of accompaniment in the bass, while (e) is developed into a 4-bar melody, closing into self-repetition, which is expanded to 6 bars, rising to a climax, and closing into tonic-and-dominant final clause on tonic pedal, (2+2+4) of tonic chord. It is not necessary to see in bars 177 foll. an allusion to (b²).

5
SONATA IN C MINOR, Op. 10, No. 1.

Allegro molto e con brio: C minor.

First Group.

Bars 1–8.—Eight-bar theme in two 4-bar steps, containing figures (a) and (b)

9–21.—Arising out of (b²) a new cantabile develops by threefold repetition of a 2-bar figure, expanded the third time to 4 bars of downward scale. At bar 17 a new 2-bar group leads in three steps, broken with rests, into the next period. The whole passage from bar 9 proves that bar 9 is unaccented, a fact not forced on the listener until the broken phrases mark the rhythmic grouping from bar 17 onwards. But theorists who tell us to carry this rhythm back to bar 1 impute a ridiculous abstruseness to Beethoven and ascribe marvellous prophetic powers to the human ear. They also fail to observe that, whatever their success in so construing the opening, they will have to admit that an odd bar or an overlap has intervened before the exposition is finished ; since otherwise the repeat, the development and the recapitulation will alternately come out on the other rhythmic basis. Meanwhile no listener is going to suppose that the bump on bar 1 represents a weaker accent than the un-supported first note of bar 2 ; nor is any intelligent player going to suppose that such an interpretation could be made appreciable to the ear. Then, since we must admit that these are odd bars and rhythmic displacements, why not assign them where they confirm the obvious facts of *forte* chords and the impressions of human listeners whose rhythmic sense recognizes that some impressions are weaker than others, and that in course of time impressions may change ?

22–31.—First theme resumed, as if to make a counter-statement, but compressed, with omission of (b²), into three 2-bar steps, followed by a new 4-bar close (the last bar silent).

Transition.

32–47.—New theme in 4-bar sequential steps, starting in A♭ (VI.) and passing through F minor (iv.) and D♭ (♭II.) and then (continuing regular descent of bass) in 4 more bars, closing on to dominant of E♭ (III.).

48–55.—Eight bars dominant preparation (4+4 with variation) leading to

Second Group : E♭ (III.).

56–93.—Large paragraph articulated as follows :

    [56-63].—Eight-bar tonic-and-dominant theme (4+4).

    [64-69].—Variation of above diverging after 6th bar into

    [70-77].—New continuation in broader single 8-bar phrase.

    [78-85].—Variation of this 8-bar phrase diverging after 4th bar into 2+2 bars carrying its rising steps twice a bar around the dominant (as ⁶₄) and followed by

    [86-93].—Further hovering around the ⁶₄ with figure (a) for 4 bars, followed by 4 bars of final ⁶₄ and resolution closing into

94–105.—Cadence theme, tonic-and-dominant in two self-repeating 4-bar phrases (2+2) with insistence twice on last 2 bars.

Exposition repeated.

Development.

106–117.—First theme in tonic major which turns out to be dominant of F minor (iv.). This being shown in 8 bars, that key is confirmed in another 4 on (a) (with an allusion to bars 28–30) closing into

118–135.—*Episode.* New cantabile in 8-bar phrases, con-

taining figure (x).  Eight bars

in F minor; repeated in B♭ minor; two bars detached so as to close into D♭.

136–157.—Sequential development of (x) starting in D♭ and passing in three 2-bar steps to B♭ minor, thence carried on in bass (retaining the crotchet flow but drifting into another figure) in three 4-bar steps, passing through F minor to the home tonic, reaching its dominant by expanding the 3rd step to 8 bars.

158–167.—Ten bars of themeless dominant preparation, consisting of 4 repeated and expanded to 6.

The two extra bars close into the

Recapitulation.

First Group.
168–188 = 1–21 unaltered.
189–190.—The short counter-statement (22–30) is omitted, the theme closing into a bare octave.

Transition.
191–214.—Starting on D♭, the first phrase of the transition is given twice in the extremely remote key of G♭, and passes thence through E♭ minor by descent of bass to dominant of F minor. The 8 bars of dominant preparation follow as for that key, the first 4 being minor and the variation major, closing into

Second Group : (IV.) and (i.).
215–228 recapitulate 56–69 in this unusual subdominant major.
229–232.—Four extra bars, starting with an F minor chord, swing the theme round to the tonic minor, closing into
233–284.—Renewed recapitulation of whole Second Group (as from bar 56) all translated into the minor mode, and all *forte* until the cadence-theme. Its final slow appoggiatura is replaced by a plain chord followed by a *fortissimo* full close.

Adagio molto : A♭ major (VI.).   Sonata form without Development.

First Group : A♭.
1–16.—Symmetrical melody: the first 8-bar strain (2+2+4) ending with half-close, the second strain recapitulating it with full close and flowing accompaniment.

Transition.
17–23.—New 2-bar figure moving in three steps through supertonic, tonic and minor tonic chord to dominant of dominant, on which an additional bar's preparation leads to

Second Group in Dominant
24–30.—New 4-bar phrase in rising sequence (2+2); repeated, in variation, which at 3rd bar closes into
31–35.—Five-bar phrase (3½ + 1½) on rising bass, closing into
36–44.—Varied repetition of the 5-bar phrase with the steps of bass urged upwards in 4th bar (where the bass formerly delayed its rise), so that the 4th bar is on augmented sixth above dominant, resolving accordingly into a 2-bar cadence, closing into its repetition and resolution in lower octave.

45.—A seventh on the home dominant leads to

Recapitulation.

First Group.
46–61 = 1–16 with new ornaments in melody and accompaniment.

Transition.
62–70.—The 3rd step of the transition-theme is to a $\frac{6}{4}$ of Fb (bVI.), from which 3 bars (instead of 1) are needed to lead to the 2 of preparation on the home dominant.

Second Group.
71–90 = 24–43 in tonic, closing into

Coda.
91–101.—First theme on flowing accompaniment, with new 4-bar second clause gliding into self-repetition, which comes to tonic close, overlapping into
102–112.—Tonic and dominant swing (2+2+2), closing into 5 bars of tonic chord.

FINALE: Prestissimo: C minor.   Sonata form.
At the outset Beethoven's notation shows that he is determined to put his initial figure before the first accent, though this produces weak cadences, besides an overlap either at bar 8 or 12. Beethoven, the naïve listener and other sensible people, know not and care not where the overlap comes.   The important fact is that both the main themes present themselves alternately at both of the two rhythmic angles.   The shifting of the first theme is unmistakable, during its own progress, in the bass at bars 23–24 foll. The possibility of an overlap at bar 8 gives an ambiguous case there, and ambiguity is a definite æsthetic fact.   The repetition of the Exposition confirms Beethoven's notation of the opening, and so does the return after the short but rhythmically involved Development.

First Group.
$\frac{6}{8}$ 1–7.—Symmetrical theme containing figure (a)

and answering (1—1—2) tonic-to-dominant by similar procedure from dominant-to-tonic, overlapping (unless the overlap is 4 bars later) into

8–16.—Four bars (2+2 self-repeating) developing (a) on tonic, with subdominant colour; closing into tonic-and-dominant run down two octaves with insistence in fourth bar, closing into pause on dominant.

Second Group : Eb (III.).

¹⁶/17–27.—New theme (B) containing figure (b)

It begins as a melody proceeding in 2-bar steps. Whichever way we choose to regard the rhythm, we shall find that the bass, with (b) answering a descending scale in treble like a free inversion, has reversed the bar-accent from bar 23 (the 7th bar) onwards. The total result, on any reading, is an 8-bar melody in 2-bar steps, expanded to 11 bars by thrice insisting on its cadence, and closing into

28–36.—Figure (a) in bass answered, after 2 bars, in treble and made into a 6-bar clause by a 3-bar run, which is repeated in the bass, closing into

37–46.—Cadence theme, a 3-bar phrase (1+2), the first bar possibly suggested by rhythm of (a²), repeated with variation, and followed by 2 bars of a new figure on tonic, and one final chord with measured pause showing rhythmic position of main theme on repeat.

Development.

⁴⁶/47–56.—Two-bar development of (a) in bass imitated in treble, answered by 2 bars overlapping at bar 50 to new 2-bar process through dominant of F minor (iv.). This process is carried 2 bars further with descending bass, reaching the home dominant on the diminished seventh, on which (a) is carried down for 4 bars, ending with pause. Though this Development is extremely short, it shows enough rhythmic and harmonic variety to earn its title; and its treatment of figure (a) is quite distinct from any incident in the Exposition.

Recapitulation.

First Group.

⁵⁶/57–73 = ⅝/1–16, with slight variation at bars 10–11.

Second Group.

^{73}/74–101 = ^{16}/17–44 in tonic, with permanent change to minor mode from bar 25½ (82½) onwards, and with (a) transferred from bass to treble at bars 28–29 (85–86) with omission of the tremolo. Note the brightness caused by transposing bars ^{16}/17–25 a sixth up instead of a third down. The final cadence-figure (bars 43–44) does not close, but is continued in the

Coda.

102–106.—The cadence-figure continued on dominant of D♭ (♭II.), culminating in 3 bars of slow melodious preparation thereon, with pause.

^{106}/107–114.—Theme (B) in ♮II, *ritardando*, pausing on dominant seventh at 6th bar. This turns enharmonically into diminished seventh (Adagio), resolving into C minor cadence at bar 114 (Tempo I.), closing into

115–123.—Combination of (b) and (a) in 2-bar cadential groups on tonic pedal with subdominant colour (hence major tonic chord); (2+2+1+1), and final 2 bars of tonic.

6

SONATA IN F MAJOR, Op. 10, No. 2.

Allegro.

The tempo is moderate; scarcely, if at all, faster than that
of the first movement of Op. 14, No. 2. An all-breve in notes
of double value would give an unmistakable idea of the tempo;
but the ⁴⁄₄ notation expressed the Haydnesque element in the
mood. There is an exquisite little quartet by Haydn in F major,
Op. 50, No. 5, the first movement of which is in just this tempo.
Haydn's design, however, is spacious and flowing, while
Beethoven is here bursting with epigram and crowding as many
different ideas into his kaleidoscope as will permit it to turn at all.
This sonata remained a favourite with Beethoven himself for
many years after it was written.

First Group : F major.

1–12.—Four-bar clause (2+2) containing iambic rhythmic
figure (a) ♪ 𝄖♪ answered by a figure (b) filling up the same
iambic foot with a triplet; followed by 8-bar continuation with
sustained melody (4+4), closing in tonic

¹²/13–18.—Counter-statement of (a, b), the 2nd step on an
augmented sixth leading to dominant of A minor (iii.), which is
insisted on by two more bars into which three iambics of the
rhythm of (b) are crowded.

Second Group in Dominant (V.).

¹⁸/19–29.—New theme in C major (instead of the expected
A minor). It moves in 4-bar phrases, of which the first is
tonic to dominant, answered by the second with dominant-to-
tonic. A third group moves to dominant of dominant; its 4th
bar overlapping with

30–37.—Eight bars (2+2+1+1+2) of dominant preparation,
as if we had not already established the new key; thus giving, in
retrospect, an introductory character to the whole previous
theme. The Recapitulation will shed further light on this.

38–54.—New 4-bar theme poised on local dominant, and
closing in tonic (C major); followed by variation in the minor,
with interrupted cadence on to A♭. An echoing chord leads
back to the dominant of C, on which four bars of dominant and

tonic (4 times 1) lead to a 4-bar cadence, beginning with three on supertonic with figure (b), and finally closing into

55–66.—Cadence-theme, a new 4-bar phrase (1+1 in treble+2 in bass) closing into varied repetition, of which the last two bars are echoed in treble, closing into a final tag (c).

 Exposition repeated.

Development.

67 68.—The tag (c) echoed on A as dominant of D.

69–76.—Four-bar phrase (2 tonic+2 dominant) in D minor, with (c) in bass and new counterpoint (x) in treble, closing into repetition in free double counterpoint, closing into

77–94.—*Episode.* A new 4-bar theme in D minor closes into 2 similar bars leading to G minor, where the 4-bar theme is repeated, slightly varied, closing into four bars leading through C minor to B♭, where another repetition of the new theme closes into

95–117.—The process of (x) over (c) and (c) over (x) resumed; starting in B♭, answered by B♭ minor. A third 4-bar group moves to dominant of F (not, in this context, revealed as the home dominant). A fourth group gives chords of F minor and D♭, from which point the bass proceeds chromatically down to A (reached after 2 bars, with enharmonic change of seventh on B♭ to augmented sixth).

Four bars and a pause on this dominant of D may be regarded as ending this very episodic Development, which has throughout pointedly avoided all connection with the Exposition except for the tag (c).

Recapitulation.

First Group.

[117]/118–129 = 1–12 in the bright key of D (VI.), a remoter region than any reached in the Exposition and Development. The discrepancy between the position of (b) in bars 120–121 and its original position in bars 3–4 is an admirable subtlety which avoids weakening the brightness until the right moment comes for clouding it over.

130–136.—After a bar's pause the group (a+b) starts again, passing wistfully through G minor (ii.) to the home dominant, on which (b) is thrice crowded into two extra bars.

[136]/137–144 = Bars ⁴/5–12 at home in the tonic. Though the bass starts its accompaniment-figure in the last bar there is no overlap; but the Second Group follows at once.

Second Group in Tonic.

[144] 145–152 = [18] 19–24 in tonic.   The second 4-bar phrase is followed by

153–161.—Two new steps with melody in bass and accompaniment in treble.   The 1st step is in the tonic minor and moves to dominant of A♭ (♭III.).   The 2nd step confirms A♭, closing into two more bars that move to the home dominant, closing into it in next bar which initiates the passage of dominant dreparation without the overlap that occurred at bar 30.

162–202 = 30–65 in tonic.   To the cadence in bars 53–54 an enhanced repetition is added, and the insistence on the last two bars (63–64) of the cadence-theme is doubled.

There is no coda; but in private playing it is worth while trying the effect of repeating the second part.   Beethoven certainly saw the point of the tag (c) rising from F to A as contrasted with its former fall; and, if we are not impatient, the contrast of the episodic development and the novel strokes of genius in the recapitulation will gain by repetition, welding the total diversity into a more lyric unity.   At all events Beethoven never wrote a repeat-mark without thought of its effect at the moment when the repetition begins and its effect on what follows upon its end; though he may forget the effect of its total length, or may disagree with our opinion on that point.

Allegretto: F minor (i.).   Menuet and Trio with varied Da Capo.

Bars 1–8.—Single strain in F minor modulating to ♭III. and repeated.   The grace note in bar 6 is probably short. Beethoven had already proved this in the Menuet of Op. 2, No. 1 by contrasting it with a written-out quaver in the next bar; and the distinction appears in the varied Da Capo of the present movement.

[8] 9–16.—Middle strain; 8 bars of imitative rising sequence on a new figure (2 – 2 – 2 – half-close), closing on to dominant with pause.

17–30.—First strain resumed.   After 4 bars a lower part imitates bars [2] 3–4, and works their figure into a 4-bar cadence (twice 1 – 2) as bass to an independent melody above.   This cadence is repeated in lower octave.

31–38.—Codetta, a new 4-bar clause with medial tonic close followed by compressed repetition closing on accented 3rd bar. This disposes of any suggestion to view the rest as beginning elsewhere than with bar 1 as main accent.

Trio, D♭ major (♭VI.).

39–54.—Sixteen-bar strain built sequentially; 4÷4÷8 in D♭, modulating to its dominant.

55–70.—Varied repetition of 39–54 with contrapuntal bass and considerable changes of harmony, replacing 2nd and 3rd steps by steps in (ii.) and (iii.), necessitating similar freedom in arriving at the dominant close.

70/71–94.—Two 4-bar steps (melody in *L.H.* with answering counterpoint in *R.*) returning through (ii.) to D♭, where the 16-bar strain is resumed (using the *L.H.* counterpoint). Its second step is in (vi.); after which 8 bars, without counterpoint, close quietly in the present tonic, ending on an accented bar.

94/95–118 = 70/71–94 with grace-notes added to treble counterpoint, and a beautiful chromatic detail just before the close (114 = 90).

119–124.—Another 4-bar step moves in bare octaves from D♭ to C, which is the home dominant. On this 2 bars of chord of seventh close into the

Da Capo (varied).

125–132 = 1–8.

132–140 = 1–8 varied. (Note the long appoggiatura in the bar representing bar 6.)

140/141–170 = 8/9–38 varied. The downward inflections in bars 141–146 are no mere discrepancy from the upward inflections of bars 9–15. Note also the contrast between the *crescendo* to *forte* at the end and the original *piano* close.

Presto: F Major.

Sonata form with archaic (or melodic) exposition, but considerable development and expanded recapitulation.

Exposition.

1–8.—Four-bar theme (twice 1÷twice 1) containing two figures, which in course of development become detached by bars instead of by metrical feet. The Greek letters *a*, *β* here illustrate the metrical view: and the letters (a), (b) show the figures that Beethoven actually develops:

The theme is announced by the bass and answered at the octave by a middle voice.

8/19–22.—A treble enters with the theme in the dominant, and carries (b) onwards into D minor, thence making a 4-bar close (2÷2) in C. This 4-bar close is repeated, expanded so as to defer its tonic chord (of C) to the next period.

23–32.—Cadence-group in C on tonic pedal, making a 4-bar group (1+1+2) of (a) in an inner part, plus a new figure (c)

with a counterpoint (x) in contrary motion above. The group closes into self-repetition, followed by two tonic bars. Exposition repeated.

Development.

³²/33–40.—Four bars of a modified compound of (a+b) rising up the chord of A♭ (♭III., or, reckoned from previous C major, ♭VI.), and closing in that key into the whole theme on a homophonic bass, closing into

41–50.—Answer in upper octave. (Note that Beethoven explicitly refrains from beginning this answer on the up quaver. He wishes bar 41 to initiate a new stage.)

The *L.H.* follows the *R.* in 3rds. The 3rd initiates a new development of (b) in imitative 4-bar groups, first closing into B♭ minor, thence into F minor, closing into

51–62.—New sequential process grouping (b) in dialogue between upper parts, while bass moves in 2-bar steps up from one dominant to the next—viz., through C minor, G minor, and D minor. The 2-bar groups fall into pairs, and the 3rd pair closes into

63–68.—Six bars preparation on dominant of D, the last 2 without theme.

69–86.—Cadence-group (a+c) in D major with (x) prominent above in contrary motion to lower part. The 4-bar theme having repeated itself, figure (c), with its inversion in treble, descends in 2-bar sequential steps, passing down the dominants. The 2nd step having reached B♭, 4 bars of descending scale reach the home dominant, on which 2 more bars close into

Recapitulation.

⁸⁶ 87–106.—Theme (a, b) in bass with new running counterpoint above, answered by treble with the new counterpoint below. The 4th bar of this answer is diverted to G minor (ii.), closing into a repetition of these 8 bars in that key, modulating at the last moment to B♭ (IV.). Here a third 4-bar clause closes into

107–124.—New version of theme in broken octaves over

homophonic bass, reducing (b) to outline. After the 4 bars of the theme, this outline is carried down the scale of B♭ minor in 4 more bars, reaching a phase of the home dominant, whence a new sequence rises in half-bar steps for 4 bars, followed by 6 that worked from (iv.) to a close into the tonic. The actual close reproduces the treble of bars 21–22, and so leads to

Cadence-Group.

125–132 = 23–29 in tonic, closing into

Coda.

133–150.—The cadence-group is continued in the shape it assumed during the Development (bars 69–75). Its 8 bars close into a 2-bar version of (c) on tonic, which, closing into itself four times in alternating parts, ends the work. The effect of repeating from the Development is to follow this end by a dramatically violent change to ♭III., but the total result is not as interesting as that of the second repeat in the First Movement.

7

SONATA IN D MAJOR, Op. 10, No. 3.

Presto: D major.   Sonata form.

First Group.
  Bars 1–4.—Four-bar unison theme (A) in tonic, ending with pause on dominant, containing figure (a)

The rhythm dates its main accent from bar 2.
  5–10.—Six-bar phrase of descending sequences of (a), harmonized below a sketchy upper part, and coming to a full close.
  [10]/11–16.—The 6-bar phrase repeated *forte*, with the upper part in bass, and with intensified close.
  [16]/17–22.—Theme (A) extended upwards in 6-bar phrase reaching F♯ (=dominant of vi.) with a pause.

Transition-Themes.
  [22]/23–30.—New 8-bar melody (4+4) in vi. (B minor) modulating to iii. (F♯ minor).
  [30]/31–53.—Sequential continuation on a new running theme, 4 bars in iii., repeated in V. (A major) and thence expanded with imitative passage arising from last bar and developed into a 14-bar close in V.   The accentuation of the whole paragraph must be dated from bar 23.   To shift the accent elsewhere leads only to confusion.   Bar 53 is extra.

Second Group : A major (V.).
  [53]/54–60.—New 7-bar theme (B) (1, 1, 1+4).   Czerny is right in urging that the grace-note is long, but is too clever in saying that the resulting figure is derived from (a).
  [60]/61–66.—Repetition of theme (B) in minor, breaking off with measured pause at 5th bar.
  [66]/67–70.—Four-bar melody with (a) in bass.
  71–92.—Modulating excursus on (a), beginning as if to repeat bars 67–70 without the new melody, but moving down in 2-bar steps by tones, thus passing through IV. (reckoned locally ; = D

major) to ♭III., where, in contrary motion, (a) is developed in
4-bar groups (1+1+1+1).   Three of these (♭III., iv. and ♭II.)
lead to a 6-bar cadence in the restored A major, figure (a) having
incidentally been drawn out into over 2½ octaves of descending
scale.

93–96.—The previous cadence has closed into a 4-bar theme in
the rhythm of A displaced by 2 bars—*i.e.*, falling on the second
of its period instead of on a preliminary bar.   The bass rises in
minim steps below an interior tonic pedal.

97–104.—The new 4-bar derivative of A, carried twice through
with the rising minim scale transferred to treble and the pedal
below, closing into

105–112.—New 4-bar theme (C) in sequential pairs of minims,
repeated with slight change an octave lower, and closing into

113–124.—Tonic-and-dominant dialogue (over tonic pedal) on
(a).   At 8th bar the 7th is flattened, thus leading in 4 bars and a
silent measure back to beginning and on to Development.   (The
rhythm has changed step; nobody knows when.)

Development.

124/125–132.—Four bars of (a), resumed in D minor (i.) lead
to the whole 4-bar theme in the minor, up to the pause on the
dominant.   This becomes leading-note to ♭VI., in which key
there appears a

133–140.—Four-bar theme on rhythm A displaced as in bars
93–96.   Call this A'.   It is repeated an octave lower, closing
into

141–148.—A' in bass, welded into 8-bar phrase with 4 bars
of new matter (x) leading to G minor (iv. from our tonic).

149–156.—The same 8-bar phrase moving from G minor to
E♭ (♭II.).   (Thus all three main steps have been a 3rd down—
viz., D minor, B♭, G minor and E♭.)

157–166.—Further step from ♭II. to dominant of home tonic,
the material of x being changed to three 2-bar steps, closing
into

167–183.—Dominant preparation for return; for 8 bars in
dialogue on rhythm of (A) (rising scale), treble answering bass in
pairs of bars; then for 9 bars without theme, the bass rising in
three 2-bar steps from dominant to leading-note, on which it
pauses.   Note the acceleration of rhythm by syncopation in bars
179–182.

Recapitulation.

First Group.

183/184–193.—Bars 1–10 unchanged.

[193]/194–204.—The restatement of the previous 6-bar phrase is diverted by upward chromatic stops in bass and expanded to 10 bars, leading to dominant of ii. (E minor), which is insisted on for the last 4 bars.

Transition-Themes and Second Group.

[204]/205–293.—Exact Recapitulation of bars 22/23–112, with the Transition-Themes in (ii.) and (vi.), leading to Second Group in Tonic. A slight change at bars 221–224 is induced by the limit of the early pianoforte, but adds point to the detail.

Coda.

294–297.—Four additional downward steps of theme (C) lead to the subdominant (G major), closing into

298–305.—Eight bars of dialogue on (a) as in bars 113–119 in subdominant.

306–326.—The last bar of the dialogue, giving an upward turn to (a), is developed in 4-bar groups, beginning with (IV.), followed by (iv.), and thence by dominant of ♭II. which appears on the 4th bar of 3rd group. (N.B.—The groups begin not in the lowest octave but in the next—viz., bars 306, 310, 314.) On this the harmony thickens, the periods overlap or break up somewhere in or before the 5 bars from 318 to 323, and the dominant 7th in ♭II. changes enharmonically to an augmented 6th, which resolves downwards into bars [322]/323–326, which make a 4-bar clause, closing into

326–332.—Six bars (2+2+2) imitative treatment of (a), in its displaced rhythmic position, on tonic pedal, closing into

333–344.—Final *crescendo* on the tonic pedal (4+4+4 bars, the final silent bar completing its period). The bass notes trace an augmentation of (a), probably intended as such by Beethoven, while the treble rises in contrary motion.

Though the manner of the end is abrupt, the matter of the coda is conspicuous for its breadth, as exemplified by these 18 bars on a tonic pedal.

Largo e mesto: D minor (i.). Sonata Form with Episodic Development.

First Group : D minor.

Bars 1–8.—Four-bar theme (A) containing figure

built up in pairs of bars repeating themselves with intensification, and closing into iv. (G minor), where a 5th bar delays an answering phrase (bars 6–9), which returns to tonic and overlaps with a new theme into which it closes.

9–16.—The new theme, a cantabile transition-theme in 2-bar phrases, begins in the middle of bar 9, closes into itself in bar 11, and modulates to ♭VII. This does not, as usual, prove to be the dominant of ♭III., but maintains itself with emphasis for 4 more bars, the melody reaching a full close at the beginning of the 5th pair of bars (reckoning from bar 9).

Second Group. A minor (v.).

17–20/²¹.—Upon the close in ♭VII. follows a 4-bar theme (1+1+2) in v. (A minor), closing into

21–25.—Repetition in lower part with antiphonal counterpoint above, and expansion of second figure (bar 19) to an extra bar, the whole closing into

26–29.—Cadence-theme in style of the transition-theme, coming to formal close.

Development.

30–35.—Broad episodic melody, starting in ♭III. (or, as from A minor, ♭VI.) and in 6th bar modulating to G minor, and there closing into

36–37.—New figure (x) etc.

alternating with previous bar, which now rises so as to close into

38–43.—Six bars on the home dominant preparing for return; figure (x) being developed into 3 steady bars, followed by 3 unaccompanied and dramatically broken, leading finally to

Recapitulation.

First Group.

44–48 = 1–5 with intensifications, notably the imitation in the bass at 3rd bar.

49–51.—Substitution of ♭II. for harmony of bar 6. A falling semitone in the bass actually deepens this to ♭ii. (E flat minor); but this merely leads to dominant of ♭VI. (B flat) in the next bar, which, with colouring of G minor (iv.) leads to

52–55.—The end of the transition-theme (bars 13½–16) transposed to ♭VI.

Second Group.
56–64.—Following the close in B♭, and consequently at a new harmonic angle (*i.e.*, from ♭VI. instead of ♭III.), the Second Group is exactly recapitulated from bar 16½ to bar 25. The cadence-phrase (26–29) is omitted, and the theme closes into

Coda.
65–71.—Theme (A), entering in extreme bass, descends through (B) (♭VI.) to G♭ (as chord of ♭ii.); and thence, obliterating the figures of (a), the bass climbs up in 12 partly chromatic steps, first 2 in a bar, then 3 and 4, until 2 final steps (bar 71) lead to
72–75.—Four tonic-and-dominant bars, on dominant bass, with figure x, closing into
76–83.—New 8-bar phrase built out of (a²), culminating with touch of ♭II. and subsiding in broken cadences, closing into
84–87.—Final cadences with plagal (subdominant) elements and a dissonant upper pedal as well as the tonic bass, which is finally left to die away in single notes.

Menuet and Trio.

Menuet : D major.
1–16.—Symmetrical melody, 8+8, answering tonic by supertonic, and closing in tonic. Repeated.
16/17–24.—New 2-bar figure (closing into next bar) in imitative dialogue for 4 steps, passing through related keys to the home dominant, leading to
25–42.—Resumption of main theme in inner part. After its 10th bar a step up to (IV.) is interpolated and carried still higher. (Perhaps Beethoven would have gone up to F♯ in bar 37 as the 3rd step, had his instrument possessed that note.) Then the phrase is expanded in 4 more bars in downward scale, closing into

Codetta.
44–54.—Twelve bars tonic-and-dominant dialogue on opening figure in lower part, rhythmically imitated by treble (2+2 = 2+2), at end of which the treble plays with the flat and natural sixth in a dying 4-bar close.

Trio : G major (IV.).
54/55–70.—Dialogue between bass and treble (*L.H.*) in symmetrical 16-bar frame (1.1.2; 1.1.2; 1.1.1.1.4), modulating to dominant (D major).

71–86.—The above repeated, with change of slurs, but with apparent intention of mere repetition. The dominant of D, however, becomes more emphatic, and persists through the last 4 bars, which break off, completing the period in silence. Thus this trio unexpectedly leads back, without a genuine second strain, to Da Capo of the Menuet.

Rondo : Allegro. D major.

Main Theme.

1–8.—Theme built of a single figure (a)

and gathered gradually together with long measured pauses and one indefinite pause (⌢) on dominant. Bar 3 develops

the figure (a').  Bars 5–6

make a phrase out of 3 steps, and a tuneful interrupted cadence into bar 7. Bar 8, giving (a) *fortissimo*, echoes the cadence as a full close. The total shape of the theme is, then, 8 bars, made of 1+1+2; 2+2, closing into

Transition-Theme and First Episode.

9–16.—New theme, a 2-bar phrase closing into itself, given thrice, the third time in an inner part with 2 additional bars completing an 8-bar period and extending the movement of the bass downward so as to reach dominant of A.

Episode in Dominant.

17–24.—New 8-bar theme 2+2; 2+2. The last couple of bars fails to maintain A major and collapses on the A chord as the home dominant ⁶₄, with a pause, closing into

First Return.

²⁴/25–32.—Main theme unaltered. Its last bar (=8) closes into

Second Episode.

33–34.—Irruption of B♭ (♭VI.) with dialogue on (a) in bass answered in free inversion above.

35–45.—Three 2-bar steps lead from B♭ through G minor to E♭, which is dwelt on for 3 bars, then moving up to E♮ as part of dominant of F minor, with a pause.   In bars 35, 37 and 39 figure (a) and its inversion are concealed in the bass.   The overlapping of harmony between treble and bass at these points is a significant feature of style.

45/46–55.—Main theme begins in F major (♭III.), turning towards home tonic minor at 3rd bar, with pause.   Then, after a silent bar, (a') is developed in 5 bars of unison in tonic minor, closing into pause on dominant.

Second Return.

55/56–64.—Main theme with additional imitations of (a) in bass.

Third Episode.

64–71.—The main theme closes into the Transition-Theme as at bar 9.   The second 2-bar step moves to subdominant (IV.), and the 3rd step, continuing in (IV.), proceeds through a modified 4th step to dominant of B minor (vi.).

72–83.—Two bars dominant preparation for (vi.), with (a) in inner part; then 2 more (without the semiquaver movement) as the 1st step in a process which in the next 2 bars changes enharmonically towards 6/4 of B♭, rising in chromatic half-bar steps to dominant of A,—with figure (a) in bass throughout. This home dominant is dwelt upon (resuming semiquaver movement) for 4 bars, ending with pause.

Third Return.

83/84–91.—Main theme, with imitative details further ornamented.   Its last bar closes into

Coda.

92–99.—New imitative development of (a) in contrary-motion dialogue between treble and inner part, with sequences rising a third each 2 bars; then, on the bass reaching the dominant, in half-bar steps on dominant pedal, culminating in dominant pause over 2 bars.

100–105.—Attempt to resume (a) in bass closely answered by treble; then in minor; then in 4 bars of chords which, preserving the rhythm of (a) (disguised to the eye, but not to the ear), pass through (♭II.) to close in the major, closing into

106–113.—Eight bars on interior tonic pedal, with (a) in tapering sequence (*i.e.*, 2+2+1+1+close) in bass.

8

SONATA IN C MINOR, Op. 13

(SONATA PATHÉTIQUE)

THE title *Pathétique* was given to this sonata by the publisher. His justification is that nothing so powerful and so full of tragic passion had hitherto been dreamt of in pianoforte music. Much of its immediate impressiveness was due to its pianoforte style, which utterly eclipsed anything Mozart could conceive. In actual depth of idea, and even in pathos, this sonata does not surpass, if it equals, Mozart's in the same key; and the pathos of Beethoven's finale is mingled with a humour which is certainly not so nearly akin to tragedy as Mozart's C minor finale. Beethoven himself was under no delusions in such matters; at about the time of this sonata he exclaimed to Ries, at a pathetic passage in one of Mozart's concertos (also in C minor), " Such ideas will never occur to the likes of us." The *Sonata Pathétique*, like the *Kreutzer Sonata* (a less consistent work, akin to it in many ways), begins with a magnificent piece of Homeric fighting; but if we overestimate the tragic quality of such fighting we shall end, like Tolstoy, in crassly underrating the rest.

Grave: Introduction.

Bars 1–4.—Theme moving in long 1-bar steps, answering tonic-to-dominant by dominant-to-tonic (medial close); then crowded into twice a bar (in dominant region), followed by a 4th bar modulating towards E♭ (III.), into which it closes in next period. All is bases on a figure (a)

5–8.—Further development of (a); thrice 1 bar, +2 half-bars. The bass, starting on E♭, descends by partially chromatic steps to F♮, which is part of the home dominant chord. Two enharmonic changes occur in the second bar (6) of this descent.

First, the $B\natural = C\flat$ when it resolves on $B\flat$; and in the next chord the $C\sharp$ is really $D\flat$ until the chord resolves upon $A\natural$, when it becomes $C\sharp$. The bass, on arriving at $F\natural$, drifts down the dominant chord, landing on to

9–10.—Two cadential bars, closing into

Allegro di molto e con brio: Sonata Form.

First Group : C minor.

1–16.—Eight-bar theme (2+2+4), closing into self-repetition with close deferred so as to lead to dominant. The theme contains two figures (b)

repeating itself in upper octave, and (c)

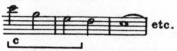

The subdominant colour of the second bar of (b) induces a major tonic triad; hence the apparent change of mode in bar 3.

17–24.—Twice 4 bars (1+1+2) on dominant, closing into

25–40.—Transition, on bass rising by semitones; 4 bars on G closing into $A\flat$; three on $A\flat$ with 4th bar on $A\natural$ rising to $B\flat$ as dominant of $E\flat$ (III.); lastly, 8 bars dominant preparation. Above this rising bass the treble builds up sequences in the style of bar 2 with an otherwise new figure (d)

Second Group : E flat minor (iii.) and major (III.).

41–78.—New theme in $E\flat$ minor, moving in 8 interlocking 4-bar groups until a final group of 6 bars arises out of the end of the 8th group. The groups all start by 1 bar in the bass, taken up by the treble. The first 2 groups represent tonic and dominant of $E\flat$ minor. The next two groups move from tonic to $D\flat$ (VII.). The next two stay in ($\flat$VII.). After this the initial figure changes, bringing about a rise back to tonic, and followed by a further rise to (ii.) in the 8th group. The last

2 bars of this group are carried further in downward sequence, coming in 6 bars to a close in E♭ major, closing into next period.

79–102.—Twelve-bar phrase (2+2+6+2) on descending bass against rising treble, closing into self-repetition with enhanced close into next period.

103–110.—New 4-bar cadence-theme closing into self-repetition, closing into

111–122.—Four bars of (b) leading to 8 bars of what would be final chords but for descent of bass down scale to F♯, leading, for the first time, to pause on home dominant, and so to repeat from bar 1. On the second time the bass remains on F♯ as part of dominant of G.

Development.

123–126.—Reappearance of Introduction in G minor (v.). Its 3rd bar echoes its 2nd bar, making therewith an enharmonic modulation (E♭ = D♯) to E minor, closing into

127–138.—*Allegro molto e con brio.* Two bars of (d), in E minor, followed by 4 of an adaptation of (a) (from the Introduction) to the quick tempo. Bass falls through E♭ to dominant of G, where a similar 6 bars, 2 of (d) and 4 of (a), lead, with fall of bass through D♭ to dominant of F.

138–156.—Development of (d) in bass below slowly falling tremolo. The figure moves in 4-bar steps (3 bars and a silence) from dominant of F minor to diminished seventh in C minor, upon which the tremolo begins to fall rapidly, passing again through F minor, and finishing an 8-bar period by closing into the home dominant.

157–184.—Thirty-two bars dominant preparation for return: first, an 8-bar clause, twice 2 of a new arpeggio figure (with a beautiful chromatic double appoggiatura), answered by 4 with (d) and a turn; closing into repetition of the whole 8 bars; closing into double echo of the last 2 bars; closing into 8 bars of unaccompanied run, proceeding in 2-bar stages down 4 octaves.

Recapitulation.

First Group.

185–196 = 1–12.

197–210.—At the point corresponding to bar 13, figure (C) digresses in 4-bar steps through a rising sequence, first through D♭ (♭II.), thence through E flat minor (iii.), lastly through F minor (iv.) on to the dominant of which it closes into 2 more preparatory bars. The rise of the bass within each step is important, and it is allowed to rise further in the last step.

Second Group.

211–242.—The first 8 bars are in (iv.); the third 4-bar group moves into the tonic (minor), where the next three groups continue. The two groups from bar 65 to bar 72 are omitted, and the 2-bar figure with the Pralltriller is carried in downward sequence into an 8-bar (not 6-bar) cadence group in the minor mode, closing into

243–278 = 79–114 translated into C minor. The rise to D♭ at the 3rd bar of the theme corresponding to that of bars 79 foll. is a master-stroke of pathos. The repetition of this 12-bar clause is identical, the 5-octave pianoforte preventing Beethoven from carrying the passage higher. We cannot carry the passage higher without mere guesswork as to how Beethoven would have translated it into the minor mode.

279–284.—Bass descends as in bars 115 foll., reaching F♯ with diminished 7th. Pause.

Coda.

285–288.—Four bars of the *Grave*, with silence on first beat. Thus (a) looms in vast spaces, first over dominant, next over tonic; lastly, in subdominant, gathering coherent rhythm over a descending bass, and coming to tonic close into

289–300.—*Allegro molto e con brio.* Main theme (b). The bass, which always used, after the 4th bar, to rise during the descent of figure (c), now falls to F♯, leading to final close in staccato chords.

Adagio cantabile: A♭ major (VI.), Rondo.

Main Theme.

1–8.—Eight-bar melody, answering dominant close at bar 4 by full close at bar 8.

9–16 = 1–8 in higher octave with fuller harmony.

First Episode.

17–23.—New theme, starting in F minor (vi.), with a bar that repeats itself twice with upward turn and downward turn; the bass meanwhile rising from E♮ at 2nd bar, and passing upwards through dominant of E♭ in 4th bar, while the melody gathers itself up for a further 2-bar close into E♭ (V.).

23–28.—Cadence phrase in E♭, a 2-bar group closing into self-repetition divided between two voices, closing into 2 bars, continuing its figure and treating E♭ as the home dominant, leading back to

First Return.

29–37 = 1–8.

Second Episode in Tonic minor and ♭VI.

[36]/37–44.—New theme in dialogue between treble and bass; twice 4 bars tonic and dominant of (i.), answered by 4 that modulate to F♭ (♭VI.), written for convenience as E♮, closing therein.

45–50.—Theme continued in (♭VI.). Its second pair of bars drops into an inverted diminished 7th on F♮; in other words, the bass rises from F♭ to the F♮. In two more bars the chord drops to the home dominant.

There has been no enharmonic change; as may be proved by transposing the whole episode up or down a semitone.

Third Return.

51–66 = 1–16 with triplet accompaniment. The appoggiatura in the last bar (66 = 16) has to give way, as a coda is to follow on the 4th quaver.

Coda.

[66]/67–73.—New 2-bar cadence-phrase, overlapping into self-repetition in upper octave, closing into 1-bar cadence given in three positions, closing into final tonic bar.

Rondo: Allegro.   C minor.

Main Theme.

$\frac{3}{8}$/1–17.—Eight-bar melody answering half-close on dominant at 4th bar by full close in tonic at 8th. Last 4 bars repeated, overlapping into a 2-bar codetta (with subdominant colour), closing into enhanced self-repetition closing into 2 bars of final chords. Bar 1 contains a figure (a) which is varied in bar 7.

First Episode : E♭ (III.).

18–24.—Taking its time from bar 17, two 4-bar steps of a new theme move downwards from (iv.) to (III.) (E♭), closing into

25–32.—New theme, 4 bars tonic-and-dominant, closing into modified self-repetition (a middle voice having entered imitatively at half-bar of 4th bar), passing through minor towards the dominant.

33–42.—Four bars (twice 1; ½+½+1) of new figure (b) in triplet quavers on dominant, closing into 4 answering bars on tonic in 2-part imitative dialogue, closing (through IV.) into 2 new cadential bars closing into tonic in next period.

43–50.—New 8-bar theme (4+4 answering dominant half-close by tonic full close) lying on 2nd bar of its period, and closing into

51–61.—Dialogue on (b) resumed, bass leading, in a 3-bar phrase, closing into self-repetition in lower octave. Here at the 3rd bar the harmony is diverted so as to reach, through a rising 4th bar, a climax on the home dominant, held for 4 bars with pause, the triplets becoming a run from a long high note down 2½ octaves.

First Return.
   ⁶¹⁄62–78 = 1–17.

Second Episode : A♭ (VI.).
   ⁷⁸⁄79–86.—New theme in A♭ (VI.) in 2-part counterpoint in contrary motion; 4 bars (1+1 in sequence + 2 with dominant close) repeated with parts reversed and upper part syncopated. (The inversion is, as far as it goes, really in the 12th, one part being a 3rd up and the other a 3rd down.) The second dominant close is stronger than the first.

87–94 = 79–86 with added 3rds and 6ths to one part or another, closing into

⁹³⁄94–97.—Four-bar interlude with new figure, initiated by bass (passing through ii.) and answered by treble, closing in dominant, and leading to

⁹⁸⁄99–106.—Resumption of A♭ upper melody with new counterpoint of descending scale in quavers; 4 bars answered by inversion in the same kind of double counterpoint in 12th as seen above; the harmony diverted through F minor towards the home dominant.

107–120.—Fourteen bars of preparation on the home dominant; at first themeless, thrice 2 bars rising by octaves, then 4 single bars rising up the dominant 7th, lastly the run down and pause as in bars 57–60.

Second Return.
   ¹²⁰⁄121–128 = ⅜ 1–8.
   ¹²ᵇ⁄129–133.—Last 4 bars taken up by bass, omitting the grace-notes and carrying the 2-bar sequence up to (iv.), from which an extra bar moves towards the home dominant.

Recapitulation of First Episode in Tonic Major.
   134–157 = 25–47 transposed (mainly a 6th upward, with effect of very high light) to tonic major, with the following changes. The second 4 bars take a happier turn, remaining in the major, and they require an extra bar in flowing into the next theme.

But very probably the extra bar is not an intrusion here at all. Beethoven may have shifted his rhythm earlier. The " extra bar " at 133 may be taken with bar 134, so as to shift the bar-accents of the present theme backwards, in which case 142 now completes a period. (These imitative self-repeating themes are easily thus shifted.)

The triplet, figure (b), takes its full imitative form from the outset, instead of arising casually as in bars 33–36.

In the final theme of the episode the slight difference between bar 156 and bar 46 is no oversight but a presage of the following pathetic new incident.

156/157–170.—The second clause of the theme becomes minor and its 2-bar group is carried up in sequence of 3rds through (III.) and dominant.   The dominant step initiates an 8-bar group, twice 1 on dominant, twice 1 on tonic, and 4 of dominant, declining into

Third Return.

171–182 = 1–12 ornamenting the repetition of the second clause and closing without overlap. (If, wishing for a strong cadence into bar 186, you read an overlap here, you will only get into an impossibly weak position over bars 188–193.)

Coda.

182/183–186.—Figure (b) in a 4-bar cadential phrase with subdominant colour (hence the major tonic harmony), closing into

186/187–192.—Expansion of the above, the figure climbing at its 3rd bar (counting from 187) up in half-bars in contrary motion with bass, till its 6th bar closes into

193–202.—New figure in 2-bar interlocking groups, twice repeated. The 3rd group flattens the supertonic, leading thence to dominant of A♭ ($\frac{6}{4}$ over G). Upon this the downward run and pause of bars 58–61 appears, explaining away the new figure from which it now seems derived.

202/203–210.—Figure (a) of main theme twice in A♭ (VI.) answered by 4 cadential bars. Of these the first has an augmented 6th, which might be a 7th in D♭, until it resolves into the tonic. The remaining 2 bars run in *fortissimo* triplet quavers slightly reminiscent of former dramatic downrushes.

9

SONATA IN E MAJOR, Op. 14, No. 1.

ONE of the most interesting documents in the history of Beethoven's art is the string-quartet in F major which, in protest against the vogue for such arrangements, he transcribed from his little E major Sonata. The string-quartet is published in Payne's Miniature Scores (No. 297) with the original sonata printed under the score. Unfortunately the sonata has been printed from an "instructive" edition with many highly destructive spurious marks of expression; so that we have no means of knowing how far the marks in the string-quartet are authentic. We only know that they are certain to differ from those in the sonata for the same reasons as the differences in notes. In particular, a sudden *piano* after a *crescendo*, as in the theme of the Rondo, is excellent on the pianoforte, but pointless in the string-quartet, especially in the thorough transformation shown in Beethoven's score. Accordingly he probably did substitute a *sforzando* there; but only shameless mendacity in the support of bad taste can account for the wide currency of that *sforzando* instead of the sudden *piano* Beethoven wrote in the sonata. There is hardly a bar of the quartet-version that does not shed some light on the nature of the pianoforte, of quartet-writing, and of the general structure of music. Quartet-players will, of course, be disappointed if they expect the result to be an important item in their repertoire. Beethoven may work a miracle, but even a miracle cannot be a contradiction in terms. He takes one of his smallest sonatas and shows the arrangement-mongers that hardly a bar of pianoforte music can be turned into good quartet-writing without quantities of new material besides drastic transformation of the old.

Allegro: E major. Sonata form.

First Group.
    Bars 1–4.—Four-bar theme on tonic pedal, containing sequential figure (a), rising to allied figure (b).

5–12.—New 1-bar figure imitated at half-bar entries down four voices, closing (note the A$\sharp$) into another 1-bar figure on dominant ($^{65}_{43}$), closing into self-repetition an octave higher, closing into 2-bar cadence, interlocking with self-repetition an octave lower, closing into

Transition.

13–22.—Figure (a) resumed. An inner part rises chromatically, followed by the treble at the 3rd bar. At end of 4th bar the bass rises to E$\sharp$, closing on to dominant of (V.), where 6 bars of. dominant preparation follow (twice $2+1+2$ of confirming chords). As the string-quartet version shows, the figure at bars 16/17 is a 2-bar figure imitated by another voice, thus:

Second Group in Dominant.

^{22}/23–30.—New 8-bar melody, sequentially answering four (moving from B to its supertonic) by 4 a step lower, closing in tonic.

^{30}/31–38.—Repetition of the melody in inner part with imitations below and above.

^{38}/39–45.—New 4-bar phrase $(1+1+2)$ with medial close, followed by repetition with full close overlapping with next period.

[The first two bars were on figure (b) in Beethoven's sketches, but he decided to keep this light work free from such thematic connexions.]

46–56.—Four bars, reiterating a single bar with an alternately minor and major 6th, are answered by two of cadential melody, closing into enhanced repetition, closing into third cadence expanded (with rests) to 3 bars, closing into

57–60.—Four-bar cadence-group on (a) in bass, below inverted pedal, leading back to repeat and on to Development.

Development.

61–64.—Figure (a) leads in 4 bars, through descending step in bass to A minor (iv.), closing into

Episode.
    65–74.—New melody in A minor proceeding in four self-repeating 2-bar steps over a bass that rises with each step, the melody remaining about its keynote with slight changes of approach.   With the last step the bass (inserting a semi-tone) approaches the dominant of C, into which key the next 2 bars close.
    75–80.—Decline of the new melody in three 2-bar groups approaching the home dominant on falling bass.
    [Beethoven's sketches indicate this episode with the words *ohne das Thema durchzuführen* (" without developing the theme "). Accordingly, critics who disapprove of episodic developments are not entitled to suppose that Beethoven was episodic by inadvertence.]
    81–90.—Resumed development of (a) in 10 bars of preparation on the home dominant for return; dialogue between tenor and treble in pairs of 2-bar groups, making 4 bars repeated, with 2 more bars, closing into

Recapitulation.
First Group.
    91–102 = 1–12, with *forte* scales as a bass counterpoint in bars 1–3.

Transition.
    103–106.—The close is interrupted by C major (♭VI.) with (a) accompanied by vestige of the new scales.   After 2 bars the tenor takes up (a) and the scales rise in treble.   The C♮, becoming the bass of an augmented 6th, resolves on to home dominant and into
    107–113 = 16–22, slightly enhanced in position, the appearance of an extra bar being due to the fact that 106 = 16 though it resembles 17.

Second Group in Tonic.
    $^{113}/114$–147 = $^{12}/23$–56 in tonic.   The early 5-octave pianoforte necessitates the alteration at bars 134–135.   Though the quartet-version is unrestricted here, the change is too neatly worked in the original sonata to deserve that it should be obliterated.

Cadence-phrase and Coda.
    148–162.—Cadence-phrase, as in bars 57–60, turned into full close with ♭II. below inverted tonic pedal, the last bar twice repeated, alternating ♭II. with normal II., closing into 8 bars, in which (a) rises in treble or tonic pedal; 2 + repetition in upper octave + 4 of close.

Allegretto in Tonic Minor with *Maggiore* (Trio) in ♭VI.

Although the *portamento* in bar 62 is strongly suggestive of a violin, this deeply pathetic movement is more untranslatable into quartet-writing than any other part of the sonata. Beethoven shows his profoundest insight in not allowing the four stringed instruments to reproduce the thick pianoforte chords, though this would be possible with quite easy double stops. He even makes bars 97–100 severely thin the first time, and obtains a fine new colour with inner octaves when these bars recur at the end of the movement.

First Strain.
1–16.—Eight-bar phrase (1+1+2+4) with half-close; answered, from new up-beat, by repetition octave higher, with full close. No repeat. Bars 1–2 contain a figure (a); bar 3 a figure (b).

Middle Strain.
17–32.—Eight bars on initial figure (2+2+4), starting on (VI.) and closing in (III.), answered by 8 similar bars, closing on home dominant with pause.

Third Strain.
33–50.—Bars 1–8 in upper octave; answered in lower octave, with a sudden swerve to (iv.) with 4th bar (b) twice insisted on, leading through another 4 bars to close into

Codetta.
51–62.—Two-bar cadence on (b) on tonic pedal with subdominant colour (hence a major tonic 3rd, but no real major mode), closing with repetitions in two higher positions, the last bar twice insisted on, closing into 3 bars of final major tonic chord, with a *portamento* leading to

Maggoire : Trio, C major (VI.).
63–78.—First strain of a new melody in C major (VI.), 4 bars closing into modified self-repetition rising to 8 bars (2+2+4), closing in dominant of present key, with a connecting link in inner part, first returning to repeat, then leading to
79–88.—Middle phrase 2+2 in sequence from (ii.) to 1 over dominant pedal; repeated in upper octave, continuing a downward scale with 2 more bars leading (like bars 77–78) to
89–100.—The 4 bars of 1st strain, rising to exact self-repetition in upper octave, rising to a sustained 4-bar cadence into E minor closing (with pause) in Da Capo from bar 1.

Coda.

101–116.—The final *portamento* leads, as before, into what might be the beginning of the Trio. But it proves to be its last strain, bars 89–100 closing without pause into final bare tonic of E minor

Rondo : Allegro commodo, E major.

Main Theme.

Bars ½/1–8.—Eight-bar theme; 4 bars rising over a descending scale and ending on dominant 7th, answered by twice 2 (self-repeating in lower octave) with two overlapping figures (a) and (b)

It is unusual for a developed Rondo in sonata style to have only a single phrase for its main theme, without even such an appendix of echoes of its last bars as may be found in the Rondo of the *Sonata Pathétique.* Accordingly, Beethoven here draws a double bar to show that the sequel is the beginning of the action.

⁸/9–14 =½/1–6.—This repetition drifts into action as follows.

First Episode in Dominant.

¹⁴/15–21.—Figure (a) in bass moves into B major (V.), answered by treble during 4 bars equivalent to ⁴/5–8, but avoiding clear presentation of (b). These 4 bars close into another 4 on rising bass with upward scales on first half of bar, coming to a full close on 4th bar.

²¹/22–29.—New 4-bar theme making a full close; repeated with variation and prolonged by extra bar (home dominant) with pause, the bass drifting down towards its first note in the main theme.

First Return.

³⁰/31–38 =½/1–8.

Transition to Second Episode.

³⁸/39–46.—Theme resumed in tonic minor, diverted towards dominant of G (♭III.), on which figure (a) prepares, in 4 bars, for Second Episode.

Second Episode, in G major (♭III.).

47–57.—New arpeggio theme, proceeding in three 4-bar (2+2) steps from G through A minor to B minor, there adding a 2-bar cadence, closing into self-repetition in lower octave, overlapping into

58–65.—Four 2-bar steps over sustained bass, descending by degrees from B to E, which is reached in next period.

66–75.—Four bars of the arpeggio theme in E minor (not yet confirmed as tonic minor), followed by three bars closing into self-repetition, with new turn leading to home dominant in next period.

76–83.—Eight bars of dominant preparation for return (2+2+ a chromatic scale filling 3+pause).

[There are many ways of transcribing such an episode for string-quartet, ranging from meticulously literal adaptation, with less or more technical common-sense, to highly ingenious translation of Beethoven's washes of pianoforte colour into dramatic tremolos. All this is nothing to Beethoven. For him the important thing is that a quartet is a quartet. As these arpeggios cannot possibly concern four individual players, something must be substituted that can. Beethoven substitutes strong transparent polyphony with figure (b) in conversation with a counterpoint in triplet runs; and he does not allow this to thicken into simpler textures until by so doing he can produce a climax. The naïve listener might be excused for not recognizing that the two versions belong to the same piece of music. Yet (allowing for the changed local key-names in the quartet, which is in F, not E) the above analysis applies accurately to both versions, and would be wrong wherever it did not.]

Second Return.
^{82}/83–91 = ½/1–8.

Recapitulation of First Episode transposed to Subdominant.
This is an unexpected feature, seldom found elsewhere.
^{91}/92–102 = ^{14}/15–25 in A major (IV.).
^{102}/103–108.—The varied repetition of the 4-bar theme is diverted at 2nd bar to F♮ (♭ VI. from A, and ♭II. from home). Two extra bars, with rise of bass to F♯ reach the home dominant.

Final Returns involved with Coda.
^{108}/109–121.—Third return of main theme in syncopated variation. But its first 4 bars are answered by repetition in bass, *fortissimo.* Hence absence here (as at bar 42) of the sudden *p* at bar 4. A treble counterpoint moves in contrary

motion on the beat. This does not correspond to the bass scale underlying the original theme. The bass, arriving at A, marches (in rhythm of original opening figure) up the chord of the diminished 7th, stopping on F♯ in the rhythm of bars ² 3-4, with pause.

¹²¹/122-131.—Final variation of main theme on original bass of bars ½/1-4. Figure (a) drifts into dialogue form of bars 14/15, starting with the treble of bar 15 in tonic and recapitulating therein up to bar 21, with slightly firmer cadence. This ends the sonata abruptly.

10

SONATA IN G MAJOR, Op. 14, No. 2.

Allegro: G major. Sonata form.

First Group : G major.

Bars ⅜/1–8.—Eight-bar melody (A) (2+2+4), closing in tonic, and built, as to bars 1–4, from figure (a).

Transition.

9–25.—New theme, a slow cantabile in 2-bar groups, at first repeating each other, and then gathering into rising sequences. The bass rises at first by 2-bar steps, then by quicker steps with occasional semitones, from bass G to A in the octave above. This A, reached in bar 19, is dominant of D, on which 7 bars of preparation lead to

Second Group : D major (V.).

26–32.—New theme (B), purporting to be an 8-bar strain (4+4); but the 7th bar closes into

33–46.—Four-bar phrase, closing in dominant; repeated in upper octave, and moving to subdominant, closing into 4-bar cadence, of which the last 2 bars are repeated, closing into

47–57.—Melody in dialogue (rhythmic imitation) between treble and bass, 8 bars+3 of echo and expansion, closing into

58–63.—Six cadence-bars on tonic pedal.

Development.

⁶³/64–73.—Four bars of theme (A) in tonic minor, followed by 2 breaking up (a) and effecting enharmonic change (F♯=G♭) to dominant of B♭, on which 4 bars, developing (a) in close imitation, lead to

74–80.—Theme (B) in B♭ (♭III.). At its 6th bar bass rises from F♮ to F♯ thence to G, and so to A♭ in next period.

81–98.—Development of (a) in bass, making sequences of 4-bar steps with the aid of new 2-bar continuation (x) in bars 84–85. First step leads from A♭ to G minor; 2nd step from G minor to F minor; thence with (x) alone to dominant of E♭, on which the remaining 6 bars insist, ending with pause.

⁹⁸/99–106.—Theme (A) in E♭ (♭VI.). Its 6th bar takes a new course, and finishes the period by closing into the home dominant.

107–124.—Eighteen bars of dominant preparation for return. The first 8 (2+2+2+1+1) are without theme; then, at bar 115, fragments of (a) appear in dialogue between bass and treble, at first once a bar, then at half-bars, and lastly compressed to pairs of notes, closing into

Recapitulation.
First Group.
¹²⁴/125–132 = 1–8.
133–152.—Three inserted bars (137–139) bring the first 4 into (IV.) with three new steps of the rising bass, thus diverting the whole transition so as to lead to the home dominant.

Second Group.
153–186.—Unaltered recapitulation in G until bar 183 = 56. Here the melody is expanded by 2 more bars (3 instead of bar 57), and the formal cadence-bars are omitted, the expanded melody closing into

Coda.
187–200.—Theme (A) set at a new rhythmic angle, combining part of its initial figure and its 5th bar in a 4-bar phrase (187–190) closing into its expanded and enhanced repetition to 6 bars (191–196),—all on tonic pedal. The 6 bars close into final cadence-bars, 1+1+2.

Andante: Theme with three Variations. C major (IV.).

Theme.
Bars 1–8.—First strain: 2+2+2+1+1. Every pair of bars ends on some form of dominant, approached with different shades of emphasis, culminating in full close in dominant key. The wit (for such it is, though solemn persons have put this tune into hymn-books) does not bear repetition; hence the direction *senza replica.*
9–20.—Second strain, consisting of 4 bars passing through (IV.) to half-close on dominant, returning to 4 bars of 1st strain

with a tonic close, followed by 4 of coda containing a modulating sequence. The repeat, here and in the variations, is essential to the whole movement.

21–40.—*Variation* 1, with plain theme in middle part and a syncopated counterpoint above; until last 4 coda-bars, where the syncopations are applied to the melody, now as top part.

41–60.—*Variation* 2, in syncopated chords.

61–64.—Four bars interlude on dominant, closing into

65–84.—*Variation* 3, in semiquavers. The whole scheme of the movement now appears as that of the old *air et doubles*; for the syncopations of Variation 1 did not, at first, concern the theme, whereas in Variation 2 the effect is that of quaver movement throughout, except at the grotesque syncopated sforzandos; and now Variation 3 duly doubles the movement again. This time the second part is not repeated.

Coda.

85–90.—Resumption of original theme, breaking away at 4th bar, with ostentatiously perfunctory cadence dispersed over different octaves.

Scherzo: Allegro assai.   G major.   Rondo form.

Main Theme.

Bars ⅓/1–8.—First strain (A), 4+4 (all on tonic except bar 7),

built of figures (a)      in cross-rhythm and

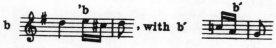 , with b′

⁸/9–16.—Second strain (B), 2+2+4 on dominant with new

figure (c)      , ending with pause.

17–22.—Third strain, compressing (A) into 6 bars (4+2) by means of ('b) and ('b'). The whole main theme appears to date from bar 1. Not until the end of the movement are its accents shifted.

First Episode : E minor (iv.).

23–42.—New theme. Four 4-bar phrases, starting on dominant of (vi.), the second phrase closing in (iii.), the third resuming in (vi.), the fourth in (ii.) (A minor). Two bars chord of home dominant and two of silence. [N.B.—There is no overlap in the rhythm. The accent is on the upper of the two dominant chords, bar 39.]

First Return of Main Theme.

⁴²/43–64 = 1–22.

Second Episode : C major (IV.).

⁶⁴/65–72.—Eight bars of strain (B); (c) in bass in subdominant, with its answering chords in *R.H.*; the latter 4 bars in cross-rhythm, imitative, with melodic lead into

73–124.—Sustained 3-strain melody. First strain an 8-bar melody (73–80), closing in tonic; repeated (81–88). Second strain on dominant, 8 bars (1, 1, 1, 1+4), repeated with minor colouring in inner part as to first 4 bars, and its half-close twice insisted on; leading to 3rd strain, a *da capo* of 1st strain with its last 4 bars insisted on, and the last 2 bars twice more.

¹²⁴/125–138.—Main theme in C for 7 bars, from the last of which a falling sequence on (b′) leads in 5 steps to home dominant, on which it dwells for 4 bars with pause.

Second Return.

¹³⁸/139–160 = 1–22.

Coda, including a Final Episode in Tonic.

¹⁶⁰/161–168.—Strain (B) treated as in bars 65–72, but in tonic, and ending in silent bar.

169–174.—Bottom note of (c) raised first to D♯, then to E (compressing the figure into partly chromatic scale).

¹⁷⁴/175–188.—The result of that rise in the bass is the entry of (A) in the paradoxical key of F (♭VII.). At 7th bar the bass climbs down again by semitones, while (b) apologizes above. The home dominant being reached, a new 4-bar cadence (185–188) closes into

New Episode, or Epilogue.

189–212.—New tonic-and-dominant theme, beginning with dialogue between treble and bass (2÷2, 2÷2, 4÷1), followed by 12 bars (8+4), containing two other ideas—a rising sequence ending in cross-rhythms, and a 4-bar cadence, closing into

213–236.—Repetition of bars 189–212, closing in tonic.

237–254.—Final return of (A) on drone-bass, followed by final echoes of (b). Here (A) is unmistakably dated from 237 which represents the full bar *before* that corresponding to bar 1. Bars 241, 245, 249, and 252 thus become accented.

11

SONATA IN B FLAT MAJOR, Op. 22.

OF this work Beethoven said, " Die Sonate hat sich gewaschen," which means literally, " This sonata has washed itself." The idiomatic translation of Beethoven's slang might be " This sonata takes the cake," Beethoven's triumph being akin to that of Stevenson when he said, " *The Master of Ballantrae* is a howling cheese." Although the next sonata, Op. 26, and the first three movements of Op. 27, No. 1 consist of less highly organized music than anything that Beethoven had hitherto put into sonata form (less even than the Serenades, Op. 8 and 25), they actually mark a new departure in that very fact. Op. 22 is the work in which Beethoven has achieved, as pure a normality as an art-form can maintain without losing its individual life. Another meaning of " hat sich gewaschen " is, " that's the way to do it." And Beethoven will not do it a second time. His next works are studies in colour, with the forms made ostentatiously simple in order that the colours may show in sections. The colours will soon come together under the stresses of new forms.

Yet Op. 22 is far from being a Mozartean work. Whatever elements in its style may be early, all are in a late stage of maturity. Many works lie between this and the complete establishment of Beethoven's " second style " (whatever we may agree to include in it); but this is the last that has removed all younger traces of conflict without anticipating new conflicts or new issues.

Allegro con brio.   B♭ major.

First Group.

Bars ¼ 1-11.—Abrupt figure (a) in disguised 3rds; a single bar given twice on tonic chord, and carried in 3rd bar up the chord into a 4-bar cantabile, 2 - 2, interlocking with self-repetition and subdominant colouring; closing into a new 4-bar group, in which the bass at last leaves the tonic, and (a) (preceded in treble by two extra notes) moves in half-bar steps to a dominant close.

Transition.

¹¹ 12–21.—Figure (a) in bass rushes up as in bar ²/3, reaching

the 5th of the tonic chord. Thence the bass descends while two upper voices initiate a rapid sequence in half-bar steps for 3 bars, finishing a 4-bar group from 12, and closing into the dominant of F (V.). On this we have 6 bars of preparation; 2 interlocking with repetition, plus insistence on last half-bar twice, plus 1 bar of scale and measured trill as a melodic link.

Second Group in Dominant.

22–26.—New 8-bar melody; twice 2 on the new tonic chord (accompanied by bass answering the previous melodic lead), followed by 4 passing through supertonic to full close into next period.

30–43.—Another new 8-bar melody (B) in sequences of a 1-bar figure in alternate versions (b) and (b′), lying across the bars and making a higher rise after its 4th step, carrying (b′) downwards to a close into a varied repetition.

44–47.—Apropos of the C♯ in the bass at the 7th bar of theme (B), the variation is cut off by 4 whole-bar arpeggios passing through (vi.) and dominant regions into

48–55.—Four-bar phrase (4 half-bars+2 bars) in broken octaves, closing into repetition in contrasted position, closing into

56–61.—Interlocking 2-bar groups of another new theme self-repeating over tonic pedal, an upper voice answering a tenor and flattening the supertonic. The last bar is twice insisted on. with the supertonic, alternately ♮ and ♭, closing into next period, [It is tempting to derive this figure by augmentation from (a); but Beethoven seems purposely to avoid establishing any such connection.]

62–68.—Cadence-phrase 4 bars of rhythmic scale-figure (C), 2 rising (A) and 2 falling (V), closing into 3 bars of cadence with (a) and final chords. Repeat.

Development.

⁶⁸/69–74.—Two bars of (a) in dialogue on chord of F, closing into theme (C), diverted so as to lead the dominant of G minor.

75–80 = 56–61 on dominant of G minor. Notice the complete absence of the tonic sense felt in 56–61. The difference does not lie in the fact that now the primary emphasis of the penultimate chord is on the flattened instead of the natural form : the passages could be interchanged without affecting the question, though the present version is best for the purposes of a dominant. But in the recapitulation this point is triumphantly tested, the supertonic being flat every time except the last but one.

81–93.—Three 4-bar steps down the dominants, (A) imitated in several voices led by bass with treble quavers (♪), answered by 2 bars on (a) plus a new running figure, passing through G minor, C minor, and F minor.

94–104.—At the end of the 3rd 4-bar step the bass has taken B♭ as the start of a descent, and the running figure has become an arpeggio (x). From 94 the bass proceeds in steps averaging 2 bars, while a+x proceeds in 2-bar steps above. The sequence is not mechanical, inasmuch as the bass delays by a bar those steps that are chromatic, recovering time by giving only one bar each to the G♭ and F♭. The 7th step (counting from bar 91) is on the dominant of A♭.

105–127.—Three 4-bar steps of a compressed version of (C) in bass, below (x) as accompaniment formula; dominant of A♭; dominant of F minor; with minor 9th above in conflict with the rising natural 6th degree of scale below (Bach-like but shocking to Beethoven's contemporaries); and then dominant of B♭ minor. This is the home dominant, which now lasts for 15 bars. In the middle of the 4th bar the minor 9th resolves (as in bar 112). The bass sustains its deep dominant, an incident which produces an overlap of rhythm, so that from this 4th bar a 12-bar passage of preparation is dated; twice 2 echoing end of (♪), plus 2 of insistence on last bar, plus 4 of rising scale (A), handed over from bass to treble, leading to 2 of pause on the dominant 7th. This is the last time Beethoven ended a development with a pause. In the finale of the quartet, Op. 59, No. 3, the long-sustained dominant at that point is a strictly measured rhythmic item.

Recapitulation.
First Group.
　127/128–138 = 1–11.

Transition.
　138/139–152.—Before rushing up to the transition, figure (a) is given in dialogue (half-bar imitation) between bass and treble for 2 bars. This produces, together with the following bar, a solid counterstatement to bars ½/1–3, and affords a perfect illustration of the view of recapitulations taken by Mozart, Beethoven, Brahms, and, when at the height of his power as far as he lived to show it, Schubert. On that view the recapitulation is not the part that is merely copied out again, but the thing now seen with both eyes whereas it was formerly seen with one.

The uprush now reaches A♭; and the following sequence must move for two further bars before it can be brought to the home dominant. This done, the 6 bars of dominant preparation follow, with a shift to a higher octave after the first pair.

153–199 = 22–68 in tonic. Note the above-mentioned use of (♭II.) in the bar corresponding to 57 as well as 2 bars later. The change is very purposeful, and the upper parts are carefully adapted to it.

Adagio con molta espressione : E♭ (IV.). Sonata Form.

First Group in E♭.

1–12.—Eight-bar melody closing into a 1-bar cadence, closing into self-repetition in lower octave, closing into triple cadence in 2 final bars. The listener will feel that the music begins on a full bar with the first note of the accompaniment, and that the melody enters with a glide into the second bar. This is true, and is confirmed by the Recapitulation. But with such long bars the clearest playing will make the listener quite content to identify the slow ⅜ time without bothering to retain his correct first impression of the rhythmic date of the melody. Thematically speaking, bars ⅓/2–5 are built up with an initial figure (a)

treated sequentially on the spot, and another figure (b)

used later on in the Development. Bars 6–12 answer 2–5 with new matter not used elsewhere.

So formal and final is the close of this theme that Beethoven marks it with a double bar—a thing he never puts at this point in any other work. It is the more odd as there is no double bar at the very similar end of the Second Group.

Transition.

¹²/13–17.—New 2-bar theme, closing in tonic, and answered in a higher position. In the answer the first bar moves towards key of dominant, in the minor mode of which 2 more bars make for a close in next period.

Second Group in Dominant.

18–21.—The chord proves to be major, and it initiates a new 2-bar melody, with imitative lower parts over tonic pedal, interlocking with enhanced repetition, closing into

22–26.—New 3-bar group (2+1), closing into 2 bars of florid melody representing a compressed repetition of the 3, closing into

27–30.—Cadence-phrase, 1 bar closing into repetition in lower octave, closing into threefold final cadence. (Same form as bars 9-12, but avoiding any definite allusion.)

Development.

31–38.—The bass announces the dominant of C minor, and the melody climbs up the chord with figure (a), making rich chromatic harmony with the very long appoggiaturas of (a²). At the 4th bar (which the ear will be equally ready to regard as the 3rd of the melody) (a) and (b) join in a compound figure (ab), which, in dialogue between two voices, moves down the dominants for 4 more bars.

39–46.—The ♯ of A♭ minor being reached, figure (b) is worked in a continuous passage for two voices in 6ths, with a soprano ejaculating a wailing figure at the turn of each bar. Two bars move from A♭ minor to E♭ minor, where the same process leads to the home dominant, on which 4 bars of preparation—twice 1 in the previous style, and 2 of melodic link on (b) in single voice—close into

Recapitulation.
First Group.

47–56 = 1–10.—As in the first movement of this Sonata the Recapitulation gained solidity by expansion, so here it gains continuity (another aspect of solidity) by compression. Instead of the formal final cadences of bars 11-12, a single bar glides in a melodious arpeggio into the Transition Theme.

Transition.

⁵⁷/58–64.—Bars 58–59 = 13–14; but the second couplet goes into the tonic minor, passing thence to (♭III.), in which the 2 bars corresponding to 16-17 seem about to close; but their cadence is interrupted by a transposition of 16-17 to our tonic minor, closing into

Second Group in Tonic.
65–77 = 18–30.

Menuetto in B♭ with *Minore* in G minor (vi.).

The appearance of semiquavers and the title *Menuetto* made

it unnecessary for Beethoven to specify a tempo. The only possible direction would have been *Tempo di Menuetto*. More feminine and without the military swing of the famous minuet of the Septet, this movement is in about the same tempo.

First Strain.

½/1-8.—Four bars (2+2), moving from tonic into dominant, answered by 4 returning from dominant 7th to close in tonic repeat.

The prominent figure (a) of semiquavers with grace-note must not be supposed to allude to the slow movement; the testimony of the eye is worth nothing in such matters.

Middle Strain.

⁸/9-16.—Two contrasted pairs of bars: dominant of (VI.) answered by close in that key; followed by similar pairs; dominant of (IV.) answered by return *via* (ii.) to home dominant.

Third Strain.

¹⁶/17-24 = 1-8, with enriched bass in second clause. The tonic close is without appoggiatura, so as to make room for a codetta.

²⁴/25-30.—Cadence-group with (a) in dialogue between treble and middle voice; 2 bars repeated in lower octave and insisted on, the rhythm tapering to two and a half groups of 2 crotchets across the bars, and thence to the 2 remaining crotchets of the penultimate bar. Repeat.

Minore : Trio, G minor (vi.).

³⁰/31-38.—Eight-bar strain of running figure in bass in G minor, answering half-close on dominant in 4th bar by modulation to dominant minor key with full close at 8th bar. Repeat.

(The resemblance of the running figure to an inversion of (a) is another mere accident.)

³⁸/39-46.—The running figure is taken up imitatively by three upper voices, in two 2-bar steps, the first in (iv.), the second in tonic; after which the bass resumes its theme in 4 bars ending in tonic. Repeat.

Menuet Da Capo.

Rondo : Allegretto. B flat major.

Main Theme.

²/1-18.—Eight-bar strain; 2+2 in sequence, on figures (a) (b), followed by 4 (1+1+2) with dominant close; the whole

answered by repetition diverted to medial tonic close, interlocking with variation of last 2 bars ended with full close.

Transition, merging into *First Episode in Dominant*.

[18]/19–22.—New 4-bar theme (C) answering 2 bars in tonic by 2 moving to dominant.

[22]/23–31.—Two bars in dominant, with stationary treble over rising bass, answered by 4-bar phrase in falling sequence, 1+1+1+accelerated descent into medial close, interlocking with repetition of the 4 bars in lower position, overlapping into

32–39.—Cadence-group on tonic pedal (of F), 2 bars closing into repetition in higher position, after which the bass moves downwards, and 4 more bars (1+1+2) land us on home dominant approached through tonic minor.

40–49.—Dialogue between bass and treble, on (a) rising on the home dominant; two steps of the antiphony; then in close imitation, arising from which the upper voice revolves on ('a) as 6 semiquavers descending thrice from F across the accents; then accelerated in mid-step (which happens to be on the beat), first to triplets, then to demisemiquavers. Raising its top note to ‿G♭, it finally mounts to G♮ as 2nd note of main theme.

First Return.

[49]/50–67.=½/1–18 with slight enhancement in 3rd bar.

Second Episode in Tonic Minor, in a completely organized recapitulatory form with a development of its own.

[67]/68–71.—Theme (C) in tonic minor, answering its first 2 bars by carrying their initial 2 notes in 2 steps into dominant minor, closing into next period.

72–80.—New 3-bar theme in F minor (v.); twice 1 plus close into repetition in higher octave closing into a cadence-figure of a single bar, closing into self-repetition in lower octave plus final chord.

[80]/81–88.—Theme (C) in bass with answering counterpoint (cx) above; 2 bars in F minor answered in tonic minor. The process repeated in tonic minor and (iv.), theme (C) in treble and (cx) in middle voice.

[88]/89–94.—Two-bar falling sequence of theme (C) in bass with allied counterpoint in contrary motion above, both parts in added 3rds; the next 2 bars continue the falling sequence with interchanged voices; and another 2 bars presses, in contrary motion, to a close into tonic minor in next period.

95–103 = 72–80 in tonic minor.

103–111.—At end of final bar the bass enters with (a+b) in G♭ (♭VI.) (note the shift of bar-rhythm), closing into A♭ minor, where sequential repetition leads to A♮ as part of home dominant. The treble takes up an appoggiatura (downward) from (b), and in 5 bars on home dominant accelerates it to demisemiquavers. Its G♭ becomes G♮ and drifts into main theme.

Second Return.

¹¹¹/112–129 = ½/1–18; the first 6 bars giving the theme to an inner part, and the rest ornamented in treble.

Recapitulation of Theme (C) and First Episode in Tonic.

¹²⁹/130–149.—The addition of 2 bars to theme (C), answering its second couple in the tonic, brings all the rest of the First Episode into the tonic. The limits of a 5-octave pianoforte prevent bars 147-148 from assuming a higher position than 145-146.

149–152.—Drift towards subdominant, parallel with 36-39, but without minor colouring.

¹⁵²/153–156.—Four bars of main theme in (IV.).

¹⁵⁶/157–164.—Figure a+b in C minor (ii.), followed by (a) alone in dialogue, punctuated with semiquaver rests veering towards home dominant. The bass prolongs (a) in a downward scale which reaches dominant at a half-bar, while the treble answers in an upward run which, becoming partially chromatic triplets, mimics the style of the lead back to First Return, but without any cross-rhythm. In 2 bars after the bar in which the bass reached the dominant, the treble arrives at the main theme.

Final Return.

¹⁶⁴/165–182 = ½/1–18 varied in triplets and with other new ornaments. The last note initiates a run, leading to

Coda.

¹⁸²/183–199.—Theme (C) built (with insistence on its first 2 crotchets) into a new 4-bar phrase on a descending bass, closing into repetition with the bass decorated in a demisemiquaver figure, closing into insistence on last 2 bars, plus final close into a quite novel 2-bar derivative of (a) in close imitation. This repeats itself in lower octave, and its end is again detached as two iambic final cadential quavers, given twice.

12

SONATA IN A FLAT MAJOR, Op. 26.

HAYDN and Mozart do not scruple to give the name of sonata to works that have no movement in a form developed beyond melodic sections. Beethoven's Sonatas Op. 26, Op. 27, No. 1, and Op. 54, are thus more exceptional for him than for earlier composers. Haydn's famous " Gipsy Trio " has even less of elaborate organization than the present work; for the " Gipsy Rondo " is an entirely sectional dance-movement, whereas the Rondo of this sonata, though apparently hardly longer than the Scherzo, is in the completest Rondo form.

The ancestry of works of this kind is not to be sought in the suite-forms. It originates in the *Divertimento*, a group of small movements in sectional forms deliberately avoiding a polyphonic or argumentative style. J. S. Bach used to say of non-polyphonic sonatas, " These are mere *divertissements*," and many of Haydn's early sonatas and quartets were published under the title of Divertimento, which afterwards became applied, like the term Serenade, to important orchestral and chamber works in a festive style, with a number of movements ranging from 2 to 8. Beethoven's Septet and Schubert's Octet are typical Divertimenti or Serenades on the largest scale.

Andante con Variazioni.   A flaᵗ major.

Theme.
   Melody in 3 strains.
   1–16.—First strain: a symmetrical 16-bar tune, 4+4 answering the half-close at 8th bar by full close at 16th.
   17–26.—Second strain: sequence in 2-bar steps answering supertonic by tonic, and followed by 4 bars modulating to dominant, with interrupted close leading to 2-bar echo with completed close, returning to
   27–34 =9–16 constituting Third strain.
   Variation 1 weaves an arpeggio figure closely into the framework of the theme.
   Variation 2.   Melody in left hand.
   Variation 3 in tonic minor.   The bass is organized as a rise

90

through 6 steps of the minor scale plus a 7th step to F♮.   Hence considerable harmonic freedom between the 3rd and 7th bars, as also in the corresponding bars near the end of the 1st strain.   In the 2nd strain the supertonic is replaced by the subdominant minor.   The minor mode has no normal harmonic centre on its supertonic, and the flat supertonic has been already emphasized as a result of the newly organized bass.

Variation 4 in the major.   In the 1st strain the rising of the bass is again developed systematically, but in the 4th and 5th bars its steps are quickened so that no liberty is taken with the harmony.   (The 5th bar completes the rise, as changes of octave do not affect this matter.)

Variation 5.   Triplet movement in the first 8 bars, accelerated to demisemiquavers in the rest of the variation.

Coda.

205–219.—With delicious effrontery an entirely new melody enters: 4 bars repeated with variation, and the last 2 bars twice sketchily echoed, closing into 4 bars of tonic chord.   There is an overlap between the end of the tune and the echoes, unless we refer the overlap back to bar 204, the end of the 5th variation.   As the difference between a strong and a weak bar is hardly appreciable in this tempo, the question is unimportant.   Meanwhile the bass slyly explains that it is justifying the new tune by harping on the first 2 notes of bar 1 of the theme, though it never gets them onto the beat.

Scherzo and Trio : Allegro molto.   A flat major.

The bar-rhythm of this movement is subtly balanced.   Yet Beethoven writes for the unprejudiced listener; and if the player trusts Beethoven and plays what is written, the unprejudiced listener will hear what Beethoven intends him to hear.   The following account is accordingly based on no theory that assumes anything not evident to the ear.   The result explains, amongst other things, a point in the Trio that has always given rise to doubts.

The *sforzandos* in bars 1 and 5 forbid the listener to regard the 1st bar as unaccented.   A *sforzando* cannot be heard to be " off the beat " before there is a beat for something else to be on.   Count, then, in 4-bar periods from bar 1.

1–8.—Four bars moving from chord of F minor to close in E♭, repeated a 4th higher, thus proving A♭ to be the tonic. (Compare the similar structure in the Allegretto of Op. 27, No. 2.)   Figures (a) and (b) may be distinguished.

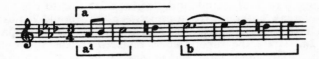

[Note that the inner part does not belong to the melody in bars 2-3. Beethoven's keyboard style in this matter differs from Bach's in the opposite way from which one would expect. Bach, the pure polyphonist, constantly allows two keyboard parts to make a composite sense more important than either; whereas Beethoven is meticulous in keeping them distinct.]

9–16.—Repetition of 1–8 with new imitative details.

Middle Strain.

16–28.—Two 4-bar steps, answering (a) by a new figure, and rising in sequence from dominant of D♭ (IV.) on chromatically rising bass, the 2nd step reaching dominant of F minor (vi.). Upon this a 3rd step breaks into a diminution of figure (a) in its 3rd and 4th bars, leading to

29–44.—Four 4-bar groups still on dominant of F minor, the bass rising up the triad, reaching its 5th (G) at the 3rd step, while the themeless upper part has tapered away from 2-bar groups to single bars, and finally to single chords. The reason why the bass clings for 8 bars to its note G is that this at last leads to the 1st note of the main theme.

Third Strain.

⁴⁴/45–52 = 1–8, with melody (with a new chromatic touch) in bass and a counterpoint in treble. The 1st chord, being that of F minor, has gained a new point from being preceded by all that dominant preparation as for a foreign key.

53–60 = 45–52 inverted in double counterpoint.

61–67.—Two echoes of (b) (twice 2 bars) and three 1-bar echoes of its last two notes. Now hold on to your 4-bar groups ! Though the bass reaches the tonic at bar 64, there is no overlap. The next accent is on 65. " But this will put us wrong when we repeat ! " Certainly bar 17 foll. will be displaced when we begin the repeat; but we need not call this " wrong." The impression of displacement will not survive bars 27–28 unless we can attain the mentality of a bell metronome. Other mentalities, human and even divine, may be supposed to have memories, and Beethoven has his *sforzandos* wherewith to propel such humble minds into the old rhythmic groove. So we again reach bar 65 as an accented bar with 67 as the next (subordinate) accent. (If the 5-octave pianoforte had allowed Beethoven to reach a top

A♭ at bar 65 this would have been unmistakable.)   And now we find that the first accent of the Trio is on its 2nd bar (69).   This does not affect the length of its periods as shown in the following analysis

Trio in D♭ (IV.).

[67]/68–75.—Eight-bar strain in D♭, closing into its dominant. Repeated.

76–91.—Sixteen bars, 4+4 on rising bass, passing to subdominant and theme in 8 bars to tonic close.   Repeated.

Now consider the accentuation: 69 being accented, the *sforzando* on 73 is in a normal position.   In the 2nd strain the main accents will be on 77, 81, 85, and 89, so that the *sforzando* on 86 will be off the accent.   By this time such a cross-accent will be quite acceptable.   The bass at bar 85 is often queried. There is a wide consensus of opinion that it ought to be A♭.   But the autograph is particularly clear on this point, and the wish for A♭ results from taking the accents from the 1st bar.   Take them as the approach from the Scherzo shows, and you will see at once that the following scheme

is an excellent independent bass, while A♭ would reduce everything to parallel thirds.

There can be no question that the Trio is much prettier in this light than in any other, nor that this is what will reach the unprejudiced ear if Beethoven's directions are followed.

Coda to Trio.

[91]/92–95.—Figure (a) twice in inner part, first reaching A♭, thence reaching home dominant.   At present, of course, the bar-accent is reversed, but the Da Capo to which this leads will soon (with Beethoven's sforzandos) recover the original poise.

Marcia funèbre sulla morte d'un Eroe.   A♭ minor (i.).

Military funeral march in tonic minor, with a Trio in major, obviously representing salutes fired over the grave.   Beethoven soon afterwards orchestrated this march for some incidental music to a play.

1–8.—Rhythmic melody concealed under a monotone; 4 bars tonic and dominant, answered by 4 passing through minor dominant to close in ♭III.

9–16.—Bars 1–4 a third higher (♭iii.).   C♭ minor written as

B minor, answered by 4 passing by its subdominant (instead of the dominant minor as in bar 6) and reaching the extreme distance of ♭V, E♭♭ written as D♮. The close is on a bare octave. The convenient change of notation is, of course, no enharmonic modulation. In orchestrating this march Beethoven transposed it to B minor, and then bars 9–13 became D minor and 15–16 became F. In fact, the whole of 9–16 is a recapitulation of 1–8, except for substituting a subdominant for a dominant in the 6th bar. We have reached the remotest possible key, but no unusual progressions have been heard.

But the way back is drastically enharmonic; startling on the pianoforte, which need not be worse than well-tempered; and dreadful when attempted by military bands, where enharmonic distinctions may outrun discretion. Here is how bars 16–18 would appear in Beethoven's B minor orchestral version if he troubled to spell his harmonies according to their sense.

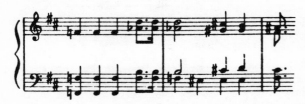

[16]/17–20.—Sudden enharmonic return, in a single bar, to home dominant. In this light the bar is twice insisted on with increasing vehemence; and a 4th bar, answering the emphasized C♭ by an F♭, leads to

21–30.—Opening strain resumed: recapitulating bars 1–4, then passing (in 4 bars through major tonic chord) to (iv.) and theme through ♭II. to 2 extra bars of cadence. This is the one place where the rhythm expands, great breadth being attained by bars 27–28, which carry forward the pauses of bars 2, 6, and parallel places.

Trio in tonic major.

31–34.—Four bars moving from tonic to dominant: twice 1 on tonic, ½ ÷ ½ ÷ 1 in key of dominant. Repeated.

35–38.—Same scheme as 31–34, moving from dominant 7th to tonic. Repeated. Drastically short as this trio is, the first sketch of it was even more perfunctory, covering the same ground in 2-bar instead of 4-bar steps.

March Da Capo.
[38]/39–68 = 1–30.

Coda.

⁶⁸/69–75.—Double melody in contrary motion over a tonic pedal, 2 bars, closing into repetition with parts reversed, closing into twice 1 bar closing into 2 of final tonic. The whole passage being coloured first by (iv.) and then by ♭II., the tonic chord is major throughout, in contrast with the minor 9ths and minor 6ths.

Allegro : Rondo.

[Note.—(♼) denotes an inverted figure, (♠) a direct one.]

Main Theme.

½/1–12.—Six-bar theme answering sequence of figure (a)

 etc.,

by scale-figure (b)

with upper part in contrary motion closing on dominant; the whole 6 bars repeated led by bass, with treble adding contrary motion to (a) and turning (b) into close in tonic. With groups of 3 bars the ear is always likely to take the 1st bar of the 2nd group for a 4th bar, whatever the melodic figures may say. And as most of the rest of this movement is in 2-bar or 4-bar groups it is doubtful whether the ear will ever think of these 6-bar phrases as twice 3.

¹²/13–20.—Three 2-bar groups in double counterpoint displayed in alternate positions, moving in sequence through (vi.) and (V.) to tonic, where the 3rd step is completed by 2 cadence-bars.

²⁰/21–28 = ¹²/13–20, with parts interchanged.

Transition and First Episode in Dominant.

²⁸/29–32.—Two-bar passage of (a) in bass, moving from (vi.) to (V.) and ended with chord on odd quaver; repeated by treble with contrary bass, moving from (iii.) to dominant of dominant.

³²/33–37.—The detached quaver gives rise to a new 2-bar figure over (♼) on dominant 7th of E♭. This is given twice *in situ*, then twice with parts exchanged and with an echo of its 2nd bar, closing into new 2-bar scale-figure closing (by interrupted cadence) into self-repetition twice, hurrying down

from successively higher notes.   With the third run the bass is
allowed to close on to E♭ in the next period.

48–51.—Five bars on E♭ as home dominant leading to return;
figure (a) struggling upwards till it hovers for 1½ bars in the right
position.

First Return.

⁵²/53–80 = ½/1–28 unaltered, except that the bass E♭ lingers
through the first 2½ bars.

Second Episode :   C minor (iii.).

⁸⁰/81–88.—New 8-bar phrase answering tonic close into 4th bar
by dominant minor close into 8th.   Repeated.

⁸⁸/89–100.—Beginning in G minor like a 2nd strain, the
episode proceeds in 2-bar steps: the first pair answers G minor
by a change to F minor; the second pair repeats the process,
moving from F minor to home dominant, whence the unaccompanied figure climbs a chromatic scale, reaching in 2 bars
the position in which it can merge into figure (a), as in bars
50–51.

Second Return.

¹⁰⁰/101–128 = ½/1–28.

Recapitulation of First Episode in Tonic.

¹²⁸/129–138.—Contrary motion is added to bars ²⁸/29–30;
the chord of B♭ minor (ii.) is substituted for the dominant
of E♭ in bar 32, and 2 further steps are added, followed by 2½
bars in which the " odd quaver " is hurried through 5 steps,
leading to

¹³⁸/139–153 = ³²/33–47 in tonic, closing into

Coda.

154–169.—On tonic pedal figure (a) makes a 4-bar phrase,
coloured by (IV.) and (ii.), closing into self-repetition in lower
octave, closing into 2 echoes of its last 2 bars, closing into 4 of
tonic chord descending to extreme bass.

13

SONATA IN E FLAT MAJOR, Op. 27, No. 1.

THIS sonata begins like the lightest divertimento that ever failed to rise beyond dance-music. Yet behind the ostentatiously silly graces of the merely sectional first movement a hidden power lurks, and makes itself dimly suspected in bright gleams and dark shadows. In the later movements the power reveals itself in terms not far remote from Beethoven's " second manner." The opinion that the first movement is " unworthy of Beethoven " represents little if any advance upon the naïve view that takes that movement " seriously." Some much too clever persons achieve a higher nonsense in the theory that the barring is " wrong " because the cadences " ought " to fall on strong beats. But perhaps the bass has its rights as well as the treble, and perhaps Beethoven might dismiss that very modern theory with the inspired words of the Fool in *King Lear* :
" This prophecy shall Merlin make; for I live before his time."
Meanwhile, Beethoven manifests his own deep thoughts about strong cadences. The coda of the first movement shows that he meant exactly what he wrote as to the barring, and the next movement shows the utmost care to place the rhythmic position of the cadences correctly.

Andante : Square tune with sectional Alternatives. E♭.

Main Theme.

Bars 1–4.—Four-bar strain of melody on a rhythmic figure (a) over a bass running during the long notes; a pair on tonic and dominant, closing into repetition crowding the 2nd bar into a cadence in tonic. Repeat.
5–8.—Second 4-bar strain; 2 bars of rhythm (a) rising on dominant, and a 3rd step (during which the bass rises further) flowing into a bar that closes in tonic. Repeat.

First Alternative in Tonic.
9–12.—New 4-bar strain with up-beat, using rhythm (a) as part of a sustained melody over thick quaver chords; 2 bars tonic, answered by 2 of dominant closing in tonic.

¹²/13–16.—A chord of C major, in rhythm (a), makes a bright colour, but proves to be merely dominant of (ii.). The melody continues in (ii.), for a 2nd bar on the lines of bar ⁹/10, imitated in next bar by the bass, upon which it runs down in semiquavers to a tonic close with imitative lower parts.

¹⁶/17–20 = ¹²/13–16, with ornaments in second figure.

First Da Capo.

²⁰/21–36 = 1–8, with up-beats to each 4 bars, and with the repeats very simply varied. The 2nd strain begins in the varied shape, which is further varied on repetition.

Second Alternative in C major (VI.). Allegro ⁶₈.

³⁶/37–44.—Eight bars in C major (VI.), with close in its dominant; 2 of tonic to dominant, answered by 2 of dominant to tonic; followed by imitative sequential run downward, with cross-rhythm on its initial 4-semiquaver figure (b) for 2 bars, leading to a 2-bar cadence into (V.) through (vi.). Repeat.

⁴⁴/45–52.—Four bars on dominant 7th, thrice 1+2 echoing half-bars, all with *sforzando* on last quaver; closing into 4 bars, recapitulating 40–44, remaining in tonic, and proceeding through (IV.) to the close.

⁵²/53–62.—Repetition of 45–48, after which the sequential run starts in tonic minor, which becomes unmistakably E♭ in the 2nd bar. This being the home dominant, figure (b) continues to revolve over it in cross-rhythm for 2 bars plus a run up to pause on dominant 7th.

Second Da Capo.

63–78 = 1–8, with the repeats inverted in double counterpoint.

Coda.

⁷⁸/79–86.—Introduced by an up-beat, the rhythm (a'), minus its last note, droops over an answering bass on tonic pedal, in 3 bars through (IV.), closing into final cadences, 1+1, ending in 3 of tonic chords, with long silences and pause. The next movement follows without break.

Allegro molto e vivace : C minor (vi.). Scherzo and Trio.

A thoughtless reader might think that Beethoven wasted space in making his repeat date from the 2nd bar when the return involved no alteration in the 1st bar. But this is Beethoven's way of showing where the rhythmic periods lie, and he takes the same trouble with the 2nd repeat. The whole movement is unintelligible unless it is read in this way. If we ask why

Beethoven did not make it more unmistakable by using ⁶⁄₄ bars, the answer is that, as he shows in all his scherzos, he attaches great importance to the prevalent harder accents of the short ³⁄₄ bars, and that no player would read this kind of accent into ⁶⁄₄ time unless it was expressly marked with > from beginning to end. And great composers have learnt, quite as soon as other people, that fussy marking produces general inattention.

Scherzo : C minor.

First Strain.

¹/2–16.—Sequences of an arpeggio-figure with bass descending from C by semitones every 2 bars. Across the bar-rhythm each pair in a lower octave is answered by one in a higher octave. The steps of the bass, being on the bar-rhythm, lie in both octaves. When the bass has reached G with ⁶⁄₄, a sudden *forte* interrupts, and the figure makes a staccato close in the dominant minor. Repeat. 17a = 1.

Middle Clause.

17b/18–24.—Four pairs on the above lines move through (iv.) back to tonic, closing into

Recapitulatory Strain.

25/26–40.—Enhanced version of 1st strain, the harmony making a chain of suspensions, with a *crescendo* leading to the staccato *forte* which now closes into tonic. Repeat. Bar 41a = 25; and 41b completes the couple.

Trio : A♭ major (VI.).

First Strain.

⁴¹/42–55.—The tonic chord of A♭ is drummed in an iambic rhythm persistently. After 2 bars an off-beat detaches itself and rises up the chord in 6 bars, reaching G♭, upon which a 2-bar trill, over A♮ in bass, leads to close in dominant. In the retrospect the first 2 bars will be found to be introductory, square periods beginning with the rising part. Repeat.

⁵⁵/56–73.—After 2 introductory bars of the persistent iambics, the melody (in complementary rhythm) enters, moving down and up the scale between F and G, prolonging its second scale down till it leads to a 4-bar full close. Note that bars 64–65 do not correspond rhythmically to 58–59; for 58–59 begin a group, and 64–65 end one. Repeat. On the second time the final appoggiatura is omitted so as to make room for bar 1 in its position of anacrusis.

Da Capo.

⁷³/74–88 = 1–16a.

⁸⁹/90–104.—The repeat is varied by legato syncopations above staccato bass.

¹⁰⁵/106–127 = 17–39 in the varied form. Instead of the final 2 bars of minor tonic chord the sequel to 39 is

Coda.

128–140.—Four-bar cadence, with subdominant colour inducing major tonic, closing into repetition in higher position, closing into final descent down major tonic chord (4 bars+pause). Adagio follows without break.

Adagio con espressione: A♭ (IV., as regards the Sonata as a whole). Lyric melody in three strains.

First Strain.

Bars 1–8.—Four bars on tonic pedal with medial tonic close, followed by 4 with moving bass and dominant accents, ending in half-close.

Second Strain in Dominant.

⁸/9–16.—Continuation with new figures in dominant, passing through (iii.) and (ii.) to full close, the last 4 bars with an unbroken flow of syncopated quavers (*i.e.*, tied semiquavers). A minute figure-analysis of these 2 strains might show various points of correspondence or " logic " in the interior rhythms; but what really matters is the immense breadth of all these various figures within their 8-bar frame. We feel the rhythmic symmetry, but we wait in vain for any figure to repeat itself, except in vague metrical outline (*e.g.*, bars 5–8, and the cadential appoggiaturas), until the 3rd strain makes a complete recapitulation. Nobody grasps less of such music than the musician who remains satisfied with taking in a whole page of an Adagio at a glance.

Third Strain.

17–24 = 1–8, with semiquaver accompaniment in first 4 bars and substitute of a tonic close, reached through (IV.), in the 7th and 8th bars. In this last bar the bass descends towards the key of the dominant.

25–26 link with Finale; 2 bars on D♮ as dominant of E♭.

Allegro vivace: E♭ major. Rondo, with Development in place of Second Episode.

Main Theme.

First Strain (A).

¼/1–8.—Symmetrical 8-bar theme over running bass, answering dominant close in bar 4 by tonic close in bar 8.   Figures (a) and (b) used in developments.

Second Strain.

9–16.—New 8-bar theme; 4 bars on dominant, closing into self-repetition, diverted into tonic at last bar.
17–24 = 9–16.

Transition.

²⁴/25–35.—Figure a+b (without the trill) initiates a development of (b) in sequence, antiphonal between 2 octaves, *forte* below, *piano* above.   The 1st downward step, to (vi.), begins an 8-bar group with its *forte*; the next step is in (V.); the next 4 bars consist of half-groups (2 quavers in cross-rhythm), making dominant preparation for (V.).

First Episode in B♭ (V.).

³⁵/36–55.—New theme (C) (arising from hint given by last bar) making a 4-bar group (twice 1+2), outlining a figure (C)

in broken 6ths  The 4-bar group

repeats itself.   An F, drumming in quavers in the midst of the 6ths, rises to F♯ while the last 2 bars are repeated.   On a further rise to G the treble rises to D♭ as its upper note, thus producing dominant of A♭, highly disturbing to the key of B♭. A fragment of figure (c) makes a cadence in A♭ twice in the next 2 bars, and then coalesces into a descent by 3 sequential modulating steps, leading to 3 more bars closing into B♭, the treble having descended along a chromatic scale the while.   Since the close into A♭ an 8-bar group has been completed here.

56–81.—The key of B♭ being restored, a new 8-bar cadence-theme rises in three 2-bar groups up the tonic chord, finishing its period by a humorous self-repeating close into the middle of the last bar.   The last 4 bars are repeated and their close expanded with a new tag in 2 more bars.   These bars also repeat themselves,

and their tag is developed into a passage of 10 bars preparation
on home dominant in tapering rhythm—*i.e.*, in pairs of bars,
single bars, half-bars, ending in a couple closing into Return.

First Return.
    82–97 = 1–16.

Development.
    98–105.—The repetition of the 2nd strain is in the tonic
minor, and its last 2 bars are on the dominant of G♭ (♭III.),
into which key they close at next period.
    106–120.—Development of a 3-bar group on (a) plus new
continuation (y), in double counterpoint with a semiquaver
theme (x) suggested by the original running bass.

    [It would not be impossible to see how (y) might be a diminu-
tion of (a). But such " logic " is not the true course of musical
events. Later on, Beethoven manifests much more ingenious
processes to the ear instead of to the eye. Musical derivations
must be heard in the making or verified in the sequel if they are
to be worth anything.]
    The 3-bar group is displayed four times in its double counter-
point; the first group is answered (*piano*) in D♭, (ay) over (x).
The 3rd group is again in G♭, and its 3rd bar groups with the
next as a 2-bar member of a rising sequence on (y). The second
2-bar step leads to the 4th complete group (x) over (ay) in B♭
minor. This closes into F minor and initiates a new process.
    121–130.—Figure (y) is reduced to 3 notes, which first descend
in 2 bars of imitative sequence. Then they continue descending
as 3-quaver steps across the ⁶₄ rhythm for 7 steps. These fill
5 bars and 1 note. The first 4 steps are *piano* and *legato*; but a
forte intervenes on the last note (before bar 126), and the next
3 steps are *f* staccato. The 6th bar is completed by notes leading
to 2 bars of vibrating semiquavers, closing into B♭ minor.
    131–138.—The close in B♭ minor (interlocking) is twice
insisted upon, and then repeated by diminution 4 times in 4 bars,
closing into next period. We cannot fail to notice the melodic
figure thus impressed upon us.
    139–166.—Drumming quavers on B♭ in treble become, after
2 bars, an accompaniment to figure (c) in unbroken quavers
below, in E♭ minor, its 3rd group coming in next period. There-

fore that emphatic B♭ minor close was figure (c) with reversed beats. In this next period the treble quavers fall a third, bringing the underlying figure (c) into C♭. A similar fall at the next corresponding point brings (c) into A♭ minor, where it remains for another 4 bars, figure (c) repeating itself once between rests (152–154). Then the upper quavers make appoggiaturas every 2 bars, while the lower part, reduced to one iambic at each 2-bar join, descends through what proves to be the chord of the home dominant. This is reached in 4 bars and dwelt upon for 8; 2+twice 1+4 ending in 2 bars of leading-note trill in bass, closing into return.

Second Return.

167–190 = 1–24, the repetition of the 2nd strain (17–24) transferring its melody to the bass.

Transition.

¹⁹⁰/191–203.—By substituting (IV.) for (V.) at the 6th and 7th bars (=30–31) and inserting 2 extra bars of the half-bar steps, passing from (ii.) through tonic minor to tonic major, Beethoven brings the last 4 bars of the Transition on to the home dominant.

Recapitulation of First Episode in Tonic.

²⁰³/204–239 = ³⁵/36–71 in tonic, unaltered but for shift of octave at 5th bar of theme (C).

Coda.

240–255.—When the aftermath of the cadence-theme reaches the 7th on dominant of (IV.) corresponding to that of home dominant at bars 72–73, it does not rise to a 9th, but the bass moves up in 4 chromatic steps, reaching the 7th of the home-dominant. With treble working its own figure in contrary motion, the bass swings twice down and back to the 7th, in twice 2 bars, and then turns a third descent into a 4-bar scale down to a pause on the dominant.

256–263 = Third Strain of *Adagio con espressione* transposed to E♭.

²⁶³/264–265.—Two florid echoes of last cadence, the second remaining on dominant, prolonged in a free-rhythmed melodic cadenza, of which the last notes anticipate, not quite accidentally, figure (a) of finale.

Presto.

266–285.—Four-bar sequential phrase on 2 notes of (a); the 4th bar breaking into quavers; and closing into repetition of whole 4 an octave higher with added 3rds. The last 2 bars are insisted on twice in rising positions, closing into a 2-bar group in which the final result of these tapering repetitions is a compound of (a) diminished and (c), closing into self-repetition, closing into 4 bars of final tonic chords.

14

SONATA IN C SHARP MINOR, Op. 27, No. 2.

(*Commonly called* " MOONLIGHT.")

Adagio sostenuto : C♯ minor.   Continuous melody on an
enormous scale with elements of development and recapitulation.

Bars 1–4.—Four-bar introduction, establishing the key
(coloured by ♭II. in bar 3) and closing into

5–8.—Four-bar period in which a melody slowly rises from
monotone on prevalent rhythmic figure (a)   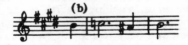   , and
modulates to (III.), closing into

9–14.—Six-bar period, modulating boldly through (iii.) and C
major (an extreme distance) and closing into ♭vii.

15–22.—The ♭vii. becomes major and proves to be the
dominant of (iii.) or (III.), on which a new figure (b) appears

and, with repetition, initiates an 8-bar period closing into (iv.).

23–27.—Clause resuming the theme of bars 5–7 in the subdominant, closing into

28–41.—Fourteen bars of "dominant preparation" for a
return to the opening.   Bars 28–31 are on a figure resembling
(b); the remaining 10 keep up the suspense without any theme.
Towards the end ♭II. appears over the dominant pedal (bar 39).

42–45.—Recapitulation of bars 5–8.

46–50.—Refraining from the former change of (III.) to (iii.),
the melody passes in 5 bars back to the tonic, closing into

51–54.—Figure (b) on tonic major chord with ♭II. on same
bass.   Note that whereas bars 15½–19 were on the dominant
of E, the same bars a tone higher have here no effect of dominant
of F♯.   They are in the tonic as modified by the ♭II.

55–59.—In continuation of bars 51–54 the melody sinks in 5 bars (containing a falling sequence) to a close into

60–69.—A coda on tonic and dominant chords, with (a) persisting in a low inner part. The overlying triplets (which have been maintained throughout the movement), allude in bars 62–65 to a new figure which they took in bars 32–37, thus enhancing the dramatic significance of that passage by treating it as no longer themeless.

Though the movement closes with complete finality, Beethoven directs that the next shall follow without break.

Allegretto : Lyric Da Capo movement in the tonic major.

1–8.—Epigrammatic couplets playing with the antithesis of tonic-to-dominant and subdominant-to-tonic.

9–16.—The repetition of the 1st strain is written in full, being varied by syncopation.

17–24.—Middle strain in descending sequences ending on half-close leading to

25–36.—Expansion of 1st strain, combining the plain and syncopated versions and insisting on bars 5–6, making a climax before the final close. Repeat bars 17–36.

Trio.

37–44.—Eight-bar self-repeating melody (4+4) with tonic closes. Repeated.

45–60.—Sixteen-bar strain, beginning with falling sequences, passing subdominant 2+2+4; the second 8 bars, of corresponding shape, grouped about the tonic.

Allegretto Da Capo.

The whole movement may be regarded in either of two rhythmic positions: (a) as if the 1st bar had the stronger

accent ♪♪ ; or (b) as if the first strong

accent came later, thus ♪♪ ; or earlier,

thus ♪♪ . Between these latter versions the difference to the ear is negligible; but it is quite possible that Beethoven had in mind the main distinction between (a) and (b), and quite certain that, as in many similar cases, he declined to decide between them. To play the movement in such a way as to compel the listener to recognize only one accentuation is to miss the point altogether. Beethoven chooses short bars in order to equalize the accents. The view of

(b) has much to recommend it, and is not impugned by the fact that it makes the *fp* in the Trio a cross-accent. But we must not expect the listener to recognize the " crossness " of the only strong accent he is allowed to hear.

Presto agitato : Sonata Form. C♯ minor.

First Group:

1–8.—Theme (A) of arpeggios punctuated by a rhythmic figure 𝆑𝆑 and moving in three 2-bar steps and 2 single bars (7 and 8) over a bass that descends conjunctly from the tonic.

9–14.—The dominant chord, reached at bar 9, is insisted on for 6 bars (2+2+1+1), with a new figure ending in a pause.

15–20.—Counterstatement of theme, moving to dominant of (v.) (G♯ minor) in three 2-bar steps, closing into

Second Group in Dominant minor.

21–24.—Four-bar melody (B), with a figure of rising appoggiaturas, closing into

25–28.—Repetition in syncopated variation, closing into

29–36.—Falling sequences touching related keys (reckoned locally), including ♭II. in passing. But at bar 33 the ♭II. arrives with a crash and fills 3 bars of a 4-bar cadence, closing into

37–42.—Interrupted close, resuming ♭II. and expanding the cadence to 6 bars, closing into

43–48.—New 6-bar theme (2+2+1+1) in quavers without the hitherto almost perpetual vibration of semiquavers, closing into

49–56.—Repetition in fuller and higher scoring, expanded to 8 bars (with touch of ♭II.), closing into

57–62.—Cadence-theme (2+2+1+1), with a figure in common with that of bar 21. (In an early sketch that theme is hardly distinguishable from this cadence-theme.)

63–64.—Two bars arpeggio-tremolo, in the first instance leading to repeat from bar 1 ; in the second instance leading to Development.

Development.

65–70.—Opening theme, starting on chord of (I.), treats it as dominant of (iv.) closing, in 3 steps, into that key.

71–74.—Theme (B) in F♯ minor, closing into

75–78.—Theme (B) in bass, leading to

79–86.—Continuation of theme (B) in G♮ major (locally ♭II.), struggling back to F♯ minor at its 4th bar, and thence developing its last figure for 4 more bars, reaching (via D as ♭II.) the dominant of our tonic C♯ minor.

87–101.—The home dominant, reached at bar 87, is maintained through a new cantabile, which it is purposeless to derive from previous themes. Its point lies in its quiescence and its proportions: 4 bars closing into 4 of varied repetition, overlapping into 2+2+2, +the 2 cadential semibreves of bars 100–101. Bar 94, the 4th bar of its period, becomes the 1st bar of 2-bar groups.

Recapitulation.

First Group.

102–115 = 1–14.

Second Group.

116–157.—Exact recapitulation in tonic of bars 21–62, except that the autograph reads (probably by oversight) A♮ in bar 135, and that the two bars 39–40 are compressed into the single bar 134.

As to the A♮ the question cannot be settled. If A♯ is right an accidental is required. If A♮ is intended an accidental is superfluous, except as a precaution. Therefore there is some presumption that in such a case the ♮ is a clerical error for ♯. On the other hand, the harmonic subtlety is attractive and by no means unparallelled.

Bars 157–200 = *Coda.*

157–166.- -The 2 bars (63–64) that led back to the beginning now lead towards the subdominant, with a descending bass over which theme (A) moves for 2 of its 2-bar steps. Two further steps are themeless and broken by pauses, while the bass continues to descend chromatically.

167–170.—Theme (B) in bass.

171–176.—Theme (B) taken up in treble, and its rising appoggiaturas developed in accelerated steps rising to climax and moving towards subdominant.

177–189.—Cadential chords (including ♭II.) spread over 13 bars and ending in quasi-recitative style, closing (*Adagio*) into

190–200.—A last resumption of cadence-theme, with final tonic arpeggio and chords.

15

SONATA IN D MAJOR, Op. 28.
(*Pastorale.*)

THE publisher, Cranz of Hamburg, gave this sonata the not inappropriate title *Pastorale*. Beethoven would not have so named it; his notions of " pastoral " style, as shown in his Pastoral Symphony, are much more definitely " racy of the soil " than anything that can be found in this rich and subtle composition, which approaches the *volkstümlich* or bucolic style only in the cadence-theme of the first movement and the main theme of the Rondo.

Allegro : D major.   Sonata form.

First Group.

Bars 1–10.—Ten-bar phrase (A), 4+2+4, on tonic pedal (bar 1 belongs to the phrase), ending with figure (a).

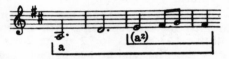

11–20.—The same repeated an octave higher.
21–38.—Continuation, with an 8-bar phrase (at the end of which the pedal is released) closing into its repetition, which is expanded by further insistence on its last 4 bars, closing into

Transition.
39–62.—New 4-bar theme (B), moving to dominant and repeated on dominant of dominant containing figure (b).

The theme begins on 2nd bar of its period, so that each phrase closes into the next.   The bass is a descending scale.   Bars 48–55 repeat bars 40–47, with imitative ornamentation, and bars 55–62

insist twice on last 2 bars over enhanced dominant.

Second Group : (V.) coloured by (iii.).

63–70.—Eight-bar phrase, beginning on dominant of (iii.) (F♯ minor) and closing in (V.).

71–76.—Repetition from 63 diverging at 5th bar, thence persisting in (iii.), and leading to

77–102.—Long cantabile moving in 4-bar steps from dominant of (iii.) into (V.). For 6 bars the bass hovers round C♯; for 8 more round B, the harmony changing to dominant of (V.) when E♯ changes to E♮; and thence descending in thirds with melody, reaching subdominant at bar 97. Two extra bars added to the sixth 4-bar group lead to

103–108.—New cadential phrase (2×2+2×1) containing figure (c)

and closing into

109–124.—Continuation of the long cantabile, clearly in (V.) with local modulations, for 16 more bars (4+4+8), leading to

125–134.—Cadential phrase, with figure (c) enhanced and expanded to 10 bars, closing into

135–143.—Cadence-theme (D), a new 8-bar phrase (4+4), beginning on 2nd bar of its period.

144–158.—The cadence-theme repeated, and its second 4 bars insisted on, the last 2 bars thrice.

159–162.—The last bar carried on in 4 bars of downward scale, leading first back to bar 1, then on to Development.

Development.

163–166.—Four bars on F♯, ♮⁶₅, closing into G major (IV.).

167–176.—Theme (A) in (IV.).

177–190.—Repetition of (A) in G minor (iv.) with imitative ornament, and with flowing bass counterpoint (x) to figure (a), followed by (a) over (x) in D minor. These last 8 bars (183–190) initiate a new process, as follows:

191–198.—Bars 183–190 inverted in double counterpoint.

199–206.—The double counterpoint continued in 2-bar groups, alternately ${a \atop x}$ and ${x \atop a}$, passing through D minor and A minor.

207–218.—${a \atop x}$ carried on in 1-bar steps, the treble rising

through E minor into B minor, and after 12 bars closing into
219–256.—Thirty-eight bars on dominant of B (vi.), the
first 8 (2 × 4) with (a²) in contrary motion in two positions. A
sudden *piano* at 9th bar initiates 12 bars exclusively on dominant
chord, with (a²) leading in extreme bass (upper imitations
continuing); then, at bar 239, the theme vanishes as soon as (a²)
in treble has reached the required top note; and the remaining
18 bars from 239 are a slow decline on the chord, ending in 2-bar
pause.

²⁵⁷/258–261.—Cadence-theme (D) at new rhythmic angle, the
melody beginning with 1st bar of its period, and figure (b) of the
transition theme guilelessly slipped in at 3rd bar; in B major.
Pause.

²⁶¹/262–266.—The same 4 bars in B minor. Pause.

²⁶⁶/267–268.—Figure (b), *Adagio*, as an unresolved question on
the home dominant, with pause.

Recapitulation.

First Group.

269–310 = 1–38.—The imitative ornaments of bars 177–178 are
used at the repetition of (A); and bars 35–38 (303–306) are
insisted on twice instead of once, with heightened detail, concluding by borrowing figure (c).

Transition.

311–336.—The 4-bar dominant phrase is answered in tonic
instead of on enhanced dominant. Thus with 2 extra bars on
home dominant (328–329) it is easily made to prepare for tonic
recapitulation of the rest.

Second Group in Tonic coloured by (vi.).

337–433 = 63–157.—Two extra bars are inserted at 403–404
(*i.e.*, between 128 and 129), thus adding emphasis to the
cadential ⁶₄.

434–437.—Arising, as before, from cadence-theme, a 4-bar
descending scale leads to

Coda.

438–461.—Theme (A). Its last 2 bars (a²) insisted on 4 times,
with a new top note rising up the tonic chord till it reaches D in
alt, where it stays to complete a seventh 2-bar group as reckoned
from the first (a²) (bars 446–447).

A final full close releases the tonic pedal. The silent bar 461
completes the period.

Andante : D minor (i.). Da Capo form, with "binary" melodies.

1–8.—First strain, 4 with half close+4 closing in dominant minor; with repeat.

9-16.—Second strain, 8 bars (2+2, +1+½+½; +2) on dominant, leading to

17–22.—Third strain, resuming 1st strain and developing bar 2 so as to close in 6 bars with a climax. Second and 3rd strains repeated.

Middle Episode or Trio in Tonic Major.

23–38.—Symmetrical 16-bar melody in 4 groups of 4 bars (1+1+2), in two sections, the first (8 bars) ending in dominant, the second passing through subdominant to similar end in tonic. Each section repeated.

Da Capo of Main Theme

39–46.—First strain unaltered.

47–54.—Repeat, varied in demisemiquavers. (Note *legato* in bass from 5th bar onwards.)

55–68.—Second and 3rd strains unaltered.

69–82.—Varied repetition of 2nd and 3rd strains.

Coda.

83–88.—First bars resumed without movement in accompaniment: bars 3 and 4 represented only by rhythm in monotone, broken by pause. These 2 bars repeated, based on G♯ instead of G, with pause.

89–99.—Allusion to Trio, on dominant with minor harmony, rising to climax at 3rd bar. The triplet figure is prolonged into a descent down the chord of the dominant 9th, from the end of which (note the passing ♭II.) arises a declamatory 4-bar close (95–99).

Scherzo and Trio : D major.

There is no need to regard this movement as beginning on an unaccented bar—*i.e.*, as in ³⁄₄ time, beginning on the half-bar. This theory is based on a rule that every close on the tonic must come upon an accent. Beethoven cannot be bound by a rule that was not invented until some seventy years after his death: and the commonsense foundation of the rule is the obvious fact that a cadence is weak when it closes on a weak beat. And why should all cadences be strong? Elementary scholarship must distinguish between strong and weak: but there is no scholarship in making rules which the classics disregard not merely occasionally but systematically. In a slow tempo the distinction between strong and weak bars vanishes because the bars are too long; and in a quick tempo with short bars it vanishes if and when every bar is equally accented. That is why classical scherzos are written in short bars: the composer wants hard and equal accents, such as Mr. Plunket Greene admires in the playing of Irish jigs by Irish fiddlers. For other reasons even so simple a movement as the Rondo of this Sonata utterly refuses to conform to the strong cadence theory. If you displace its bars by half a bar at the beginning you will have to replace them later, and it is perfectly clear that Beethoven would consider your theory mere nonsense. If it amuses you to read the Scherzo and Trio with its 1st bar off the accent, by all means do so. It is unlikely that Beethoven thought of bars 45–48 in that way; nor does the doubled chord in bar 58 settle the question, while bars 68–70 are whimsical on any theory. Hence the term Scherzo.

1–16.—Symmetrical strain 4+4 in tonic, 4+4 in dominant. The 1st note, F♯, reasserts D major after the previous D minor movement.

17–32.—Repetition of 1–16 with new detail.

33–48.—Sequence rising in three 4-bar steps, with initial figure in bass; the remaining 4 bars complete the rise in shorter steps, reaching dominant chord.

49–70.—Eight bars of 1st strain (as in 9–16, *piano* throughout), answered in tonic by 14 bars; 4, +4 closing viâ (ii.), + cadential 2+2+2.

Trio : B minor (vi.).

71–78.—Eight-bar strain, 4+4 in 2-part counterpoint, the melody repeating itself with modulation to D (♭III.). Repeated.

79–86.—The same melody reharmonized first in D, then returning to B minor.

87–94.—Reharmonized repetition of 79–86, with rising contrapuntal bass.

Scherzo Da Capo; its first F♯ now sounding like dominant of B minor.

Rondo : Allegro ma non troppo. D major.

Main Theme.

1–8.—Four-bar theme (2+2), self-repeating to 8 bars, the main figure (a) persisting in bass

while treble intervenes in alternate 2-bar phrases.

9–16.—Tonic-and-dominant continuation, with 4-bar phrase built of single bars in treble, while (a) persists in bass; repeated with variation. [As (a) is rooted on the tonic, the whole main theme is on a tonic pedal.]

Transition.

[16]/17–28.—New theme (B) of arpeggios on a descending scale (2 steps a bar); 4 bars ending on half-close, repeated, with 3rd and 4th bars diverted to dominant of A, and expansion for 4 more bars of dominant preparation.

First Episode in Dominant.

[28]/29–42.—New theme, a 4-bar phrase in 3-part imitation on chord of A with close; repeated with variation, the close insisted on for 4 more bars, with 2 of slow final cadence closing into

43–51.—Cadence-theme (C), a 2-bar figure (c) given 3 times, the 3rd time with G$\natural$, so as to return to D, leading by the 3 notes F$\sharp$, G, G$\sharp$, with measured pauses, to

First Return.

52–67 = 1–16, with new counterpoint in bars 5–6.

Second Episode in Subdominant.

68–78.—Figure (a) in treble makes dominant preparation for G major in 4-bar phrases (with bass in contrary motion and complementary rhythm). The second 4-bar phrase closes in G (with overlap of rhythm at bar 75), and the close is insisted on, leading to

79–100.—New 4-bar theme in G major (IV.) in double counterpoint, with a lower theme in added thirds; answered by middle voice in dominant (D) returning to tonic. The third entry, in bass with new counterpoint, remains in G and closes into a fourth entry in G minor with thicker harmony closing into D minor. Here a fifth entry, in bass, expands into 6 bars of rising sequence, the last 2 steps accelerated, leading to

101–113.—Preparation for return with theme (C) on home dominant; 2+2+2+1+1+5; and pause.

Second Return.

114–129 = 1–16 = 52–67, with the new counterpoint varied in bars 5–6.

Transition.

[129]/130–144.—Theme (B), diverted at 6th bar through subdominant on to home dominant.

Tonic Recapitulation of First Episode.

$^{144}/145-168 = 29-51$, the insistence on 8th bar being expanded from 4 to 5 bars.   The cadence-theme (C) leads to subdominant.

Coda.

$^{168}/169-176$.—Bass of main theme (a) with syncopated chords throughout instead of the original intermittent melody; in G major diverging at 6th bar and rising chromatically, closing into

177–192.—Crescendo on home dominant pedal, with (a) in bass and sequence of ½-bar steps rising for 4 bars in treble, poised at top for 2 bars, and descending at 3 steps a bar for 4 more, ending with 6 bars $(2+2+1+1)$ on figure of (B) on dominant 7th, with pause.

Più allegro.

193–210.—Figure (a) in bass, with brilliant new running counterpoint; $4+4+2+2+1+1$; $+4$ bars of final close.

16

SONATA IN G MAJOR, Op. 31, No. 1.

In its treatment of keys this sonata closely foreshadows the *Waldstein* sonata. In both works the first movement begins by treating the nearer keys as if they were mere local chords, attacking the subdominant from the flat 7th by way of repeating the opening phrase (which modulated to the dominant) a tone lower. In both works such bold treatment of the nearer keys makes the dominant ineffective as a key for a contrasted section, and leads to the choice of (III.) for the Second Group. In the present sonata the slow movement presents us with a self-conscious reaction, being the most diffuse and ornate ABA movement in all Beethoven's works. In the *Waldstein* sonata the slow movement was originally the long and ornate rondo afterwards published without opus-number as *Andante in F*. The G major sonata states its bold harmonies with a nervous and jocular air of paradox. There is almost a touch of humour in following its first movement with a reactionary slow movement. The *Waldstein* sonata is too serious for any such reaction, and so the *Andante in F* was extruded and replaced by one of Beethoven's profoundest pages. Both sonatas end with a brilliant and luxurious rondo, but that of the G major sonata laughs at itself in its last page.

Allegro vivace : Sonata form.
First Group : G major.

Bars 1–11.—Theme, 2 bars closing into 3 times 2, closing into cadence *in* (not *on*) dominant; containing figures

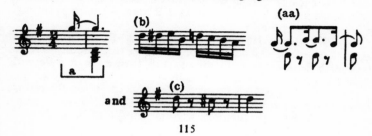

12–22.—Bars 1–11 repeated a tone lower, thus starting in ♭VII. and reaching subdominant.

23–29.—Last 3 bars, (aa) and (c), repeated in tonic, with twofold insistence on (c), closing into

30–45.—Long extension of (b) on tonic and dominant, culminating in 6 bars of dominant chord ending with pause.

46–65.—Counterstatement of main theme, diverted at end of 8th bar to dominant of (iii.) (B minor). This turn (bars 52–56) is reiterated and extended, through figure (c), by 5 more bars, thus leading to

Second Group : (III.) and (iii.) (B major and minor).

66–73.—Symmetrical 8-bar theme in B major, closing with figure (d)

74–87.—Counterstatement of the new melody in bass, in B minor, expanded to 14 bars. At its 5th bar it takes a new course in rising sequences of 2-bar steps of its syncopated rhythm+figure (d). The 3rd step of these falls back in 1-bar sequences (chain of 7ths), closing in 5 bars into the next clause.

88–97.—The last 10 bars repeated in treble, closing into

98–111.—Cadence-theme, consisting of tonic-and-dominant swing, alternately minor and major (only once major); 3 times 2 bars, and 4 times 1 bar. Final chords in rhythm (a) followed by 2 notes (x)

which lead back to bar 1, and on to the Development.

Development.

112–133.—Beginning in tonic with bars 1–7, the development proceeds to carry (aa) in 4 bars into C minor (iv.). Resuming from bar 4 in that key, it proceeds in 2 more 4-bar steps through F into B♭, closing into

134–157.—Long run on (b) starting in B♭ with an 8-bar series (4 couples). which at 3rd couple moves to C minor. Thence another 8 bars lead to D minor, and thence, in 8 differently turned bars, to the home dominant.

158–193.—Thirty-six bars of dominant preparation for return. After the first 4, the arpeggio-form of bars 39–43 appears, expanded to 8 bars; then the rhythm (a) fills 12 bars (thrice 4)

and dwindles for the remaining 12 bars first to once a bar and then to once in 2 bars, at last closing into

Recapitulation.

First Group in Tonic.

194–217.—Bars 1–11 intact.   The answer in ♭VII. is omitted and bars 23–26 follow at once.   These, however, are followed by bars 52–65, transposed a fourth higher so as to lead to (VI.).

Second Group : (VI.), (vi.) and Tonic Major.

218–233.—The 8-bar melody reproduced in (VI.).   Its counter-statement in bass diverges at its 5th bar and moves (without expansion) to G, closing into

234–279.—Complete recapitulation of the whole Second Group in the tonic, remaining major throughout.   As a consequence the major bars (100–101) of the cadence-phrase become minor to preserve their contrast.   The 2 notes (x) follow in their original position, leading to

Coda.

280–295.—Final appearance of (ab), with (b) expanded to the passage (bars 30–45) that ends on pause on dominant.

296–299.—The combination of (a) with (x) fills 4 bars, with a whimsical query on the dominant. (A publisher, Nägeli, enraged Beethoven by inserting a ⁶₄ answer to that query !)

300–325.—An 8-bar tonic-and-dominant development of (a) (twice 2+4, with gaps) arises in reply; is repeated with new point; its last 4 bars are twice reaffirmed; and the movement flickers out.

Adagio grazioso : ABA form with coda.   C major (IV.).

Bars 1–8.—Sustained 8-bar melody (2+2+4) in C, closing in tonic.

9–16.—Counterstatement, with bars 1–4 in bass and running ornaments in alternate bars above.   The next 4 bars are led by the treble, and modulate to (V.), closing therein.

17–26.—A new figure moves in 3 bars to (ii.), and thence in 3 more (a step lower) to the home dominant, on which there are 4 bars of preparation, 1+1+three thirds+pause with cadenza, leading to

27–34.—Resumption of bars 1–8, with increased ornamentation.   The last chord changes to the minor, leading to

Middle Episode.

35–40.—A new melody, entering on 2nd bar of its period, moves from (i.) to ♭VI. in six bars (thrice 2) over a bass slowly rising by semitones; closing into

41–52.—New semiquaver theme, moving in four 2-bar steps (alternately treble and bass) from A♭ to F minor (iv.). Thence the bass descends 2 steps in a bar, and in 4 bars reaches, through ♭II., the home dominant.

53–64.—Twelve bars (1+1+3+3+4) of dominant preparation lead to *Da Capo.*

65–98.—Complete recapitulation of bars 1–34, with livelier accompaniment and enhanced ornaments; closing into

Coda.

99–103.—Arising from bar 98, the trills of the main theme are turned into a 4-bar cadential phrase (1+1+2), closing into

[103]/104–107.—Intensified repetition of this 4-bar phrase in bass, closing into

108–119.—Theme of bars 1–2 in bass, witn new melody in dialogue with it. Two bars of this repeated with intensification, then compressed into twice 1, then expanded into dying cadences on tonic pedal (2 bars, 1 bar, 1 bar in three thirds, and twice 1 bar).

Rondo : G major. Sonata-rondo, recapitulating its First Episode like a Second Group, and containing much development in its Second Episode.

Main Theme.

½/1–8.—Symmetrical 8-bar melody (A) (4+4) containing

figure (a)      and closing in

tonic.

8/9–16.—Second strain, (B), making 4 bars into 8 by plain repetition, containing figures (b), (c).

16/17–32.—Repetition of both strains in an inner part, with counterpoints above. [Figure (c) emerges in treble at one point.]

Transition.

32/33–41.—Figure (c) developed, passing in 2-bar steps through (vi.) in treble to (V.) in bass, and thence expanded in a passage of dominant preparation lasting for two 2-bar and $2\frac{1}{2}$ single-bar steps.

First Episode (quasi Second Group), (V.).

42–51.—New tonic-and-dominant 4-bar theme (1+1+2), expanded by insistent reiteration to 10 bars, closing into

52–57.—A 6-bar phrase (2+4) closing into itself.

58–66.—The repetition of the 6-bar phrase fails to close, and impinges upon the home-dominant 7th, on which it dwells for 4 more bars. The bass glides away into a descending counterpoint to

Return of Rondo-strains.

66/67–82.—Strains (A) and (B) with new flowing accompaniment.

Middle Episode, quasi Development, chiefly in ♭VI.

82/83–86.—Strain (A), with its treble counterpoint in triplets, as at bar 17 foll., is given in tonic minor, intact for 4 bars—

87–97—after which it is developed in 2-part canon in upper octave at 1 bar, for 4 bars, passing to (iv.) (C minor); whereupon an upper part and an extreme bass turn the canon into one in the lower octave (3 octaves apart), passing to ♭VI., with 4 more bars to establish that key, closing into

98–105.—New theme (D) in ♭VI., 4 bars closing into 2 of main theme, which are repeated in (iv.) (C minor), together making an 8-bar phrase, closing into

106–113.—The same process in (iv.), with the last 2 bars diverted towards F minor. (The sforzandos in bars 106–108 were perhaps omitted by accident in bars 98–100; but it is at least equally reasonable to interpret the whole process as a growth to a climax.)

114–120.—A 3rd step, passing into B♭ minor, drifts in its 3rd bar into a new 2-bar sequence with (a) and the sforzando notes, falling through A♭ into G minor (i.).

121–124.—Four more bars of theme (D) in G minor, closing into the home dominant.

125–132.—Eight bars (the last 4 reduced to the underlying tremolo) of dominant preparation for the return.

Recapitulation.

132 133–164.—Second return of Rondo-theme, with new scoring and ornament.

Recapitulation, in Tonic, of Transition and First Episode.

¹⁶⁴/165–177.—The transition, beginning as in bars 32½–33½, substitutes (IV.) for (V.) and then passes in 5 extra bars through (ii.) (bars 168½–171) to the home dominant. This being reached at bar 172, the rest of the dominant preparation follows, transposed from bars 36½–41.

178–195.—Recapitulation, in tonic, of bars 42–59.

Coda.

196–205.—The bar corresponding to 60 gravitates, as before, to its subdominant; but the passage is not allowed to drift thither, but is carried upwards towards chords hovering around the home ⁶₄, which, after 6 bars urgent insistance, arrives at bar 206.

206–219.—Cadenza-like imitative development of figure (b) on dominant pedal, *quasi* in 4 parts; first, 3 bars imitation in lower 4th; then the same 3 bars in upper 5th; then (abandoning the pedal) the same imitation in lower 4th, but a 5th higher and expanded by 2 bars; leading to 8 bars of dominant, twice 2 in dialogue, and the last 4 unharmonized, with rise of 7th to C♯ leading to

²²⁴/225–243.—Main theme (strain A) broken up by extravagant pauses and an *Adagio* tempo for its alternate figures. Its 7th and 8th bars (as originally reckoned) take an upward turn (at bar 236) and are repeated, extending the penultimate note to 3 *Adagio* bars of cadential trill. (The *fp* chord in bar 240 is the real last note of the melody, the beautiful bass cantabile that strays across it being accessory until it reaches the trill.)

²⁴³/244–247.—Over the 3rd bar of the trill figure (c) enters *Presto* and twirls for 4 bars, closing into tonic at bar 248.

248–275.—Playful dialogue on (c), as between augmented 6th and plain full close: first 2+2, then 4+4; then, from bar 260, in skeleton harmony, 1+1+2+4 (dominant). Chords intervene at these last 2 bars, closing into 8 bars of tonic chord punctuated by gaps, the silent last bar completing the period. (The *crescendo* at bar 264 marks the beginning of the 4-bar period.)

17

SONATA IN D MINOR, Op. 31, No. 2.

THE inquirer who asked Beethoven what his music " meant " usually received an answer according to his folly. Hence the yellowhammer with a compass of two octaves in the *Pastoral Symphony*, and hence the lack of time to finish the Sonata Op. 111 with a triumphant finale. There is more illumination in Beethoven's advice to " read Shakespeare's *Tempest* " in connection with the D minor Sonata, though the two works have not a single course of events on any parallel lines and though each contains much that would be violently out of place in the other. But there is a mood that is common to both. Beethoven would never have posed as a Shakespeare-scholar; but neither would he have been misled by the fairy-tale element in Shakespeare's last plays into regarding them as consisting only of mellow sunset and milk of human kindness. With all the tragic power of its first movement the D minor Sonata is, like Prospero, almost as far beyond tragedy as it is beyond mere foul weather. It will do you no harm to think of Miranda at bars 31–38 of the slow movement; but people who want to identify Ariel and Caliban and the castaways, good and villainous, may as well confine their attention to the exploits of the Scarlet Pimpernel when the *Eroica* of the C minor Symphony is being played.

Largo and Allegro: D minor.

First Group.

Bars 1–6.—A figure (a) on c$\sharp$ announced in *Largo* tempo with a pause, is answered by a 4-bar Allegro theme (b) in D minor, twice 1+2, including *Adagio* pause on dominant. The tendency of the bass to rise, as shown in bar 3 and developed in 3+^{3}/4-5, governs the whole first movement.

7–20.—Counterstatement, giving the *Largo* figure on $_{\text{E}}^{6}$, which unexpected chord proves to be dominant of (III.). The Allegro figure (b) again proceeds for 4 bars (twice 1,+2) on a bass rising by semitones till at 5th bar it reaches the home dominant, on which 7½ bars of $^6_4$ are completed by a final ½-bar's dominant

7th closing into

Transition.

21–40.—Starting on the first fundamental tonic chord yet heard in this movement, figure (a) in the Allegro tempo enters in the bass, in dialogue with a new 2-bar figure in treble, making a 4-bar clause. The bass carries this in sequence up the steps of the scales of D minor and A minor, using the augmented 2nd at each juncture. From the 3rd step onwards the sequence is in 2-bar steps, and the 7th step leaps another augmented 2nd to D$\sharp$. Two more bars on this D$\sharp$ complete a period, closing into

Second Group in Dominant Minor.

41–54.—Three interlocking 4-bar groups (1+thrice 1,+interlock) on a new theme in rhythm of (b) with gaps; all on dominant of A minor (v.): viz., $\sharp\,^5_3$, $^6_4$, $^9_7$.

Hence the effect is that of dominant preparation, and a conscientious theorist might prefer to date the Second Group from the following theme. So long as we avoid the wretched term Second *Subject*, and so long as we can tell a dominant from a tonic, the rest of our terminology cannot do much harm. The last 4-bar group is prolonged by 2 bars of further descent on the dominant 9th.

55–62.—New 8-bar theme (C) strongly emphasizing $\flat$II. in a 2-bar group interlocking with two repetitions rising by octaves, the 3rd step being diverted into a rising sequence, leading through (iv.), to close into next period.

63–74.—Repetition of theme (C) in extreme bass, with antiphonal treble and major tonic 3rd. The 3rd group does not rise, but its G$\sharp$ behaves as A$\flat$ resolving on to G, where it begins a 6-bar running passage, rising in 2-bar sequence back to A minor, while the treble descends in iambics cut off from theme (C.). The third 2-bar group closes into

Cadence Theme.

75–90.—Two-bar double counterpoint in a $^6_4$+$^5_3$ position closing into its inversion, and the 4 bars repeated in syncopated variation closing into compressed repetition in 2 bars, closing into 4 of rhythmic final bare tonic, leading to a 4-bar melodic link, returning first to the repeat. The link is afterwards represented by a single 2-bar step down to G leading to

Development.
93–98.—The *Largo* figure (a) with its pauses, first on F$\sharp$, then

on a diminished 7th, which might be anywhere, but which resolves into F♯ major $^{\sharp 6}_{\sharp 4}$ $_{c\sharp}$.

99–120.—The $^6_4$ never resolves ; figure (a) in the Allegro tempo, with its answering figure as in bars 21-24, bursts out in F♯ minor and rises up by steps as before. The steps modulate, and the 2-bar steps group in pairs. Hence the appearance of a halt where B♭ (the 2nd of a pair) $^{\sharp 5}$ is followed by B♮ ^{6}. The sixth 2-bar step (the 8th from the start) having reached a chord of D minor, 2 single bars descend to the home dominant, which is reached in the next period.

121–142.—Twenty-two bars of dominant preparation avoiding all thematic allusion: 4 (2—twice 1) repeated twice in lower positions, closing into 4 semibreves descending to a 6-bar melodic lead (with a ♭II.) into the recapitulation. (Take the tied semibreves together with the following self-repeating 2—2 bars.)

Recapitulation.

First Group.

143–158 = 1–12, with the addition of 4 bars of recitative to each of the *Largo*. The first recitative is continuous with figure (a). The second is separated from (a) by a pause. The last bar in both recitatives implies a tonic close in its key.

159–170.—Three themeless 4-bar steps (four ½-bars+2) rising by semitones from dominant of F minor towards the home dominant. The final A♭ of the recitative implied F minor. The F♯ minor is thus really G♭ minor. There is no enharmonic change at that moment, for such changes of the name of a key as a whole are mere changes of notation. But the whole passage has either made an enharmonic circle or there is (as is always possible with diminished 7ths) a compensating enharmonic change somewhere in the 3rd step (bars 166-169). At all events the ear will not be worried by any doubt that the following recapitulation is in the home tonic. Its pitch suffices to indicate a tonic relation to the dominant key in which its whole contents were given in the exposition.

Second Group in Tonic.

171–218 = 41–88 in tonic.

Coda.

217–227.—Tonic chord, 4, −4 half-bars ; 4 sustained final bars.

Adagio: B♭ major (VI.). Sonata Form without Development.

It is not length, but harmonic and rhythmic content that constitutes a development.   There are developments hardly longer than the passage comprised in bars 38¼-42 of the present movement. For instance, the 8 bars in the corresponding part of the slow movement of the D major Trio, Op. 70, No. 1, are within a few quavers of the same length by the tick of the metronome. But that passage develops two different themes in two different sequences passing through 5 keys, with two different polyphonic methods, and then has leisure for an entire themeless bar at the end. This is very different from spending 5 bars over one ascent of the home dominant chord.

The present movement gives an unusually clear impression of grand proportions, and the student will be well advised to listen to it from that point of view. First then, as an example of the proportion-values of a slow tempo, the first paragraph, bars 1-16 closing into 17, will take exactly one minute at the fairly acceptable tempo of ♪ = 96.   A properly moderate tempo for the finale is ♩. = 72.   One minute of this takes us through two pages into the middle of one of the later themes of the Second Group ! Slowness means bigness.

Again, in the slow movement the theme of the Second Group repeats itself after 4 bars. Many later composers, old as well as young, despise such tunes as too petty for the Wagnerian spaces the composer delights in. The designs of people who hold this view are apt to sag. The point is easily tested, and is well worth testing. Supposing we substitute the following turn at bar 34:

We need go no further: the mischief is done, and we know that the patient listener is condemned to 4 bars ending on the dominant, and a pair of complementary 4-bar groups further expanded by echoes. Instead of the contrast between human dimensions and the Matterhorn, we have Mark Twain's unfortunate photograph in which the donkey's ears obstructed the view.

But the grandest lesson in proportion is at the end, when an entirely new theme occupies 2 bars, repeats itself, and then dies away in crotchet groups leading to a final bar which compels us actually to think of its 6th quaver as an ultimate unit. Nothing can be more futile than to seek a " logical " connexion in the melodic figures. Even the misplaced ingenuity that traces a resemblance between common forms of ornament has no explanation why the composer avoids unmistakable allusions. The all-sufficient " logic " lies in the fact that this new theme draws the scale as no old theme could have drawn it. The human figure at the foot of the Great Pyramid would be none the better for being so shaped and draped as to present a pyramidal outline.

First Group : Bb.

1–16.—Symmetrical and sequential melody in 4-bar groups, 2+2 interlocking, answered by 4 (third 2-bar step+2) half-closing on dominant. The reciprocal 8 bars (connected by anacrusis in bar 8) use the figure of bar 2

as an inner part in the initial bar of each pair, and ornament it in the melody. A dominant 9th in the 2nd pair contrasts with a diminished 7th in the 3rd pair resolving up to (vi.). The close is broadened so as to arrive in next period.

Transition.

17–22.—A drum-figure, (b) impinging on each crotchet, supports a new melody moving in interlocking 2-bar steps lying across the 2-bar periods. The 3rd step approaches the dominant of (V.), reaching it in next period.

23–30.—Eight bars of dominant preparation (4 times 1,+ twice 1,+2), with sequence of 6 quavers lying across the bar and rising for 3½ steps; closing into twice 1 cadential bar and 2 of unmixed dominant chord, with melodic final links in bass and treble; figure (b) above as well as below.

Second Group in Dominant.

31–38.—New self-repeating 8-bar melody, answering medial close at 4th bar by full close in 7th and 8th.

38/39–42.—Figure (b) enters in last bar of previous melody and continues while *R.H.* rises in four 1-bar steps up the home-dominant chord of minor 9th, culminating in florid descending link, closing into Recapitulation.

Recapitulation.

First Group.
43–58 = 1–16.—Figure (a) is from the outset present in the inner parts at the 1st bar of each couple; and a new demi-semi-quaver accompaniment floats down from above through 5 octaves during the last 8 bars.

Transition.
59–72.—The first 2 couplets of the transition lie a melodic step higher, and are harmonized with a subdominant turn which the bass confirms. This brings the rest into exact transposition to tonic from the point corresponding to bar 22.

Second Group in Tonic.
73 80 = 31–38 in tonic.

Coda.
80/81–88.—Eight bars (1+1+2, + another 2 repeated) closing into next period. Proceeding on the lines of the link-passage 38/39-42, and accompanied throughout by (b) in bass, this passage ascends the minor 9th of B♭ in the first 4 bars, leading naturally to the subdominant (as ⁶₄ on B♭) and following it by self-repeating tonic cadences over the tonic pedal, closing at last into
89 90.—Figure (a) rounded into a 2-bar group in *L.H.*, answered (with anacrusis) at 1 bar by treble. The bass, answering the anacrusis, leads to
91–97 =9–16 in dialogue between bass and treble, closing into
98–103.—Entirely new 2-bar theme on tonic pedal closing into repetition in inner part with upper counterpoint, closing into 3 echoing crotchets, closing into a melodious bar ending on last quaver.

Allegretto: D minor. Sonata Form, in almost perpetual semiquaver movement.
First Group.
½ 1–30.—Theme built up of a single figure (a) into 16 bars, with curtailed repetition, the last 8 overlapping, with a codetta of twice 4 interlocking. The first 8 bars are in a reciprocal tonic-and-dominant form (T T T D, D D D T). The other 8, passing through ♭II., close with 2 continuous bars of tonic chord, which, on the repetition, are replaced by the first 2 of the codetta, which introduces a new chromatic figure repeated in higher position at the interlocking repetition 2 bars later. The codetta breaks the perpetual motion twice, to the extent of 1 quaver.

Transition.

⁸⁰/31–42.—At the end of bar 30 the bass enters with the main theme, substituting dominant of C at 4th bar, closing into a new 4-bar arpeggio figure (b) on C. An answering quatrain of figure (a) in C impinges on dominant of A minor (v.), reached in next period.

Second Group in Dominant Minor.

(Perpetual motion broken to the extent of 1 semiquaver.)

43–66.—New 8-bar theme in A minor; 4 on dominant repeating a 2-quaver group 6 times across the bars, the 7th time prolonged so as to initiate a 4-bar cadence into next period, which repeats the whole 8, closing into two repetitions of its last 4 bars in two different harmonizations, closing into

67–78.—New 6-bar theme, 4 tonic, 2 dominant (⁶₄, ⁶₃), closing into varied repetition, closing into

79–94.—Four-bar cadence-theme, with imitation at 2 bars in lower voice (2+1+1) closing into varied repetition, closing into 4 bars of tonic containing six repetitions of a 2-quaver group across the accents. Suddenly the home-dominant 9th appears, leading in 4 bars back to the beginning and afterwards on to the Development.

Development.

95–110.—The expected tonic is replaced by diminished 7th of (iv.), initiating a rise by 4 semitone steps, 1 step every 4 bars, alternating *piano* with a *forte* distributed in 4 octaves. Figure (a) pervades this and the whole following development. These 16 bars, beginning on dominant of (iv.), have reached A minor (v.) again.

¹¹⁰/111–126.—The bass takes up (a) and climbs a diminished 7th in D minor for 4 bars, following it by the tonic chord (⁶₄) for another 4. But this 4th bar suddenly flattens the A, and the treble answers with figure (a) inverted (ᘛ), descending a diminished 7th in C minor for 4 bars, followed by 4 of C minor tonic. Now watch the bottom note of the bass of each of the following 4-bar and 2-bar steps.

¹²⁶/127–150.—The 4-bar steps rise from C up the scale of B♭ minor. On reaching G♭ the steps proceed by semitones every 2 bars up to the leading-note. Figure (a) is in the bass during the first two 4-bar steps, and (ᘛ) is in the treble for the rest of the passage.

¹⁵⁰/151–172.—Eight bars of main theme in B♭ minor; followed by harmonies rising upon B♭, the top note of the minor triad

128

A COMPANION TO

sharpening at every 2 bars till, on its attaining a minor 7th or augmented 6th, the 3rd rises also. The augmented 6th is held for 2 extra bars before resolving into the next period. At some point in the who'ᵉ process there must have been an enharmonic change. The ear has no reason to suspect it until the last chord resolves as an augmented 6th. The ear first heard it as a dominant 7th. Beethoven seldom explains such points by his notation; and, when he does, his explanation is as likely to mislead as not. The augmented 6th resolves on to the home dominant. Starting upon this, another 4 bars (twice 2) swing (with melodic use of the G♯) into a passage of dominant preparation.

173–198.—With a sudden *piano* the dominant preparation begins in two interlocking 4-bar groups. Suddenly the dominant of (iv.) intervenes, and the 8 bars are repeated in that key. The last 2 bars are repeated gently in the tonic, and again with *sforzando* in (iv.). Then the tonic version is insisted on thrice, with two *sforzandos* culminating in a *forte* at beginning of next period.

199–214.—Sixteen bars (four 2-bar steps, twice 2, and 4) descending the home-dominant chord of 9th in the figure of bars 87–90, closing into

Recapitulation.

First Group.
²¹⁴/215–230 = ½/1–16.
231–242.—On repeating the 4th quatrain the ♭II. of bar 18 takes itself to be the subdominant of B♭ (VI.), and the quatrain closes into 4 bars, making a medial close in that key, followed by repetition making a full close

Transition.
²⁴²/243–270.—The bass enters in B♭ minor with the main theme, with its 4th bar on dominant of F minor closing into the 4-bar arpeggio group (b) in that key. Two similar 8-bar steps follow, F minor to C minor, C minor to G minor; then 4 bars bring (a) from G minor to an augmented 6th leading to home dominant in next period.

Second Group in Tonic.
271–318 = 43–90 in tonic.
It is by no means certain that the change in bars 307-314 was necessitated by the 5-octave pianoforte. An immediate jump to a higher octave at 307 would be awkward, and the present effect of an entry of another voice is beautiful. More difficult, and obviously not depending on any practical question, is the absence

of the enhancement of the inner part at bar 313. Yet this is not incompatible with Beethoven's ways of thinking. When he wishes a recapitulation to advance to an energetic coda he will retain what makes for energy in its details. Here the coda is to be pathetically retrospective and quiet, so that there is nothing inexplicable in a loss of energy at this point, and the listener will not be worried by it.

Coda.

319–350.—The minor 9th of (iv.), corresponding to the home dominant at bar 91, leads in 4 bars to the same rise by semitone as that in bars 95-106, but with quiet swells in varied harmonies instead of the *forte* outbursts. The home dominant is reached (instead of A minor); and 16 bars of preparation (4-bar groups like those of the previous swells) lead to

^{350}/351–384.—Rondo-like repetition of whole main theme ($\frac{1}{2}$/1-30) entering with sudden *fortissimo*, subsiding to sudden *piano* during 8th bar. The codetta (which had been eliminated in the recapitulation) is heard in full, with the addition of a third insistence on a still higher note from which the descent and cadence fill the remainder of a 4-bar group, closing into

385–399.—Final tonic-and-dominant swing, 8 bars (twice 2 in alternate octaves, the 2 pairs repeated) closing into 8 of tonic chord, in motion till the last note, which occupies half the penultimate bar of the period. (Supply a silent last bar.)

18

SONATA IN E FLAT MAJOR, Op. 31, No. 3.

THE finale has earned this sonata the title of *La Chasse* or *Jagd-Sonate*: as inappropriate to the rest of the work as *Moonlight* is to the finale of Op. 27, No. 2.

The power of Beethoven's " second manner," nervously self-assertive and liable to relapses in Op. 31, No. 1, has ripened to tragic pathos in Op. 31, No. 2, and is already in such perfect poise that in the present work it serves the finest purposes of graceful comedy and lyric beauty.

Allegro: E♭.   Sonata Form.

First Group.

Bars 1–16.—The honest old empiric name of " Added Sixth " correctly describes the chord on which the first figure (a) is announced twice. Its present bass is A♭, which, in the judgment of human ears, as distinguished from abstract theories, may pass for its " root." At all events its root is emphatically not the dominant, for the whole point of the sequel is that the bass proceeds by semitones in order to reach the dominant as a totally different centre. Music being an art manifested in works of art, not an exact *a priori* science like Palmistry or Judicial Astrology, the only correct theory of chords is an account of the way in which they happen. Here the chord is an " added 6th " to what proves to be the subdominant, inasmuch as the 6th and the bass alike proceed to rise by semitones till they reach a cadential ⁶₄–⁵₃ on the dominant.

It does not matter whether Beethoven spells his first rise with a G♭ or an F♯. He has his reason, right or wrong, for preferring G♭ here, in contrast to later passages.

Assign the letter (b) to the rhythmic figure of bars 3-4. The result of the *crescendo* to a *sforzando* at the pause is that bar 6 (pause and all) becomes the starting-point of a 4-bar group which leads to a repetition of the whole theme (1-7), distributed over 3 octaves and closing into the next period. Call 1-7 Theme (A).

17–24.—Four-bar treatment of a+b on tonic pedal, the melody running from 2nd bar into next period, where it repeats itself

130

with a variation, closing into another period. Figure (a) is ornamented the 1st time with grace-notes, the 2nd time with trills. Figure (b) is outlined in a " diminution " of (a). That this derivation is not far-fetched may be seen from the following reduction of the scheme:

Call the whole phrase Theme (B), and the Scotch-snap figure (b').

25–32.—New 2-bar theme (C). Beethoven systematically avoids· connecting its first figure with the turn in bar 7. He intends no such derivations unless he puts the versions into juxtaposition. Then, as he has just shown in 17–24, he can be very subtle. But it would be against his principles to make a common ornament bear any structural weight whatever. The new theme contains whole-bar figures (c) and (d), closing into self-repetition, followed by continuation of (d) for 4 bars which modulate to (V.) and hover there, leading to

Transition.

33–45.—New start of theme (A) in tonic minor, without *ritardando*, figure (b) taking a new direction in 2-bar groups repeated at upper octave. The 2nd pair, a step higher, moves about dominant of (ii.). Its bass-note, G, drops to G♭, the treble asking a question over the resulting augmented 6th. The question is answered by 5 octaves of dominant of (V.) descending in two bars.

Second Group in Dominant.

45/46–63.—New 8-bar melody, 4 ending on (ii.) answered by 4 closing in tonic, the whole on a bass rising slowly by semitones from 6/♭ to G in 7th bar. The 8th bar initiates a 4-bar un-accompanied run which winds its way up to a varied repetition of the whole theme, of which the 7th bar closes with overlap into

64–82.—New theme, a 2-bar group closing into self-repetition in higher octave. From this point its cadential trill and resolution are carried down the scale (with convenient modulations) in 2-crotchet steps across the bar-accents. Reaching its own key in the lower octave, it is there insisted upon, with *sforzandos*, until the current 4-bar group is completed, whereupon it closes into a tonic semiquaver arpeggio curling upwards for 3 bars, followed by another 3 of staccato quavers in groups of 4 across the beats. The lowest note of this being now the dominant, the effect has become that of a 6/4, which accordingly resolves into a 4-bar dominant trill, below which the staccato quavers continue with their cross-rhythm, playing with the 7th and minor 9th. The tonic follows in an extra bar. Casual and cadential as the figures of this 11-bar full close may have seemed, it will prove convenient to call the semiquavers of 72–75 (e) and the quavers of 75–80 (f).

83–88.—From the isolated tonic bar a chromatic link has led to a new 4-bar phrase (2+2). Beginning on the sub-dominant, it moves to a full close not unlike a plain version of that of theme (A); and its initial falling 6th also has a familiar air. The chromatic link invites it to repeat itself. Discovering that its sub-dominant is the home tonic, it makes its first 2 bars lead back to the beginning and afterwards on to the

Development.

89–99.—Theme (A) rises at figure (b) as to the melody, but the bass will not at first move. When it does move, it falls. Hence, whether G♭ was right or wrong in the treble at bar 4, the note is certainly F♯ now. The augmented 6th follows its nature—downwards in the bass, upwards in the treble. The next step takes us to F♯ as bass of a diminished 7th. Ceasing the *ritardando*, the bass continues to resolve downwards (in convenient different octaves), while (a), displaced by a beat and carried down 4 octaves, makes a 4-bar cadence into the key of C, reached in next period.

100–107.—Theme (B) in C major, with its variation, closing into

108–136.—Figure (b′) in bass (with new antiphonal treble) grouped into 8-bar phrases with the aid of a 2-bar compound of (e) and (f), the latter filling a normal bar without cross-accent. A flattened bass-note to (b′) has turned the C major into dominant of F. The 8 bars hence close into dominant of B♭ minor, where, the process being repeated, the 2 bars before it would lead to the home dominant. But the minor B♭ triad is substituted in this next step, which consists only of the last 2 bars (e+f), which, passing through the major B♭ triad, reach E♭ as dominant of A♭. Into this key figure (f) closes and proceeds to sharpen the 5th of its tonic triad to E♮ resolving on F. This being reached at the 3rd bar of the current period, the figure is reduced to its original 4 notes; the right hand takes it up *legato* in dialogue with the left, and with the old cross-accents. Both hands join and the figure revolves till the current 8 bars are completed.

Recapitulation.

First Group.

137–160 = 1–24.—Figure (a) floats in over the F minor 6th on

A♭. So the famous opening chord now becomes a chord of the added 5th. The only other changes are in ornamental detail.

161–169.—Theme (C) carries its 7th bar upwards so as to reach the descent of the home dominant down the octaves as in bars 44–45. The bass adds a melodic step through A♭ to the tonic 3rd that underlies the beginning of the Second Group.

Second Group in Tonic.

[169]/170–219 = [45]/46–88 in tonic with the following additions: The 2nd quatrain of the 8-bar theme is in a lower octave, not because of the limits of the 5-octave pianoforte, but in order that the following 3-bar run may have occasion to expand to 6 bars in winding its way back to the beginning of the theme. Similarly, in the passage corresponding to 68–71, the sequence of trills has another octave to descend. This expands the descent by 2¾ bars and gives occasion for a pretty alternation of octaves for 3 more bars when the tonic position is reached. The 11-bar cadence with (e) and (f) is vast enough without expanding, but it has 3 octaves to play with instead of 2, and it makes good use of an extra bar.

The cadence-theme will, of course, make the Coda begin in (IV.).

Coda.

220–245.—Theme (A) begins in (IV.) and proceeds as in bars 1–5, but without *ritardando*. At the 6th bar a further southward tendency shows that the rise is going to continue. It does so by semitones in cadential iambics at every bar. Four such steps lead to the original position of bar 3 (but as a plain 6th). From this point, with the original *ritardandos*, theme (A) is once more recapitulated in tonic up to bar 15. There, instead of a pause, the last 2 notes are twice echoed; and a period is finished by 2 bars of a florid cadence which avoids the shape of bar 7 lest it should forestall theme (C), into which it closes in next period.

245–252.—Theme (C) led by bass in dialogue with treble. Its twice 2 bars close into the climbing of (d) up the tonic chord, finished by a sudden full close into a 4th bar.

Scherzo: Allegretto vivace. A♭ major (IV.). Sonata Form.

As its title implies, this is a playful piece. But it is not what Beethoven usually means by a scherzo. This sonata presents the paradox that what takes the place of its slow movement is quick, while its dance-movement is slow.

First Group.

1–9.—First strain (A) of a rondo-like theme: 4 bars with

half-close, self-repeating with full close. The full close is echoed in a higher octave. Bars 1–2 contain a figure (a):

 etc.

The staccato semiquavers of the bass set up a motion that pervades the whole Allegretto, except in the following strain.

⁹/10–19.—Second strain (B) on dominant of (vi.). Four bars, 2+2 of a new 2-bar figure, in sequence. The effect of the previous echo is that the period dates from bar ⁸/9, and the phrase closes on dominant of (vi.) at the beginning of a group. This bare dominant is insisted on, *ritardando*, by a rhythmic figure (c), occupying the 2nd-to-3rd bars of the group. With the 4th bar the figure rises a semitone, proving to be at top of the home-dominant 7th, down which chord the next 2 bars descend with pause.

¹⁹/20–34.—With a new anacrusis (d) the 1st strain is repeated with its echo, and the 2nd strain (in a higher octave) is also given as far as its dwelling on dominant of F with figure (c).

Transition.

³⁴/35–42.—In one flash, figure (c) bounces into F major (VI.) as the send-off for a new staccato semiquaver formula, moving in 4 bars (twice 1+2) to B♭, where, with a single crash, the same 4-bar clause leads up the dominant 9th of E♭ (V.) and, avoiding cadential tendency, drifts into Second Group.

Second Group in Dominant.

(Themes of self-repeating dominant-to-tonic type with main stress on dominant are so characteristic of Beethoven's second groups from this period onwards that it is inconvenient to regard anything of the kind as mere dominant preparation. See Rondo of Op. 31, No. 1; first movement and finale of Op. 31, No. 2; finale of the present sonata, finale of Quartet, Op. 59, No. 3; finale of 7th Symphony; etc., the type being especially characteristic of movements that have any reason to put a rondo-like stress on their first group.)

⁴²/43–49.—Self-repeating dominant-to-tonic 7-bar theme (C): twice 2 bars, +twice 1 bar, +cadence overlapping with next phrase. Figure (c) in bass, with semiquavers above, continued from the previous transition-passage.

50–61.—New 2-bar cadence-theme, self-repeating, and its 2nd bar detached in 'two echoes, closing into a 1-bar tonic-and-dominant, repeating itself in lower octave, closing into tonic chord, which, after 2 bars, augments itself so as to lead in 2 more bars first back to beginning and afterwards on to Development.

[The iambic semiquavers of 50–54 are *not* derived from (c) with its sharp demisemiquaver raps. The mutilation forced upon Beethoven by the 5-octave pianoforte at bar 54 is a mere nuisance, though his way of dealing with it is not what would have occurred to everybody.]

Development.   6

62–63.—The previous augmented triad is tuned up to E♮ as dominant of F, leading to

64–69.—Theme (A) in F major (without the *sforzandos*) diverted at 6th bar towards B♭ minor, and interrupted by

70–82.—Theme (C) for 4 bars (twice 2) in B♭ minor, rising a tone to twice 1 in C minor, thence descending its tonic chord for 3 bars. A *sforzando* in the 3rd bar helps the rhythm to change its step, not to the up-beat but to the dating of the next period from the arrival on the dominant, where 4 bars preparation (twice 1+2 of rising scale) lead to C major in next period.

83–89.—Theme (A) in C major proceeding for 6 bars as in the previous F major passage, but using the anacrusis-figure (d) before both the 4th and the 6th bar.

90–95.—The anacrusis (d) is played with for twice 2 bars on a diminished 7th implying dominant of F minor. Then the E♮ resolves on to E♭, showing that it must be F♭, though Beethoven persists in spelling it E♮ when the bar is repeated. This enharmonic change has, then, established the home dominant.

96–105.—Ten bars of dominant preparation: twice 2+4 of downward scale, arising from 2nd bar detached and continued, with 2 *ritardando* bars finishing the scale slowly with chromatic steps. Resemblance to any definite theme is avoided, so as to throw the return into higher relief.

Recapitulation.

First Group.

106–139 = 1–34, with slight ornament in return of 1st strain after the pause.

Transition.

139/140–147.—The explosion arising from (c) is on a bare D♭, a semitone higher. This is dominant of G♭, in which key the rest of the quatrain follows. It contrives to lead to E♭, the home dominant, which corresponds to the B♭ of bar 39, so that the rest follows by exact transposition.

Second Group in Tonic.
¹⁴⁷/148–162 ³⁹/40–57 in tonic closing into

Coda.
163–171.—The cadence-passage is continued in a run in octaves assuming a new shape in 2 bars of rising sequence continuous with a 4-bar group (rising scale breaking into descent in terms of previous sequence), of which the movement stops at last bar, with bass from bare dominant to bare tonic. This close is twice echoed in fourfold octaves, once, and again with variation.

Menuetto: Moderató e grazioso. E♭ major, with Trio in same key.

Those who attach the wrong kind of importance to the function of thematic figure-work in the " logical development " of music may learn a useful lesson from this movement. As Sir Henry Hadow pointed out long ago, the melody of this menuet is remarkable for taking beautiful shape without clearly recapitulating any of its figures. Self-repetition on the spot, as in bars 8-9, contributes nothing but its length to the symmetry of the whole; and the appoggiaturas that are distributed in a symmetrical way are so little essential to that purpose that in the carefully written out Da Capo Beethoven removes the last one, lest the entry of a genuine though unexpected symmetry should be crowded. Apart from this, the main purport of the whole movement is the vivid contrast between a flowing melody and the melodic form of the Trio built " logically " (more or less) out of detachable figures. To Beethoven both types are equally important, and to ordinary mortals the " logical " type is infinitely easier to " construct." Both require invention, but it seems easier to invent figures of 2 notes than melodies of 16 bars.

Menuet.

¾/1–8.—Strain answering 4 bars ending on medial tonic close by 4 different bars ending on half-close. Repeated, with new ornament in first bar.

⁸/9–16.—Second strain emphasizing minor 9th on dominant in a repeated 2-bar group leading to 4 (recalling melodic rhythm of bars 5-6) ending in full close. Repeat.

Trio.

¹⁶/17–24.—Eight-bar phrase built of 1+1 of iambic figure in rising sequence leading to 2-bar half-close, and answered by a similar quatrain harmonizing the rise so as to lead to (V.), with full close therein in bare octaves.

²⁴/25–30.—Six bars of the iambic figure on minor 9th of dominant—the first 2 bars being followed by 4 compressing the figure into crotchets lying in 6 pairs across the rhythm, the last pair falling in octaves on bare dominant.

³⁰/31–38.—Recapitulation of 1st strain (of Trio) giving upward turn to its 3rd and 4th bars and substituting harmonized close in tonic at the end. Repeat.

³⁸/39–54.—Da Capo of Menuet written in full for two reasons: first that Beethoven insists on both repeats, and secondly in order to prepare for a Coda by the following slight but careful changes in the last bar. At the first time the quaver movement is stopped; so that at the second time a plain note may replace the original appoggiatura without making too abrupt a change of manner. The result draws attention to the second beat in the bass, which sets up a resultant rhythm of its own in the following Coda.

Coda.

⁵⁴/55–62.—The pathetic 9th of bars ⁸/9–10 finds its yet more pathetic answer in 2 bars giving the same figure on the tonic with ♭II. The 2 bars are repeated and the 2nd bar twice echoed, closing into 2 tonic bars, with the last melodic inflection spinning down to a final chord.

Presto con fuoco: Sonata Form.

First Group.

Bars ½/1–12.—Four-bar theme with a 2-bar echo, the bass announcing a figure (a) with interlocking self-repetitions,

etc.,

while a treble enters with a 2-bar figure (b) on the short anacrusis of the 3rd bar, closing with an echo in lower octave. The whole 6 bars are repeated. Beethoven indicates by his accents at bars 3 and 5 that he is quite aware that the cadences are " weak." The next theme begins with a strong enough beat for pile-driving; yet it is that theme which will ultimately change its step.

¹²/13–28.—New theme (C); beginning with 8 bars (twice 4) on the tonic-and-dominant formula T T T D, answered by D D D T, and continued with other harmonies for 8 bars of the form 2+repetition+3rd time with 2-bar cadence.

Transition.

²⁸/29–33.—Beginning by repeating the last 8 bars in tonic minor,

theme (C) diverts the bass of 3rd step towards dominant. [This is not easy to make clear in performance.] It overlaps into next group. Bar 6 of theme (C) = 1 of next theme.

Second Group in Dominant.

34–63.—New theme beginning with 4 bars in an extreme form of the dominant-to-tonic species—viz., D D D D D D D T, leading to repetition. But on repetition the dominant refuses to move. It gives way only in the 1st bar of a third 8-bar group, so that it there becomes the beginning of a modulating sequence, descending in four 1-bar steps of thirds, followed by 4 bars (2+1+2 halves) of cadence closing into repetition of this third 8-bar group. On repetition the cadence is expanded from 4 bars to 10, of which 9 are on its first harmony (ii.). At last it closes into

64–79.—Cadence-theme, a 6-bar phrase allied in internal rhythm to C. It is on the tonic-to-dominant formula, T T T T T D, closing into self-repetition. But, like the dominant in the previous theme, on repetition the tonic refuses to give way. The treble continues to descend the tonic chord, which then behaves as the home dominant, the top parts moving in 3rds to a dominant 7th with pause. Repeat.

Development.

80–84.—Last 4 bars repeated on dominant of G♭ (♭III.) with pause. Note that in order to establish this foreign key the passing 3rd in the middle of bar 81 is diatonic, not chromatic as at bar 77.

84/85–91.—First 8 bars of theme (C) in G♭, followed by

91/92–119.—Sequence of 8-bar clauses, the 8 being made of 4 bars of figure (c) as dominant to 4 of a new figure (x). The 1st of these 8-bar steps lands, without any real enharmonic change, in C♭ minor, written as B minor not only for convenience but because the development as a whole will prove to have moved in an enharmonic circle. We shall recognize our tonic E♭ by the fact that we shall hear the First Group in it; and, even if the movement were played in mathematically exact intonation, the difference of pitch between E♭ and what would " really " be F♭♭ could not worry us. Meanwhile it will save trouble to accept Beethoven's notation and names of the following keys. The second 8-bar step is in C minor. After this the steps are of 4 bars, with (x) alone, all grouped as belonging to C minor—viz., (VI.), (♭II.) (Neapolitan 6th), and (V.), closing into

120–127.—Theme (C) for 8 bars in C major.

127/128–144.—Sequence in 4-bar steps, with figure of (C) in bass, with treble arpeggios in double counterpoint, proceeding, for 4 steps of dominant 9ths with interchange of parts, through dominants of F minor, B♭ minor, E♭ minor, and A♭ minor, closing into chord of A♭ in next period.

145–171.—Chord of A♭ for 8 themeless bars—4 resembling bars of figure (x), a fact which should not be stressed, and 4 of solid chord breaking into light arpeggio at 2nd bar. Similar 8 bars on chord of F minor. Then 4 on ⁶₄ of home dominant, the bass reaching the root at the 1st of 8 bars of preparation for return, the imperfect triad quivering in the position for closing into figure (a).

Recapitulation.
First Group.

¹⁷¹/172–199 = ½/1–28, with the first 2 bars *forte*, and an ornamental variation in (b) during the repetition of the 6-bar clause.

Transition.

¹⁹⁹/200–208.—On repeating the latter part of theme (C) in the tonic minor, its 4th bar is followed by 4 in G♭ (♭III.), and these by a new turn of the bass towards the dominant of that key, leading to

Second Group in G♭ (♭III.).

209–244 = 34–69 in G♭.

Re-establishment of Tonic.

245–262.—When the 6-bar cadence-theme repeats itself, its tonic chord, no longer obstinate, makes way for a modulation to E♭ minor, in which key the whole 12 bars are given again, the 12th closing on to home dominant in next period.

263–278.—Sixteen bars dominant preparation: 8 (twice 4) of (a) in dialogue between treble and bass, and 8 halves, and the remainder (as at bars 164 foll. but more thematically) merely quivering in position for theme (A).

[Notice that the figure always runs from beginning of bar, a warning against over-articulation of metrical feet both in playing and in analysis.]

Final Return and Coda.

²⁷⁸/279–290.—The arpeggio drifts imperceptibly into (a) in a higher octave, to which (b) is added alternately above and below as the first 12 bars of theme (A) proceed.

²⁹⁰/291–302.—A new course is taken by the rise of the
⎰b ⎰a
⎱a + ⎱b groups to (ii.), 4 bars in which key are followed by 4 in A♭ (IV.), whereupon (b) is insisted upon for 4 bars of dominant,

closing into a new period.

303–322.—Four bars chord of A♭ with figure (a) lead to a pause on ♭⁷, followed by a 4-bar cadence made by (b) in bass in A♮ dialogue with treble. The whole 10 bars repeated in a lower octave, and the dialogue on (b) led by treble, *ritardando*, using the recapitulation-variant given at bars 180 and 182.

³²²/323–333.—Final development of (b) into an 8-bar cadence-group, the last 2 bars containing only staccato chords, twice a bar, closing into next period, which contains the 3 final chords. (Supply a silent last bar.)

19

SONATA IN G MINOR, Op. 49, No. 1.

WE may be grateful to Beethoven's brother Kaspar for sending the two early sonatas known as Op. 49 to a publisher without the composer's consent, as we might otherwise have been deprived of the two most beautiful sonatinas within the range of small hands and young players. That in G minor is a highly finished little work with many interesting details of invention and structure.

Andante.

First Group.

Bars 1–8.—First clause of a symmetrical melody (2+2+4, or +1+1+2), ending on half-close.

9–16.—Answering clause, repeating bars 1-4 and thence diverging into B♭ (III.) and overlapping into Second Group. There is no irregularity in the rhythm; for bar 16 at this moment belongs to the previous period. In the Recapitulation Beethoven proceeds otherwise, and shows that he knows what he is doing in both cases.

Second Group : B♭ (III.).

16–24.—Bar 16 is preliminary to an 8-bar phrase (2+2+4), coming to a medial tonic close and containing figure (a)

allied in rhythm to that of bar 1 in main theme.

25–28.—Repetition of last 4 bars expanded so as to defer close till next clause. The phrase accordingly closes into

29–33.—Cadence-group, making (a) into a 2-bar clause that repeats itself and adds a full close. Repeat from bar 1.

Development.

34–37.—Figure (a) developed into a 4-bar phrase closing into E♭.

38–45.—Episode in E♭, consisting of a new 4-bar theme

(1+1+2), closing into varied repetition, which closes into

46-53.—Three steps of (a) as in the cadence-group, moving from E♭ through C minor to G minor (the tonic), and there finished with 2 new bars closing into

54-63.—Passage of dominant preparation for return: 4 bars (2+2) rhythmically resembling the episode, and then thrice 2 bars of a cantabile that rises the third time up through C♯ to D, which is taken instead of B♭ as the 1st note of bar 1.

Recapitulation.
First Group.
64–72 = 1–8, with the above-mentioned change.
⁷²/73–79.—The counterstatement is given to the bass with a flowing counterpoint above. After its 4th bar it spends a complete 4 in returning to the home dominant.

Second Group : G minor throughout.
80–84.—Accordingly the first 5 bars on (a) are now poised on their 1st instead of their 2nd bar. The listener, remembering his first impression of this theme, has no difficulty in swallowing the extra bar that results from Beethoven's making no change in the size of the next clause.

85–88.—The translation of the whole Second Group into the minor brings with it other changes, and the medial close of bars 23-24 is lost in a broader phrasing that closes into the next clause.

89–96.—Expansion of bars 25-28 to an 8-bar passage (4+2+2) rising to a climax and closing into

97–102.—Cadence-group represented by 3 repetitions of (a) in bass with partial echo in treble, closing into

Coda.
103–110.—The prevalent quaver motion swings cadentially in a half-major mode (♮3rd and ♭6th) over a tonic pedal, in tapering rhythm (pairs of bars, single bars, and half-bars) to the end.

Rondo : Allegro.
[In a peculiar form, only once partially adopted by Beethoven later on in the slow movement of Op. 2, No. 3.]
Main Theme.
⁶⁄₈/1–8.—Symmetrical self-repeating melody (1+1+2, repeated) answering half-close at bar 4 by full close at bar 8, and containing figure (a)

which is treated sequentially. Its rhythm is also used in later **and** different themes. Another figure (b)

is developed in the recapitulation and coda.

⁸/9–16.—New 4-bar clause hovering on dominant ($1+1+\frac{1}{2}$ $+\frac{1}{2}+\frown$), followed by bars ⁴/5–8 an octave higher to finish.

Episode in Tonic Minor.

¹⁶/17–20.—Four-bar phrase in G minor, with rhythm of (a) in a new figure (c)

closing, with overlap, into

20–31.—New theme on figure (c) (at first without its grace-note) in 4-bar phrases. The first of these closes in dominant minor with a more violent contradiction of the rule against cadences on weak beats than Beethoven allows himself in later works. The rule is not as valid as some modern theorists would make it, but here its violation undoubtedly has a curious effect. But the sequel shows that Beethoven would not wish the passage rebarred, for the next 4 bars close quite normally into B♭ (♭III.), and insist on their cadence for 2 more bars+2 on B♭ tonic chord, leading to *Second Group* in B♭.

32–47.—Broad cantabile, using figure (c) : 16 bars answering half-close into 9th bar by full close into 17th bar, closing into

48–64.—Answering strain: 4 bars (2+2) of new clause, using (c), followed by 4 on material of former strain, closing into repetition of the whole 8, and thence closing into next period. The whole dates from bar 32.

• *Return of Episode* in G minor.

64–67 = 16–19, returning from B♭ to G minor and balanced a bar earlier than at first—*i.e.*, the 4 quavers of bar 16 now complete the 1st bar of the period instead of being preliminary. Thus there is no longer an overlap in what follows.

68–77.—Recapitulation of Episode-theme, diverging after 7th bar, which is carried in falling sequence down to a close in tonic minor, closing into

78–80.—Two steps of (a) in the minor, resting on D. A 3rd **step**, becoming major, proves to be the beginning of the main theme. Accordingly

Return.

⁸⁰/81–96 = 1–16.

⁹⁶/97–102.—Figure (b) is developed imitatively in 2-bar steps, passing to E minor (VI.) and C major (IV.), thence, in three 1-bar steps (figure of close of theme) and two ½-bars, to the home dominant, there closing into

Recapitulation of Second Group.

103–135 = 32–64 in G major, with slight alterations, closing into

Coda.

¹³⁵/136–148.—Development of (a); first for 4 bars (2+2), treble answered by bass, in tonic-to-dominant harmony; then in sequence, as in bars 1+2, upon which figure (b), following, as in bar 3, is taken up in dialogue between treble and bass, and its last 2 notes worked up (from their accompaniment in treble) to a climax, pausing on the dominant.

¹⁴⁸/149–152.—Figure (a), arising in bass, leads to a quiet 4-bar cadence closing into

153–164.—Final tonic-and-dominant swing, with (a) in treble, over a tonic pedal. Upon this the tonic-and-dominant chords move in 4-bar groups thus: T, D, D, T; T, D, D, T; then in ½-bars for 2 bars; then 2 final tonic bars.

Throughout the sonata the bar-rhythms, though not quite convincing, show promise of Beethoven's later freedom and variety.

20

SONATA IN G MAJOR, Op. 49, No. 2.

Allegro ma non troppo: G major. Sonata Form.

First Group.

Bars 1-4.—Four-bar melody; bar 1 closing into 2; the rest of bar 2 leading to a pair of bars with medial close. A link of 3 quavers in bass leads to

5-8.—Bars 1-4 in higher octave, with chromatic link into

⁸/9-14.—New 4-bar phrase (1+1+2) with tonic close, linking with repetition in lower octave, the 3rd bar replaced by modulation to dominant, with overlap into next period.

15-20.—Six bars *on* the dominant (not *in* it); twice 2, then one, repeating itself in ½-bars and closing into next bar. Call this passage (A). (It would be far-fetched to derive the triplets in these bars from the triplets in bar 1. The student cannot too soon be warned against judging of musical form by eye instead of by ear. When Beethoven wants the listener to recognize an allusion he gives plenty of help at the moment itself. The student had far better miss a dozen genuine subtleties than make one false point.)

Second Group in Dominant.

Although the previous dominant was not a key in its own right, it is followed up as if it were genuinely D major. This is an old joke in sonatas, and was originally meant as such in comic opera—as when a person believes that the words " I am glad to see you " are always true.

²⁰/21-28.—New melody in D major: 8 bars, 2 answered by 2 in sequence, then twice one, overlapping into 2, in which the interlock is a sequence in two ½-bars leading to a dominant half-close. Notice, first, that as far as bars are concerned, *everything* interlocks in such a melody, because each idea begins before its bar; and secondly, that the dominant half-close is, in spite of the G♯, *not* the key of A major. The most foolish musical idea could not suppose that this melody would be " glad to see A major " coming to stay.

29-35.—Counterstatement; that is to say, restatement of the melody, making a " second part " to it and substituting tonic close for the dominant close. And here comes a real overlap shortening the number of bars, not a mere interlock resulting from an " anacrusis " in the melody.

36–42.—The 8th bar of the last phrase overlaps with the 1st of a new 8-bar theme, in three 2-bar phrases, of which the 2nd pair substitutes a rising scale for the first falling scale. (So now you know what the Formidable Theorist means when he talks of Treatment by Inversion). The 3rd pair moves to the subdominant, and is followed by a close in our present tonic. Call the whole passage (B). Notice that the subdominant produces not the slightest effect of a return to our *home* tonic G major. Quotations of a few bars can tell us nothing trustworthy about the real values of keys and key-relations; and no student is too young to learn to appreciate keys as they are shown in large form. It is this large aspect that is clear and true, and it is in the small details (beyond bare grammatical elements) that the theorists themselves are in danger of losing their way.

43–48.—The last (8th) bar of theme (B) overlaps with the 1st of a 3-bar group on the same scale-figure: 1 bar in treble, answered on (IV.) by bass and followed by a cadence-bar, the cadence being interrupted by repetition of the whole 3 bars, substituting descending scale in the 1st bar. This repetition closes into

49–52.—Final cadence-group in the shape of (A) unmistakably *in* D major. Repeat the whole Exposition.

Development.

53–58.—First theme, outlined in the rhythm of its first 2 bars, and cast into a 3-bar group starting in D minor and modulating to A minor, closing there into a similar 3-bar group, closing on to dominant of E minor in next period.

59–66.—Two bars (new matter) on dominant of E minor interlocking with repetition, closing into 4 bars, in which the bass starts a new figure moving from bar to bar down steps of a 5th (followed at 3rd bar by treble in 3rds) so as to reach the home dominant, which closes into the tonic at next period.

Recapitulation.

First Group.

67–73 = 1–7.

73/74.—The 8th bar takes an unexpected turn into C major (IV.), closing into

75–81.—Theme (B) in (IV.) diverted at 5th bar into A minor (ii.) for 2 bars. In a 7th bar the bass rises by semitones towards the home dominant, closing there with overlap into next period.

82–87.—The dominant passage (A), as in 15–20.

Second Group in Tonic.

[87]/88–122.—Following (A), now according to its proper sense of home dominant, the whole Second Group is recapitulated in G from [20]/21 to 52. Into the tonic version of (A) 2 bars are inserted by adding echoes in a lower octave to each of the first 2 bars. A more dignified close in 2 bars is substituted for bar 52.

Tempo di Menuetto: Rondo, on a theme afterwards used in the Menuet of the Septet.

Main Theme: G major.

$\frac{1}{3}$/1–8.—Self-repeating 8-bar melody (twice 1+2) ending with half-close, answered by repetition of the whole 4 ending with full close. The rhythmic figure (a) of the anacrusis recurs in other themes.

[8]/9–20.—Four bars (twice 1+2) starting in (iii.) and half-closing on dominant, followed by repetition of $\frac{1}{3}$/1–8, the melody in a higher octave, with variation in 7th bar.

First Episode : modulating to (V.).

[20]/21–27.—New 4-bar phrase in tonic in double counterpoint. This term means that its bass and its treble may exchange places; which happens in the next 3 bars, which lead to the dominant of the dominant. (The " inversion " of this double counterpoint is not at the octave. As one of the parts is doubled in 3rds, and as the specimen is in any case very small, it would be pedantic to give the device its full name; but your ear will tell you that while the part in 3rds does not seem in a hurry to leave G, the other part is already in D. The effect is that of double counterpoint in the 12th.)

28–35.—New theme entering with overlap; on dominant of (V.), with 4 bars (2 of falling sequence+twice 1 in rising sequence) closing into repetition modified by cadence into next period.

36–46.—Three-bar cadence-theme closing into varied self-repetition, closing into 2-bar phrase in rhythm allied to (a) on tonic pedal interlocking with repeat, interlocking with a 3rd round, of which the intervals widen down to 1st note of main theme, its rhythmic figure being already latent.

First Return.

[47]/48–67 = $\frac{1}{3}$/1–20.

Second Episode in Subdominant.

[67]/68–87.—New 8-bar melody: twice 2+1+1 rising to 2-bar half-close; answered by repetition until its 6th bar, which is followed (continuously) by a further rise for 2 bars through the

dominant of our present key—*not* as yet felt as the home tonic. But when the climax of this rise turns into 2 octaves of scale descending over $^6_5$ while the rest of the 4-bar group swings into F♯ position for the accompaniment of the main theme, the weight of such a dominant is too strong for C major, and we expect the return of G.

Second Return.

[87]/88–107 = $\frac{1}{3}$/1–20.

Coda.

[107]/108–120.—New 8-bar phrase, carrying (a) in downward sequence in 4 bars through (IV.) and (ii.), and finishing with 4 new bars (twice 1, + a 2-bar full close), with a run leading to a variation of these 4 bars an octave higher. An extra bar provides a final cadence.

21

SONATA IN C MAJOR, Op. 53.

THE Waldstein Sonata marks the point at which Beethoven's style grew finally incompatible with that of his " first period." In Op. 32 the powerful D minor Sonata, and the E♭ Sonata, with its vein of subtle comedy, already showed in two contrasted ways that Beethoven had become perfectly at home in a style which he himself felt and avowed to be new. But he had not yet found that it forbade him to allow something of his early nervous abruptness in stating new ideas and something of luxury in the indulgence of old ideas. Both tendencies were extremely obvious in Op. 31, No. 1; the luxuriant quality is evident both in the Second Symphony, Op. 36, and the C minor Concerto, Op. 37; the three Violin Sonatas of Op. 30 and the Kreutzer Sonata all show the alternating traces of a reactionary and a provocative manner; and even the eminently Olympian Quintet, Op. 29, has a rather abruptly formal transition-theme in its first movement. The chronology of all these works is inextricably mixed; and, besides the well-known case of the finale of the Kreutzer Sonata, the sketch-books show several examples of the transference of material, at early stages, from one work to another. But in none of these works are the conflicting elements irreconcilable: the conflict is a feature of style pleasant in itself as well as historically interesting.

In the Waldstein Sonata Beethoven crossed the Rubicon. This allusion is excusable as representing more of the facts than a mere ornamental phrase. Crossing the Rubicon was an irrevocable act of war, the first act after long hesitation in hopes of compromise with the old régime.

The Andante of the *Waldstein* Sonata was a luxurious rondo with a rich Clementi-like pianoforte style. It had grown up with the sonata from the earliest sketches, and it was at first to have been in E major, like the Adagio of the other C major Sonata, Op. 2, No. 3. This contrast of keys is brilliant if, and only if, it has not been forestalled within the first movement itself. But at a very early stage of the sketches for the *Waldstein* Sonata the key of E major was assigned to the 2nd group of the first movement, and there was no longer any point in putting the slow movement in any key on that side of C, or necessarily in any remote key at all. The subdominant would give a sufficient contrast and would be the nearest in pitch to the idea of the andante as already conceived. And so the sonata was not only sketched, but finished to the last detail, and played by Beethoven to his friends with a slow movement in rondo-form on as large a scale as the finale. The criticism that the sonata was " too long " merely annoyed Beethoven, and was the last thing in the world that would have induced him to alter his work, conscious as he was of being a master of instrumental music on a larger scale than anything known before. But he soon came to realize that, whether long or short, this andante was quite out of touch with the harmonic style of the rest. Its richest modulations were indeed beautiful, but they were stated as if they were strange. This might be true within the limits of that one movement, but it was entirely false after the view of harmony displayed in the first 13 bars of the first movement. That view of harmony (with the same results in choice of key for a 2nd group) had already been propounded in Op. 31, No. 1; but propounded as a paradox thrust at the listener in a provocative jocular manner. Now the *Waldstein* Sonata has no more business than sunsets and sunrises to be paradoxical, provocative or jocular. A return to a simpler beauty may be a refreshing reaction from paradoxes. But the *Andante in F* prefaces its finest modulations with clauses to the effect that " strange and even incredible as this may seem, it is nevertheless true "; whereas these strange and incredible things seem to be entirely normal in the previous and following movements. For this reason, and not for its length nor even for the danger of putting two full-sized rondos in juxtaposition, Beethoven cut the *Andante in F* out from the completed manuscript, allowed it to be published without opus-number as a separate work, and replaced it by the present *Introduzione*, one of the profoundest things in all his " second period," and harmonically at once the boldest and the calmest thing in the whole sonata. The final Rondo itself, though un-altered, acquires a deeper meaning after the wonderful page that now leads up to it.

Allegro con brio : C major.   Sonata Form.

First Group.

Bars 1–13.—Main theme (A) in two 4-bar steps (2+1+1) of sequence, the 1st moving from tonic to (V.), the 2nd from (♭VII.) to (IV.), followed by 4 bars on minor home dominant closing into pause as extra bar. The whole structure is supported by descent of bass by semitones in 2-bar steps, accelerating the 4th step by a semitone that changes the sub-dominant from major to minor.

The theme contains figures (a)

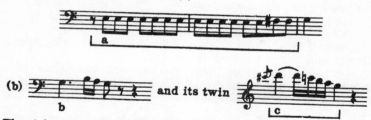

(b) and its twin

The 4 bars on the home dominant expand (c) to a long self-repeating run, closing after 3 bars into 4 beats descending the tonic minor chord down to the dominant pause. Call this close (D).

14–22.—Counterstatement of main theme in semiquaver tremolo, substituting a rising step for the fall at 5th bar. This rising step leads from (ii.) to (vi.). In an extra bar, repeating figure (c), the chord of the 6th becomes augmented and resolves into

23–34.—Dominant preparation (C) on dominant of (iii.); 2-bar clause suggested by running extension of (c), closing into self-repetition, closing into compressed version in 1 bar, followed by further compression twice into 1 bar, an 8-bar group being completed by 2 bars of dominant chord leading to a new 4-bar group, rising up the scale in dialogue between the two hands in staccato quaver broken octaves. The latter part of this scale shows that (III.), and not (iii.), is the object of this dominant preparation.

Second Group in (III.).

35–49.—New 8-bar melody (E) in (III.): 4+4 self-repeating, answering half-close at 4th bar by full close at 8th, the whole being repeated in a variation in triplet quavers arising as link from 8th bar. Note that at the 4th bar of the plain theme a new voice enters with the dotted minim, and that it is this voice that carries out the remaining 4 bars as well as the whole variation.

50–61.—The 8th bar of the previous theme overlaps with a new 2-bar tonic-and-dominant theme (F) in primitive double counter-

point [triplets (e) over or under syncopated minims (f) ♩ ♩|♩]

revolving 3 times, with the triplets in contrary motion in both voices the 3rd time; insisted upon in rhythm tapering from single bars to half-bars and quarter-bars. Two bars leading to subdominant compete a 4-bar group, closing into

62–73.—Cadence expanded to enormous size in contrast to the previous compressions; thus:

IV	IV♯	$\overset{6}{4}$ V	dom. chords V
2 bars	2 bars	4 bars (4 halves+2 bars)	4 bars (twice 2) and

closing into

74–85.—Cadence-group, with subdominant and minor harmony, making a 4-bar phrase of (C), together with a bar and a half of a new sequential figure (g)

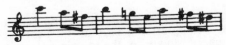

closing into repetition of the whole 4 in lower octave, followed by insistence on (g) with an anacrusis from above, and with flat supertonic in its first group, closing into C major (the home tonic), in which key a further repetition closes, in the first place, into the repeat.

Development.

86–89.—Figure (g) insists twice more in F (IV.), closing into next period. (This further insistence has been severely criticized, but it sounds quite natural to an unprejudiced ear if the repeat of the exposition has not been omitted. If the figure has first led to the main theme in the tonic we shall not take offence at its making a further effort next time.)

90–95.—Theme (A) in (IV.). The 4th bar, like bar 8, is darkened by an extra step in the bass. Coming, however, in the 4th bar instead of the 8th, it does not help to confirm the key, but diverts it towards dominant of G minor. Two extra bars, repeating (b) and (c), confirm this, closing into that key in the next period.

96–103.—Figures (b+c) compressed into 1 bar grouped into 4 (twice 1, +2), thus b+c | b+c | b+c+ | c+c, moving from G minor to C minor, where the 4 are repeated, leading to F minor, reached in next period.

104–111.—While the bass slowly descends in steps of the scale according to the harmony of the moment, figure (c) is grouped in a new sequence of 2-bar limbs, passing from F minor through B♭ minor (the C♭ in 105 is its ♭II.) to A♭, thence again into F minor (again with a ♭II.), the last note of this 3rd step being raised in warning of a climax. Two more bars confirm F minor, the bass hurrying at last in chromatic steps, closing into

112–135.—Theme (E) on dominant of F, partially minor (*not* C major), proceeding in 4-bar steps through the dominants of B♭ and E♭, and thence in the following 2-bar steps, with B♭ as bass—

viz., E♭ minor dominant of C♭ with bass as leading-note; then, with rise of bass, C♭ minor written as B♮; then again, with bass as leading-note, raising to C minor, and so in 2 single bars through its ♭II. and a diminished 7th to its dominant, reached in next period. There is no moment at which an enharmonic change happens; there is only a convenient change of notation from G♭, etc., to F♯, etc., at 126. But the sequel will show that we have moved in an enharmonic circle.

136–155.—Twenty bars of dominant preparation. As it eventually leads to theme (A) at a pitch identical on the pianoforte with the original pitch, and wholly indistinguishable from it in mathematically exact intonation after all these intervening events, we may in the retrospect consider that this preparation was on the home dominant, and not on that of D♭♭. The preparation first continues with (e) for twice 2 bars, plus 2 compressed bars. Then it closes into a themeless passage of 14 bars on a distantly thunderous bass, at first in dialogue with R.H. for 4 bars, then gathered into a continuous roll below rising short runs in three 2-bar groups, each with its series of rhythmic compressions, and a fourth group fixed at the highest point and coalescing in 2 bars that finally run in contrary motion into the main theme.

Recapitulation.

First Group.

156–166 = 1–10, except for the fact that the previous *ff* crushed the 1st note.

167–173.—The incident (D) undergoes a mysterious accident, for instead of arriving at the dominant it lands a semi-tone too high.

The only thing to be done is to treat this as the dominant of (♭II.), and to try again, hoping not to go further astray. This device reaches B♭, which is the dominant of (♭III.). A third effort helps itself with arpeggios and, risking no further plunges, modulates back to the tonic, closing with an *fp* into

174–183.—Counterstatement of (A) exactly as in bars 14-21. At this point the bass shifts to F and, proceeding there from ⁶₅ to ⁶₃ in one extra bar, with (c) in treble, reaches the augmented 6th of bar 22 transposed to the threshold of (vi.), thus leading to the dominant preparation applied now to that key instead of to (iii.).

184–195 = 23–34 on dominant of (vi.).

Second Group, beginning in (VI.), swerving at once to tonic.

196–199 = 35–38 in (VI.).

200–234.—The 5th bar of theme (E) veers through (vi.) round

to the home tonic, in which all the rest of the Second Group is recapitulated.

235–248.—In the cadence-theme (g) has at the outset a ♭II., which originally it had reserved for its repetition. This is no oversight, for the repetition is now fully in the major mode, together with the first extra insistence on (g). Then (g) is given in (IV.) and (iv.), closing into the Coda with an unexpected modulation.

Coda.

249–260.—Theme (A) in (♭II.). At its 4th bar the bass, still on C, supplies the leading-note of B♭, and from this point, instead of its habitual fall, proceeds to rise, first by semitones for 2 bars of (b)+(c); whereupon, the tonic minor being reached, it proceeds up that scale in ½-bar steps, while (a)+(b) is compressed into single bars. The bass, having passed the dominant, falls back to it from A♮ through A♭ in 2 more bars, with (c) in treble. On reaching it, the treble has the rhythm (a) for 2 bars, the 2nd bar with a chromatic chord closing into the following new device.

261–268.—Theme (A) in bass in tonal sequence for two complete 4-bar steps. Hitherto it had always been in real sequence; that is to say, in steps that are more or less transpositions to other keys. A tonal sequence moves up or down different degrees of (more or less) the same key. Here, for instance, in spite of an obvious admixture of (ii.) and (vi.), the total impression of these 8 bars is that of C major, with 4 bars typically dominant answered by 4 typically tonic; little more than the following scheme, 4

times as slow,  to which a

dominant pedal could be added without revolutionizing the sense. It is easy to see that the transformation of a real sequence to a tonal sequence produces an enormous increase of breadth, and is a powerful means of climax in a big coda, where one object is to assert the tonic spaciously.

269–283.—Arising from the tonal sequence, figures (a)+(b) are detached, with their counterpoint, and repeated a step higher. Figure (b) continues the rise in the next bar, and afterwards in ½-bars, completing a 4-bar group by one further themeless step leading to (IV.). Two bars on this lead to the dominant, where a full close is spread over 6 bars thus

$$\begin{matrix} 6 \\ 4 \end{matrix} \qquad\qquad 7 \;\curvearrowright\curvearrowright$$
4 bars (2½+thrice ½) 2 (1+1), closing into

284–294.—Theme (E) distributed over 3 octaves, and its close twice interrupted, first, after pause, by repeating bar 7, with minor 9th, augmented to 2 bars, with pause, and then again with major 9th in 2 bars, closed at last into

295-302.—Theme (a) with (b) compressed thrice into 2 bars, the bass proceeding with its extra A♭ down to dominant, whence comes a final close in 4 bars. The scales in bar 299 imply the

chords $\overset{7}{G} \overset{\overset{5}{3}}{A}$.

Introduzione : Adagio molto. Lyric melody between chromatic prelude and postlude; the whole in F major (IV.) and leading to the finale.

1-9.—Three 2-bar steps in sequence on bass descending by semitones from tonic F to dominant; followed by two bars completing a period and closing into an extra final tonic bar. The first bar contains a figure (a) in two positions; the second, a rhythm (b) with a hiatus on first beat. At the 3rd bar the bass does not descend (an immediate descent would result in the same harmonic design as that at the opening of the first movement), but uses E as the beginning of its next step. The remaining steps towards (V.) are, as in the first movement, compressed. But the total result has been a phrase with an immense range of modula-tion, the augmented 6th at the end of 1st bar already drifting far away from a key only just defined by the outline of its common-chord; while bars 3-4 (in E minor with enhanced dominant) are nearly at the antipodes of the tonic, to which nevertheless the continued descent of the bass easily leads back. The three cadence-bars arise from (b).

9/10-16.—Lyric melody connected with prelude only by use of (a) as anacrusis. Two bars move from tonic to dominant, the second filled by 2-part imitations on a scale of four semiquavers repeated in different octaves across the ⅜ time. Two similar bars answer, moving from dominant to tonic. A bar of new melody, distributing rhythm (a) in pairs across the ⅜ time, interlocks, with repetition diverting the last chord and followed by bar 8 of the prelude. This makes the 7th bar of this melody; and the 8th overlaps with

17-28.—Recapitulation of prelude, filling up the gaps in the rhythm by repercussion of (b) and by a new arpeggio linking the steps of the bass. From the 5th bar the bass continues to descend, and the harmony moves towards dominant of (V.), the bass marking this tendency by falling an augmented 2nd from B to A♭ on the way to the new dominant. The treble has risen with (a) to the 7th, on which it insists. The bass, rising again from the new dominant to the A♭, sets the arpeggio swinging on it for the rest of the bar, and spends another whole bar on the dominant while the treble descends. Then, with rhythm B, the bass rises its semitone again. But this proves to be G♯, not A♭. It resolves upon (vi.) (of C); and one more bar closes, with pause, into the next movement.

Rondo: Allegretto moderato; with *Prestissimo* Coda.

1–8.—Eight-bar strain on tonic pedal, 4+4 self-repeating, the last note of 4 having the effect of weakening the cadence so that bar 8 provides a full close in contrast to the previous medial close.

The last note of the Introduction draws the listener's attention entirely to the first note of this melody as the starting-point of the theme. But, as Bülow points out, the bass-note on the first beat is treated as an integral part of the first figure. Accordingly figure (a) is

and any development of the figure that omits the bass-note must be indicated by ('a). Bars 3-4 contain a figure (b), which in 7-8 becomes (b').

9–30.—Middle strain, entirely on dominant: 4 bars of (ab) in dominant position, repeated in minor, (b) echoed again in major (2 bars) and once more in minor with upward turn; reiterating ('a) with reversed accent in a bar echoed twice, with half-minor harmonies leading to an 8-bar soprano run, twice 1+2, interlocking with twice 1 interlocking with four ½-bars in sequence falling into da capo of 1st strain. The interlocking at bar 20 gives, in the event, no ground for supposing either that there is an overlap at that point or that the theme should date its period from bar 2 in order to make the cadences " strong." Throughout the movement the main theme always begins on a strong bar and closes in a weak one, and no surprise is felt when its diminution in the *Prestissimo* enforces this sense to the exclusion of any other possibility. As in all Beethoven's works, we shall find here plenty of contrast between weak cadences and strong, with plenty of obvious changes of step, and (as may be admitted in listening to bars 19-22) a certain amount of ambiguity which has at least as high æsthetic value as any rigid accentual feature.

31–52 = 1–22 rescored.

53–62.—The repeated notes in the treble having broken into a long trill, the 8-bar link 23-30 is replaced by a 2-bar descent of bass, leading to final restatement of 1-8 *fortissimo* over an inner trill and a running bass.

First Episode, starting in tonic and moving at once to (vi.).

⁶²/63–70.—New 8-bar theme: 4 bars in 2-bar sequence over tonic, answered by 4 similar bars a 3rd higher, still with tonic as centre.

⁷⁰/71–85.—Continuous with the foregoing, a new 4-bar phrase in (vi.) goes in 4 bars up to its dominant and down again, the whole 4 being then repeated in higher octave and answered by another 4-bar phrase with tonic close into varied repetition. A series of *sforzandos* is gradually changing the step of the rhythm, until the change is achieved with 5 successive *sforzandos* beginning in bar 78, which bring bar 80 on to a main accent, confirmed by repeating the procedure in bars 82-83.

86–97.—New cadence-theme on tonic pedal, 2 *forte* bars interlocking with 2 *piano* bars, closing into repetition of the 4, with echo of last 2 and 2 bars dwindling echo of the last, closing into

98–113.—Figures (ab') in bare octaves in the present key (vi.), then in (IV.); then for 8 bars descending the home-dominant 7th and closing into

First Return.

114–175 = 1–62.

Second Episode in Tonic Minor.

¹⁷⁵/176–183.—New 8-bar theme in 2-bar sequences rising from (i.) through (iv.) to (♭vii.) as supertonic of (♭VI.), into which the 2 remaining bars close by prolonging the figure in a downward scale. There is a strong suspicion that by an overlap the theme dates from 175, but Beethoven does not as yet prescribe or wish for any decisive *sforzando*.

¹⁸³/184–191 = 175–183, with new counterpoint in bass.

¹⁹¹/192–199.—Answering strain, reversing the sequence—viz., starting in (♭VI.), followed by (iv.), followed by descent to home leading-note (here Beethoven has a *sforzando* confirming the change of step), and concluding with close into tonic. The counterpoint of 191–198 is reversed, the new running figure being in treble, with a slight but deliberate alteration avoiding certain harmonic weaknesses that would have resulted from exact transcription.

199–206 = 191–198, inverted in double counterpoint, restoring the bass version of the running figure, and closing into

207–220.—Repetition of last 4 bars with parts again interchanged, closing into insistence on last 2 bars twice, with 2 more of compressed close, leading to final tonic octaves. These last (217-218) are the end of the episode and should not be taken together with the following 2 echoes, which lead to the next event.

Finding the Way Home.

221–238.—Figures (ab') proceed in full harmony on tonic pedals, distributing (a) in different octaves, in 4-bar steps as in 97–112. They start in (♭VI.). The next step is in (iv.), and the next is in D♭, which will not, in such a series of changes, be felt as (♭II.). Accordingly figure (b) decides that at this distance from home there is no use in hurrying. It repeats itself in a lower octave, and, in yet a lower octave, turns twice round in 2 more bars closing into the next period.

239–250.—New sequence feeling its way in 4-bar steps by tones from D♭ to E♭ minor, and thence to F minor, from which the 4th bar does not move but leads to the next process. [It is unnecessary to derive this from other themes. Of course, all repeated crotchets are suspiciously reminiscent of (a), but Beethoven has here marked them with dashes instead of dots; and the previous sequence, by distributing (a) over different octaves, has removed any immediate connexion. The main point of the passage is precisely that it is new, and thus emphasizes the acquiescence in taking D♭ as an altogether remote starting-point from which further progress must be made by casting about for a new line.]

251–286.—Figure (a) climbs up 9 steps, in 3 groups of 3 bars, the first on dominant of F minor, the second on dominant of B♭ minor, and the third on dominant of E♭ minor. Then it descends in steps of twice 2 bars through D♭ to C minor, the tonic of which is given in 2 bars (as if to begin a 3rd step); after which (a) is represented by single bars (a') carried down in dominant-and-tonic alternation for 6 bars, completed by two of themeless arpeggio in a sudden quickly damped *forte*, as if in startled and belated recognition of the home dominant.

287–312.—Twenty-six bars of dominant preparation. For twice 4 bars figure (a), with an extra crotchet, alternately overshoots and falls short of its note. Then, without the extra crotchet, it mounts the dominant 7th during 8 bars, broken into isolated up-beats in the last 2. Hesitating for 2 extra bars on the 7th, it then begins a new 8-bar group, with ('a) in anacrusis answered by dominant plus 9th in bass. These 8 bars date from ³⁰⁴/305. The first 4 consist of this dialogue twice; the remainder, beginning like a 3rd pair, break up into up-beats again, again touching a 9th on their fall downward to a sudden triumphant close into

Second Return.

313–344 = 31–61, the first 8 bars *ff*, with sudden return to *pp* at 9th bar.

Coda.

[344]/345.—The beginning of the First Episode is given as far as its 8th bar, and its theme is continued without modulation in higher positions for another 8 bars, and then carried in cadential harmonies for 4 more bars, which are repeated in higher position and diverted into key of dominant. Herein the figure continues in 2-bar dominant-tonic closes, alternately *forte* and, in higher position, *piano*. These last 4 bars are repeated, expanded by 2 extra bars echoing the last, with *crescendo* closing into next period.

[This passage illustrates why the dominant is so little evident as a key in this sonata. The plausible view that Beethoven, or any sensible composer, was " tired " of the dominant or " wanted to get away from it " is as inadequate as are all attempts to regard boredom as the guide of life. The plain fact is that if in a major movement *any* other key has been chosen for the second group, the dominant loses all value as an independent key-centre. This Rondo has used no remote keys at all in positions of functional theme; and it has treated (♭II.) as a very remote region, not to be explained away as a " Neapolitan 6th " until we are within sight of home. But in the Rondo, no less than in the first movement, (V.) sank permanently to the position of " home dominant " as soon as the First Episode settled in (vi.). Few works, if any, have more extensive passages of " dominant preparation." In a later period Beethoven brings out key-contrasts in ways which restrict opportunity for even preparatory dominants.]

378–402.—Dominant preparation during 25 bars with paus,e carrying (a) for 8 bars up 7th; then, reduced to (a'), down 2 octaves of minor 9th for twice 4, closing into chords gliding every 2 bars chromatically to 7th, over and under which the note G descends with air of alluding to theme.

Prestissimo.

403–410.—Bars 1-8 diminished and repeated with ornamental variation (*αβ*). (Diminution and augmentation concern the ear, not the eye. Though this theme is still written in crotchets, it is in rhythmic units of half-size quite apart from the faster tempo, which does not by itself affect the question.)

411–427.—Figure (*β*) repeated, and its end carried down the scale in 4 bars, closing into repetition in lower octave, closing into a new 4-bar cadence-group. This also closes into repetition in higher octave, but, finding that its 3rd bar is on (IV.), stays there for the 4th bar.

428–430.—Theme (ab) in (IV.), diminished and its self-repetition given in the ornamented form (*αβ*).

431–440.—As if in answer to (IV.), the dominant phrase of

(ab), as in 11-16, appears, diminished, in its proper position. Its self-repetition does not use the minor colour of bar 15, and its last bar (on present basis) is carried further down the scale for 2 whole bars and eight $\frac{1}{2}$-bars, closing into

441-464.—Sequence of (a) in bass, undiminished, in 4-bar steps—2 occupied by (a), the others by (a') twice—starting in ($\flat$VI.), moving thence to (iv.), and thence to D$\flat$ (in such a context no longer felt as ($\flat$II.): compare 228 foll.), which leads to B$\flat$ minor, whence the bass proceeds in four 2-bar steps back towards the tonic minor. It reaches $\flat^{\overset{\sharp^6}{5}}_{A\natural}$, on which a 4-bar arpeggio leads to

465-484.—Cadenza in strict time: 4 bars $^6_4$ to $^5_3$, repeated, and begun a 3rd time, when the $^6_4$ lasts out the 4th bar, its resolution being inferred during the following 4 bars of scale rising in bass below dominant trill. The scale reaches the 7th, on which its tucked-in finish is twice echoed, leaving the trill alone for a 4th bar.

485-514.—Bars 1-8 undiminished, over the trill; the 4 latter bars (with b') carried down in sequence of thirds through (i.), ($\flat$VI.), and (iv.); in which last key a 2-bar echo leads back to tonic minor, with 4 bars reaching dominant for final 4-bar shake.

515-528.—Diminution of (a+b), ff and p in alternate octaves on tonic pedal, the whole 4 bars. repeated in variation ($a\beta$); (β) echoed twice, and then carried up dominant chord over the tonic pedal for 4 bars, closing into

529-543.—Four 4-bar periods of tonic chord, the first period filled with crotchets, the rest in detached rhythms dying away to pp until a *fortissimo* breaks in before last period, of which the 4th bar (544) is represented by pause at the end of 543. The figure of the whole 16-bar process is reminiscent of the falling 3rd of the main theme.

22

SONATA IN F MAJOR, Op, 54.

THE neglect of this subtle and deeply humorous work comes not so much from its being overshadowed between its gigantic neighbours, as from the fact that it is almost, if not quite, as difficult as either of them. Moreover, it is utterly unlike any other work of Beethoven, just as *Meistersinger* is utterly unlike any other work of Wagner. The enormous size of *Meistersinger* compels the enthusiast to recognize that without a knowledge of it a whole aspect of Wagner's mind, and that perhaps the wisest, remains unknown and hardly suspected. Beethoven's Op. 54 represents only what can be comprised in ten minutes of his most Socratic humour; but that is too important to deserve neglect. The humour is not bitter: Socratic irony approaches it nearly. But its purport is not philosophic. The two movements speak naïvely in their own characters, and Beethoven does not intrude with any indication that he could write a different kind of music with his fuller knowledge. The first movement seems quite happy with a main theme that cannot get through 4 bars without a full close, and prefers to sit down after 2. The finale, on the other hand, cannot stop at all, though its initial range of sentence is only 2 bars, with a hiccough at the 3rd. It does not seem to have heard of any other texture than 2-part writing, with occasional nodules of double notes, nor of much internal rhythm beyond perpetual motion; nor, strangest of all, does it seem to have heard of counterpoint beyond note against note, or rather arpeggio against arpeggio, with an occasional syncopated figure in monotone. Hence we can hardly explain it as a reversion to Bach, though nobody but Bach and Beethoven can have had anything to do with it. So much, then, for what it is not. It resembles all Beethoven's other works, great and small, late, middle, and early, in this,—that it can be properly understood only on its own terms. If Beethoven uses an old convention, we must find out how it fits the use he makes of it, instead of imagining that its origin elsewhere explains its presence here. If Beethoven writes in a form and style which cannot be found elsewhere, we must, as Hans Sachs says, find its own rules without worrying because it does not fit ours.

Beethoven's contemporaries knew their Haydn better than we

do; and they probably saw nothing unorthodox in the outward aspect of a sonata consisting merely of a Menuet and the sort of *perpetuum mobile* which by some obscure process had, since the time of Paradies, acquired the name of *toccata*. Bach's toccata-form is too sacred a thing to allow us willingly to acquiesce in this later use of the term; but the contemporaries of Beethoven and Clementi would probably have said that Beethoven's Op. 54 was a small work consisting of a minuet and a toccata; and they would see nothing calling for further explanation in the title *Sonata* for a group of two movements in the same key, in mani-festly good contrast of form, and by no means lyric in style.

In tempo d'un Menuetto: Minuet, with modulating Trio, part of which recurs between two repetitions of Minuet with progressive variation.

Main Theme.
    Bars ¾/1–8.—Four-bar melody distributed over 3 octaves on bass rising from (I.) to (V.); 1+1; +2. The whole 4 bars are repeated, the repetition being part of the form, inasmuch as the single phrase would not be ready to proceed to a 2nd strain. Moreover, a feminine* cadence in the first clause—*i.e.*, one extra note on the 2nd beat of bar 4, not reproduced in bar 8—would suffice to make the whole 8 bars a single theme of manifestly the same type as the Rondo-themes of the *Waldstein* Sonata and Op. 90.
    The theme contains figures (a):

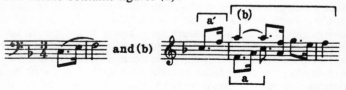

and (b)

*In musical analysis this term of prosody will be found very useful. A line that ends with a strong syllable—*e.g.*, a normal blank-verse line—is masculine; *e.g.*:
        Of man's first disobedience, and the fruit.
An additional weak syllable makes the ending feminine, *e.g.*:
        To be or not to be: that is the question.
For musical purposes the size of the strong note is unimportant. It may be a whole bar, as in what we have elsewhere called " weak cadences," or a semiquaver, as in bar 3 of the *Allegro* of this sonata.

⁸/9–16.—Second strain, 8 bars, distributed in 3 octaves like the 1st strain, and moving twice as slow; viz., 2+2+4; the first couples being on the tonic, and the 4-bar group beginning like a third couple and breaking away into sequence descending with

local modulation to full close.   The material is derived from
(a'+b), with (b) shifted on to a later beat.
^{16}/17–24 = ^{8}/9–16, with a few new ornaments.

Trio.
    ^{24}/25–38.—New 4-bar theme in triplet quavers on dominant,
led by bass and imitated by treble, its figure drifting into sequential descent in steps filling crotchets across the ¾ time.   At end of
4th bar the treble takes the lead in a continuation for 10 bars,
the sequential figure taking another shape and the harmony
becoming 4-part instead of pairs of octaves.   The sequence,
having got astride of D minor in relation to C major, oscillates
on this pair twice across 2⅔ bars and passes into a scale of C (our
dominant) in contrary motion, rotating in cross-rhythm again at
the highest point till, on a main accent, the bass rises in a new
partly chromatic legato, and the treble, after hesitating for 3 beats,
makes up its mind to come down to a close.   The last triplet of the
close constitutes a figure (c) which is echoed in a low octave in the
next beat.
    ^{38}/39–54.—Bars 25–38 repeated in A♭ (♭III.) with the addition
of two further downward steps at the point corresponding to 31⅔.
This not only brings the cross-rhythm sequence in relation to A♭
instead of to its dominant, but displaces its beat so that it has to
repeat its last 2-crotchet group before running into the scale that
leads to its climax.
    [By all means correct the second *R.H.* group of 49 to 6ths in
conformity with 33 if this sort of discrepancy worries you.   It
does not worry Beethoven; and the listener who could detect it
by ear, without having it expressly pointed out, is very unlikely
to have an ear for real subtleties.   It would be the height of
pedantry to burden one's memory with such mere differences
between six and half-a-dozen.   But it is hardly less pedantic to
correct them in the text, and it leads, as experience shows, to
almost limitless falsification.]
    ^{54}/55–69.—The last two bars are carried in sequence down by
3rds, through F minor to D♭, closing into 4 bars in which figure
(c) hovers upon D♭ while the harmony approaches the home
dominant.   This is reached with the next period, in which (c),
with minor 6th, finds its way up to a soprano region in which it
pipes its query till, in the next 4 bars, in the deep bass it growls
its way home, discovering first that its 6th should be major, and
then that it must stretch itself before it can run down to its tonic.
During that run the Minuet returns.

First Da Capo.
    ^{69}/70–93 = ⅓/1–24, with progressive increase of ornament.

Allusion to Trio.

⁹³/94–105.—The first 4 bars of the Trio lead to a new 2-beat sequence across the ¾ time, led by treble and followed by bass at distance of 4 beats; remaining entirely in tonic (over dominant origin), and coalescing after 4th step in a scale rising to the top of the dominant 7th, reached in 4th bar and dwelt upon for 2 more with pause. The bass moves down to 7th while these 2 bars are echoed *piano*, with pause.

Second Da Capo.

¹⁰⁶/107–128 = 1–22, with progressive variation arriving at continuous sextole semiquaver movement. [There is reason to believe that Beethoven distinguished the sextole from the double triplet. This, apart from the special merits of the present case, justifies the modern editor in making the notation unmistakably thrice 2 instead of twice 3.]

In the bars corresponding to 1–2 and 5–6, the bass, having to resolve its 7th in bar 106, is now a third higher.

128–136.—At the penultimate bar of the theme (= 23) the sequence is urged forward into a descent in 2-crotchet steps across the ¾ time till, after 2 more bars, it breaks into 5 bars of expanded cadence, closing, with freely declamatory cadenza and pauses, into the following Coda.

Coda.

¹³⁶/137–154.—Figure (b) on tonic pedal with the extra note which (as argued above) *might* have been present at bar 4, and with an answering pair of bars making it into a new 4-bar phrase. This is repeated in a variation. Then (a') climbs up the tonic chord, hastening at the 3rd bar. At the outset of this climb an overlap may be suspected, because the bass begins to stir at the 4th bar of the past period. But bar 148, in which the dominant minor 9th bursts out over the tonic pedal, may equally well be a 4th bar, not the first of the new group. The ear does not interest itself in the question where the overlap occurs, or whether there is any such thing. But there is good rhythmic sense in dating a new 4-bar period from 149, the point where the throbbing triplets slacken to duple quavers. This makes the dominant 9th resolve on to a weak bar, after which the rest of the chord resolves on to the tonic in the next bar, which is the 1st of 4 final bars, with 2 full closes, the one plain, the other feminine.

Allegretto : *Perpetuum mobile* in 2-part polyphony on a single theme, with short archaic (melodic) Exposition, but extensive Development and Coda ; running at a uniform pace which nothing can stop.

Exposition.

1–8.—Subject for 2-part polyphony; 2 bars (A) in bass climbing up the scale of F and closing into a sudden jerk in 3rd bar, while a treble answers at the upper octave. (The omission of the 1st note by this answer does not constitute a variant of the theme, being merely a practical necessity that would vanish with two instruments.) In the treble the sudden jerk has an extra note, with the result that, whereas the bass held the tonic throughout the answer, the treble holds the dominant while the bass again climbs up with the subject, initiating a repetition of 1–4 an octave higher. Figures:

9–12.—The " jerk " becomes a steady figure descending in a sequence, falling in crotchet steps by thirds (B) for 2 bars, followed by 2 more completing the period and closing into dominant. Though no new figure is propounded, it will be convenient to call these last 2 bars (C).

13–20.—Eight bars in dominant. (The dimensions and style of this Exposition give no room for distinctions between *on* the dominant and *in* it, when once the new leading-note has been given. But this is the only solid dominant *key* in the whole piece. As soon as the movement has launched out into deeper water the distinction appears in full force.) The jerk (b), as a rising octave, marks the rhythm in the bass (and marks it out of time) as a tonic pedal in the present key, in a period of twice 1 bar followed by 4 half-bars, while ($a^1 + a^2$) in analogous distribution climbs up in treble. This leads to 4 bars of scale in which the two voices pull in opposite ways rhythmically as well as melodically. At the 3rd bar the treble drops a cadential chord, and at the 4th bar the bass finds its way back to F the first time. After the repeat, it takes a new direction through a trill, which does duty for the perpetual motion, and leads to

Development.

21–28.—Theme (A) for 8 bars *on* A major. Approached from

the previous B♭ this, though for 7 bars it is an exact transposition of 1–7, cannot possibly be anything more than the dominant of D, (VI.) or (vi.); and into (vi.) the 8th bar accordingly closes.

29–36.—Theme (B) in D minor, its 4-bar descent repeated in lower octave, closing into the next incident. [The treble is throughout in a new position. Similar changes will not be mentioned in the rest of this analysis. They disguise appearances to the eye, and the student will find the analysis more useful if it ignores the disguise. Inversion in double counterpoint, though apparently the same kind of change, must always be mentioned, since it is an important structural principle.]

37–44.—The expected tonic (vi.) is replaced by a sudden drop of the bass to a lower semitone A♭, starting a descent by semitones to the dominant of G, a key which we need no longer trouble to connect with our tonic.

45–60.—Theme (A) enters in G in extreme bass, *forte*, with a new syncopated monotone (x) for countersubject, which naturally joins itself to the " jerk " in the bass when the treble answers. The answer is *piano*, and (as in the Exposition) the duet is resumed in a higher octave: alternately *f* and *p*. Here the answer descends with (a²) into C minor (thus retrospectively turning all the G major into a mere dominant). A similar 8 bars in C minor leads, in its last answer, to F minor.

61–74.—Theme (B) descends in 4 bars from F minor into D♭, where the end of its group (C) develops into a new 2-bar sequence. (The interrupted cadence is not the same as that at 37.) The new sequence falls in 2-bar steps by tones (the bass moving in semitones) from dominant of C minor to dominant of B♭ minor. Then the steps proceed once a bar by 5ths, lying across the bar. Four such steps reach the threshold of D♭, and one extra bar closes into the dominant thereof.

75–82.—On dominant of D♭ the bass traces a plaintive cantabile on the outline of (a), answering 4 bars (1+1+2) of dominant by 4 of tonic, closing towards repetition from the beginning of the 8.

83–98.—The repetition gives the first 4 bars and breaks away, repeating the last 2 on dominant of G♭, and proceeding thence in 1-bar steps down the dominants. G♭ is written as F♯; the remainder as B, E, A, D, G, C, and F, all represented with minor 9ths. The dominant of F initiates a 4-bar phrase, descending to a close into the following passage of preparation. There are many enharmonic circles in Beethoven's works—that is to say, many developments that return to the tonic by a road that contains no actual enharmonic modulation that would stand the test of transposition, but which has, as here, changed the notation at a convenient point and then ignored the theoretical names of the subsequent keys. But this is the only case where circle is actually the whole " circle of 5ths." The infantile " Two Preludes in all the Major Keys," published without Beethoven's consent as Op. 39, should be ignored ; though some textbooks are still in use which recommend them for study. Poorer models could hardly be imagined. But here we have the highest art. The very outset of the development, 20–21, the incidents at 37 and 65, and the beautiful expanse of lyric relaxation from 75 onwards, all completely remove from our minds any suspicion that the course of modulation has been from the G major of 45 straight down 24 steps from subdominant to subdominant.

99–114.—Dominant preparation for return. Six bars of (A), with (x) and with its own usual permutations *in* C, are now in effect merely *on* the home dominant. Figure (a²) is then worked into a new type of sequence in dialogue between treble and bass in 2-bar steps, the 2nd step starting higher up the triad, and the 3rd step starting from the dominant 7th and descending the scale into 2 extra bars, closing into the

Recapitulation.

115–122.—Theme (A) climbs 2 octaves in treble over vibrating tonic bass, which answers the theme at 5th bar. The remaining 2 bars of the period carry the theme (in both voices in harmony) into (IV.).

123–133.—Theme (B) in (IV.). It closes into repetition in lower octave, which passes through (iv.) and ♭VI., where (c) is interrupted by an overlapping 4-bar group, the bass having risen to D♮ and descending again by semitones, the incident being reminiscent of that at 37. It closes into home dominant.

134–152.—New sequence of (a) in 4-bar steps (1+1+2) descending by tones from home dominant to dominant of E♭ and dominant of D♭. From this point the last 2 bars are detached for the next step, where the sequence becomes tonal—*i.e.*, instead of modulating it passes along the lines of the prevalent key. This is here construed as E♭ minor during 2 bars in which the sequence is hurried into ½-bar steps. Then it reaches an augmented 6th, impinging on the home dominant, into which, accordingly, the next 2 bars close. Meanwhile, the top notes of the sequence have been outlining a new figure (y)

153–161.—The new figure (y) is given as a quaver cantabile in a tenor part amid homophonic chords on dominant of tonic minor. Four bars of this lead to 4 in which (y) is clipped into a ½-bar figure with cross-accent. During 4 bars this contracts its interval and then becomes a 2-bar trill on the 7th. It closes in the first instance (like bar 20) on to a chord of (A), beginning the repeat of the Development. In the second instance the trill makes a normal full close into the Coda.

Coda : Più Allegro.

162–188.—Abandoning 2-part polyphony, theme (A) rushes up 3 octaves over vibrating tonic pedal and makes an 8-bar phrase with the aid of 4 more bars on rising bass with zigzag treble, closing with a bar like (C), which closes into repetition of the whole 8, with insistence twice upon the 8th bar. This closes into 4 tonic bars of (A) below (x) (3 bars+two ½ bars); repeated, with (A) in treble rising up the chord over (x) in bass, followed by 2 abrupt chords within 1 final bar.

23

SONATA IN F MINOR, Op. 57.
(Appassionata.)

The title *Appassionata* was given by the publisher without waiting for Beethoven's consent. It is justified by the eminently tragic tone of the whole work. No other work by Beethoven maintains a tragic solemnity throughout all its movements. The first movement of a sonata tells a complete story which no later movement can falsify: hence Beethoven is under no compulsion to follow up even the most tragic first movement by a tragic finale. Opinions as to tragic expression in music are apt to outrun musical knowledge; and when writers refer to the " cheerful vivacity " of the end of Beethoven's C minor Trio, Op. 1, No. 3, or the " triumphant end " of the C♯ minor Quartet, we mere musicians can only treat such criticisms as the young man was advised to treat more serious difficulties in preparing for his profession—we " look them boldly in the face and pass on." The finales of the C minor Trio, of the *Sonata Appassionata*, of the C♯ minor Sonata, Op. 27, No. 2 (which we will *not* call " Moonlight "), and of the C♯ minor Quartet, are Beethoven's only tragic finales. All his other pathetic finales show either an epilogue in some legendary or later world far away from the tragic scene (the quartets in F minor and A minor) or a temper, fighting, humorous, or resigned, that does not carry with it a sense of tragic doom. That sense is surely present in the quiet end of the C minor Trio; the harmonies are major only at the very end, and there as the result of deep minor subdominant colour. In the *Sonata Appassionata* the very beginning of the finale is in itself a final stroke of fate, after which there is not a moment's doubt that the tragic passion is rushing deathwards. The slow movement itself is, like the other sublime variation-movements in that position in Beethoven's works at this period, a dream that must be shattered at the first hint of action; for it cannot move away from the harmonies of its theme, and its range of key is merely melodic. Nowhere else has Beethoven confined his theme not merely to its key but to tonic closes in every pair of bars. In earlier works he has been witty in showing how many dominant closes can be tolerated in succession (the slow movement of Op. 1, No. 3, and Op. 14, No. 2). But in Op. 57 the tonic closes are no more witty

169

than the similar monotony in the lines of the melody. The conception is sublime and may be taken as representing the ultimate faith underlying the tragic emotion. At the opposite end of the emotional scale, the realization of that which was feared, comes the entirely new theme of the *Presto* at the end of the finale.

Beethoven had gone some way in the sketching of the first movement before he thought of putting any major mode into it at all. It was to have been more like the D minor Sonata, with both groups wholly in the minor, and in this case with the second group in the extremely dark key of (♭iii.); in short, the second group began with bar 51, even when the huge transition-passage 24-34 was almost in mature shape. The glorious afterthought converted the whole movement from the gloom of a storm to the active passions of a tragedy.

Allegro assai: F minor. Sonata form.

Bars ⅟1-4.—Theme (AB) of 2-bar figure (a) on chord of F minor, followed by 2-bar figure (b) on and around dominant.

⁴/5-8.—Repetition of theme (AB) on (♭II.), with (VI.) as its dominant. (This is what becomes of a sequential opening with tonic and supertonic when the mode is minor instead of major. Beethoven's contemporaries were shocked.)

9-16.—Eight bars on the home dominant. This is its first entry as a bass-note, since (b) is always centred on a ♯. Figure (b) is now repeated; with a new rhythmic figure (c) in the bass, falling by a semitone on to the dominant during the 2nd bar, both here and in answer to a higher position of (b) in next 2 bars. After this the treble takes up the rhythm (c) in dialogue with bass, and suddenly bursts into an arpeggio, filling a bar and a half, followed by a half-close from (♭VI.) to dominant, both in chords of ♯ Pause.

¹⁶/17-23.—Counterstatement of (AB), interrupted at 1st main beat by crashing tonic chords (d) filling nearly 2 bars. A bar of similar crashes on dominant (♯) precedes and follows figure (b). Then (b) is repeated. Its base E♮ suddenly resolves (as F♭) on to E♭, dominant of (III.)

24-34.—Ten bars of dominant preparation for (iii.), consisting of 4 bars repeated with variation, and continued with further decline of their half-close in 4 more bars (2+twice 1), closing into

Second Group in (III.), afterwards (iii.).

35-50.—New theme (E), allied to (a) in rhythm and in the feature of a tonic arpeggio: but such derivations must not be stretched when the composer keeps the themes apart. The melody enters at end of 1st bar and lies in a 4-bar phrase (2+2 with medial close) across its period. The bass rises by step from tonic to dominant. (This quite normal feature has important results later.) The melody repeats its first 2 bars in a higher octave, then breaks down, replacing its medial close by an enormously expanded minor cadence filling the next 8 bars themelessly (1 bar of minor $^6_4$ and 7 bars of dominant), closing into

51–60.—New theme in (iii.): a 4-bar phrase; two half-bars self-repeating, on tonic, the whole repeated on (♭VI.) on same base; and two whole bars proceeding from (♭II) to dominant; closing into repetition of the whole 4 an octave higher. The penultimate dominant, in two positions, is insisted on for an extra bar, grouping with a final whole-bar close into

61–66.—Cadence-theme; three interlocking statements of a single bar, with descending bass in successively lower octaves, while treble rises again to top octave. A 4th tonic bar closes into a bare tonic, initiating another 2-bar period. In this period the first 3 notes of (a) move from an A♭ minor $^6_4$ to an F♭ major triad, written as E major.

Development.

⁶⁶/67–78.—Theme (AB) in F♭ major, which, for the purposes of the enharmonic circle traversed by this development, may be called E major, as written for present convenience by Beethoven. Figure (b) is answered, unexpectedly and questioningly, in the supertonic of this key, in a higher octave. The question is settled in the lower octave by a calm 3-bar cadence in the tonic—(b)+2 new bars—closing into repetition in the upper octave.

⁷⁸/79–92.—Figure (a) moves in 4-bar steps (2+2) over 5 octaves, with a new accompaniment of descending arpeggios; passing from E minor into C minor, and thence to A♭. The steps are not the mere 2-bar interchanges that appear on paper; the parts cross, and each part takes actually 8 bars to complete its pattern. Thus the line started by the bass at ⁷⁸/79 passes into the treble at 81. Here you understand F sustained for 3 beats, concealed by the quintoles around it, and continued by *R.H.* In the same way the quintoles descend from the top G of 83 down to the extreme bass, closing into the next step at 87. Meanwhile the other part, starting with the tremolo at 79, executes the converse design.

The chord of A♭ begins the next stage. It changes into a diminished 7th on A. What the momentary intention of this chord may be is never divulged. The A♮ proceeds to behave as B♭♭ 4 times in the next 2 bars. It may thus be unwinding the previous enharmonic circle—*i.e.*, it may have brought us (in mathematically ideal tuning) " really " on to the dominant of D♭

instead of on to that of E♭♭♭, which is where we are now in
theory. On the other hand, it may be doing nothing at all; which
is just as good drama, and is exactly what our ears tell us. Beethoven is taking extraordinary measures to emphasize this dominant,
whatever it may be. The previous modulations are as vast in their
range as any that appeal to key-relation at all, and infinitely
wider than any that do not. And a still greater journey awaits us
hereafter.

93–104 = 24–32 transposed, with slight changes, to dominant
of D♭.

105–108.—As if the whole transition-passage were not enough
bars 33–34 are replaced by 4 bars (1+1+2) on an entirely new
figure started by a bass below the dominant pedal and imitated
by the treble. It is idle to try to derive this from previous
material. It is new because the old transition-material, already
severely simple, is exhausted, and any allusion to other known
themes would be distracting; and it is melodious because the
moment is not ripe for a themeless arpeggio. Lastly, it is
thoroughly introductory and urgent. Interpreters who detach it
from its surroundings or slacken its pace have no right to talk
disrespectfully of old Italian operas where the sentiment " our
only hope is in instant flight " is represented by flights of coloratura in ten minutes of dacapo aria. The effect of these 4 bars is,
" the path winds further up the hill; shall I be in time?" And the
time is inexorable, not more to us than to the adversary.

109–122.—Theme (E) enters calmly in D♭. But at the 4th bar
its bass *continues* to rise. Nothing stops it; the theme is driven
(in its 4-bar groups) through B♭ minor and G♭ by this rising
bass. After the 2nd bar in G♭ it is reduced to insisting on its last
2 notes. The bass is on C♭ = B♮. The next 2 bars bring it to C.
The key of C♭ minor is written as B minor; once more we are in
an enharmonic circle—in the same direction as the previous one—
so we will not enquire into the relation of E♭♭♭♭ to the home
dominant, but will attend to serious matters.

123–135.—With one more semitone the bass has reached D♭.
The passion is beyond articulate utterance; and the next 7 bars
(note the odd number) are filled with a diminished 7th in arpeggios
entirely void of any theme. After 7 bars the rhythm (c) emerges in
treble and bass, for 2 bars on D♭ only, then for 2 bars in its
proper shape of D♭ to C. Quite suddenly it becomes a subdued
continual muttering on the home dominant (as we may now
recognize); and at the end of 2 more bars the Recapitulation
begins.

Recapitulation.

First Group.

$^{135}/136-151 = \frac{1}{4}/1-16$ above the continued muttering on dominant, which rises with the rise to (♭II.), and returns through ♮B back to home dominant during the rest of the paragraph, the original figure (d) entering in due course in the next available octaves. There is no *ritardando* during the bars corresponding to 12–13. The new bass obviously sheds a dramatic light on the avoidance of root-positions during 1–16.

$^{151}/152-162$.—The counterstatement now bursts out in the tonic major. This overwhelming stroke of tragic irony was twice again achieved by Beethoven in passages externally quite unlike the present case: first at the same juncture of form in the slow movement of the Trio, Op. 70, No. 1, and secondly in the Coda of the first movement of the Ninth Symphony. The point is not to be confused with the inevitable irony of a major recapitulation in a minor movement: it is an independent action, not a normal feature of the form.

Only the tonic chord is major. Figure (b) mounts up in four successive phases of its dominant chord, all with minor bearings and all preceded by the crashing chords (d).

163–173 = 24–34, with a more explicitly minor cadence in the last 2 bars.

Second Group in Tonic.

174–203 = 35–64 in F major and minor.

Coda.

204–209—The last descent of the bass proves to be the 1st notes of (a), which rises from the extreme bass and passes in 2 steps of 2 bars and 2 of 1 bar into (VI.). [The autograph is perfectly clear in making the treble flicker in sympathy with the theme below. The passage is misprinted in many editions.] It is often asked how Beethoven is able to visit D♭ again after he had made it so conspicuous in the development. The answer is that the key that was so conspicuous in the development was either E♭♭♭ or some other region lying between two enharmonic circles; whereas we are now in the submediant of our own tonic, and have reached it in the straightest possible way.

210–217.—Theme (E) enters in a high octave in (VI.). Its bass lacks energy to rise; the tonic chord ($^6_4$) remains in the 3rd bar; and when the bass rises in the middle of the 4th bar, it immediately falls back again; the key changes towards the home dominant, reaching the tonic minor chord in 2 more bars, the bass no longer conjunct.

218–238.—Suddenly the bass plunges into the depths, or a new bass enters. There is no more theme. Arpeggios rise in harmonies moving first in 2-bar steps from (♭II.) (⁶₄ on B♭) to (iv.), then in half-bar steps up the scale of the tonic for 2 octaves, reaching D♭. This chord, reached at a half-bar, lasts for 2 more bars, after which 2 on D♮ lead to the home dominant, on which a ⁶–⁵₄–₃ cadence is spread over 4 bars. Through the dominant chord sustained by the pedal, articulate utterance returns (as at the end of the development) with figure (c), which fills 4 bars in dialogue, *ritardando* to *Adagio*.

Più Allegro.

²³⁸/239–248.—With a sudden full close figure (c) concludes in a quicker tempo. Theme (E) enters in the tonic minor. It has lost all calm; its bass rises no further than in flow and ebb between A♭ and C; while the melody repeats its first 2 bars with passionate interruptions on the dominant 9th of (iv.), into which it closes in its swing back to repeat itself. When this has happened twice, the last notes are taken up in the following groups.

249–256.—The melody ended with three C's. These become a 3-bar cadence-group in dialogue between *R.* and *L.*, closing into self-repetition in lower octave, and repeating the last bar twice in higher octaves, closing into a final tonic chord in a new period.

257–262.—Through 4 bars of the final tonic chord the ghost of (a) rises through 2 octaves and sinks through 5 octaves. The whole is sustained by pedal, and the enormous *pianissimo* 5-octave triad dies away in 6 bars with pause.

Andante con moto: D♭ major (VI.). Theme with 4 Variations.

Theme.

1–8.—*First Strain*, 4+4, with tonic cadences every 2 bars, the bass confirming the subordinate cadences (bars 2 and 6) and undermining the main ones (³/4 and 8).

9–16.—*Second Strain:* 3 pairs of bars, each pair with the same 1st bar (on dominant), and a 2nd in which the melody reaches the tonic in the 1st pair, the mediant in the 2nd pair, and the 5th in the 3rd pair, the last quaver being always a tonic harmony. A fourth pair of bars gives a final cadence stronger than bars 7-8 and undermined in the same way.

The first 3 variations are *doubles*, dividing the beats in systematic progress.

17–32.—*First Double:* division by halves; syncopated bass.

33–48.—*Second Double* in steady semiquavers.

⁴⁸/49–80.—*Third Double* in demisemiquavers. The demisemiquavers are first below the melody; and in the repeats they are

above it, or they outline it in their top notes.

81–96.—*Variation* 4.   The unvaried melody is distributed, in its natural articulations, between 2 octaves, giving the bass room for a broader flow in bars 3-4 and 7-8.   At the last moment a diminished 7th appears instead of the final tonic.

97.—The diminished 7th is answered *fortissimo* in a higher octave, and leads to the finale.   [The autograph very clearly indicates, with word and sign, *arpeggio* for the left hand and *secco* (*i.e.*, dry, or unbroken) for the right.   The purport of the word *arpeggio* has been made quite unintelligible by the omission of the *secco* in most editions.]

Allegro ma non troppo :   F minor.   Sonata Form.

Introduction.

1–19.—Dominant preparation; 4 bars (twice 2) of rhythm marking the new tempo on the previous chord, closing into a period in which a figure (a) descends that chord in 2-bar steps from a high octave to lower octave, then gathering itself into a 4-bar run down to the dominant.   The rhythm changes its step somewhere, for the next 6 bars have evidently dated their periods from 10.   As this was the beginning of the continuous run, the change of step is not unnatural.

First Group.

20–35.—Eight-bar theme (A) on (a), with a prefix (b)

grouped into 2 tonic bars, repeated, and 2 passing through (♭II.) to close into repetition of the whole 8 with a new figure above.

36–62.—The new figure establishes a rhythm ♪|♩ which
(C)
is grouped into a 14-bar theme (C) in three 4-bar steps, with 2 more bars closing into repetition of the whole 14.   Meanwhile, figure (b) has become an accompaniment formula, with sustained crotchets on the verge of melody at each join.   On repetition the new theme is in the treble: the bass rolls in semiquavers, the origin of which it would be pedantic to trace.   The theme now closes into

63–75.—Three repeated pairs from theme (A), on tonic. dominant of C minor (v.), and C minor itself.

Second Group in Dominant Minor.

76–95.—Ten-bar theme: 2 bars, emphasizing ♭II., repeated, and the 3rd time carried down scale for 4 bars to 2 cadence-bars closing into varied repetition of the whole 10, closing into next period. [Note the D♮ at end of bar 80.]

96–111.—Cadence-theme on theme (A) imitated in lower octave at the ½-bar and worked into a new 4-bar phrase with a rhythmic figure (d), closing into repetition in higher octave. The 2 bars with (d) are detached and twice insisted on; then the bass descends towards home tonic in 4 more bars, with (d) in corresponding positions above.

112–117.—Instead of the expected tonic, an explosion on G♭, with diminished 7th, reverberates through 6 bars.

Development.

118–125.—Figures (b+a) on dominant of (iv.) for 8 bars, twice 2, then new imitative treatment of (a) for 3 bars, with a 4th bar closing into

126–141.—Theme (A) in (iv.), the bass avoiding root positions. The whole 8 bars are given, and repeated *crescendo* enhanced by a fragment of dialogue in crotchets above and below the first 4 bars.

142–157.—*Episode.* New 4-bar theme (1+1+2) closing into *forte* repetition; followed immediately by repetition of the whole 8 in tonic, with, however, no recognition of the fact as yet. The repetition substitutes a downward inflection for the upward one in bar 142. The last bar closes into

158–167.—Resumed development of (b+a) in rising sequences imitated below at half-bar and passing in three 2-bar steps from (i.) through (♭II.) and ᶜ⁶ to (iv.), where a 4-bar down-rush turns
                                    C
at last moment towards home dominant.

168–211.—Forty-four bars of preparation for return: 8 theme-less bars (4 repeated) on home dominant; then arpeggios on figure (b) in two 4-bar groups of 3+silent 4th; first on Neapolitan 6th, then on dominant 7th. Then 22 bars of diminished 7th (4 times 2; 8 unbroken; 4 minims and a semibreve). The period is finished by 2 of dominant 7th, on which chord an extra 4-bar group leads at last to the tonic.

Recapitulation.
First Group.

212–255 = 20–63, with the following new touches. From the 3rd bar of theme (A) onwards, the counterpoint of its second statement is applied, and the second statement is given to the bass with a new counterpoint above. [To derive this counterpoint from an augmentation of the end of the 2nd bar of (b+a) is far-fetched.] The *ritardando* indicated in most editions at the close of this restatement is a misreading of Beethoven's *rinforzando*.

256–267.—In the transition (corresponding to 64-75) the three 4-bar stages are (i.), dominant of (VI.) and (VI.). These last 8 bars give the only touch of a major key as yet heard in this movement.

Second Group in Tonic.

268–299 = 76–197.

300a.—At this point Beethoven leads in 2 bars back to the explosion in bars 112–117, with the intention of repeating the Development and Recapitulation. Now, whatever may be said against it, this is not conventional. No other sonata movement has ever repeated its second half when it did not repeat its first. Beethoven has two purposes vividly in mind here. First, he values the interrupted close and the effect of the subdominant that will follow; secondly, he wishes to delay the appearance of an entirely new theme in his Coda. This second point is really important. But it is not an absolute necessity. And Beethoven has un-questionably overlooked the difficulty ordinary mortals must feel in enjoying such a crisis as 168–211 twice in one performance !

It is at least significant that the two points here mentioned do certainly concern the moments at the double bar—viz., the impact of the first explosion, and the surprise of the new theme after the repeat is over. Beethoven may easily have considered such present moments to the neglect of the total effect.

Coda.

300b–307.—The cadences continue for 8 more bars with (*d*) in bass (2+2, with 4 all on dominant) *accelerando*, closing into

Presto.

308–325a.—Entirely new theme in two repeated strains. The first consists of 8 bars: 2 whole-bar chords, + a quaver group of 2 bars repeating itself and adding a close in (v.). The second consists of 10 bars beginning by transposing the first 6 of the first strain to (III.), the only other patch of major tonality besides bars 260–267 in the whole movement. The remaining 4 bars return through (iv.) to close in tonic. On repetition the last bar overlaps with the resumed main theme.

325b–361.—Theme (AB) in 8-bar phrases (2+2+4), with (b) as accompaniment in first half of every bar; closing into repetition in higher octave; closing into four reiterated 2-bar groups +3 single bars, 2 half-bars; and 8 bars of final tonic chord, the last an unwritten silence.

24

SONATA IN F SHARP MAJOR, Op. 78.

BEETHOVEN was quite in earnest when he said he preferred this sonata to the C♯ minor, Op. 27, No. 2. It is a complete contrast to that earlier work, not only in mood but in qualities that foreshadow Beethoven's 3rd period and lie complétely beyond the scope of the works that led to his second period. Within less than ten minutes the Sonata Op. 78 shows us proportions that range from a single isolated bar to whole pages, and welds half a dozen totally different figures into paragraphs that make indivisible melodies out of whole sections. To derive one figure from another here is a harmful waste of energy. The "logic" is in the varied proportions of the paragraphs; and where the figures do not resemble one another they are intended to be nothing but themselves, except in so far as they are parts of the whole. It is possible to analyze the phrasing more completely than is done here, but not necessary to carry this out beyond the point at which its subtleties become manifest. They belong to those things which we "can understand perfectly so long as you don't explain."

Introduction: F♯ major   Adagio cantabile.

Four bars of melody on a tonic bass, potentially the first clause of a big slow movement. But the 4th bar dies away with a pause. (Bülow has no justification for sustaining the 3rd of the chord; the bare 5th is essential to the point.)

Allegro ma non troppo: F♯ major.   Sonata form.

First Group.

Bars 1–8.—Eight-bar melody (4+2+2) containing several contrasted figures

and

178

9–13.—From (c) arises a continuation, leading, with allusion to (b), to dominant of (vi.).

14–23.—Ten bars (2+2+2+4) of transition, with semi-quaver movement derived from (b) in treble, passing from (vi.) to dominant of (V.), and preparing there to close into

Second Group : C♯ major (V.).

24–34a.—Starting on half-bar after close of transition, a new 2-bar theme closes into itself, and on repetition takes a turn through (ii.) (reckoning from the present key), to half-close on dominant. Repeating this half-close with a new semiquaver figure suggestive of (b), the paragraph concludes by developing the semiquaver figure into a steady flow for 4 (or 3½) bars. The semi-quavers having reached the bass, an additional bar (34a) returns to the repeat from bar 1. (The whole paragraph of the Second Group amounts to 2+2+2+5, the 5 being 1+1+2+1.)

Development.

34b.—In this version the extra bar leads to F♯ minor (i.).

35–37.—Starting in (i.) the main theme (a¹ and a²) moves to ♭III. (A major).

38–40.—Bass drops from A♮ through G♯ to F× as dominant of G♯ minor. Figure (A¹⁺²) appears, displaced by a half-bar, in bass in that key, answered at half-bar in treble, and leading to

41–50.—Ten bars development of (a¹) in inner part in dialogue with bass. After 2 bars on dominant of D♯ minor, the procedure is by sequences falling a tone every two bars, the steps not exactly alike. When B is reached, the *L.H.* merges into the semiquavers of *R.H.*, and the harmony approximates to that of the home dominant which is reached with emphasis at bar 51.

51–52.—Two bars of home dominant returning to Recapitulation. The ⁶₄ position at the beginning of bar 52 is a feature of style which Bülow unjustifiably deletes by retaining C♯ in the bass.

Recapitulation.

First Group.

53–58 = 1–6.

59–70.—Figure (b) is carried a step higher to the super-tonic. This harmless procedure causes the next bars (corresponding to 9–10) to burst out in the unexpected and unorthodox key of (♭VII.) (see Introduction, p. 10, last paragraph). The continuation of (c) thereupon passes through keys unrecognizable in this context, though really our own tonic minor and subdominant

minor. But this last, changing to major, becomes recognizable as our subdominant when—
71–82 the whole transition-passage (bars 12–13) is reproduced a 5th higher, closing into

Second Group.
83–92.—Exact Recapitulation of bars 24–33 merging into coda.
93–101.—The running bass continues to the end of the movement, turning the tonic into dominant 7th of (IV.). Upon this figure (a¹) appears, checked by a rest, and then resumed with development of (a²), passing through (iv.), and so back (with climax) to home dominant. The tonic arrives half a bar before its time (an incident definitely foreshadowing Beethoven's later style), and persists to the end. The whole last paragraph may be dated from bar 93.
Bar 101a leads back to repeat from beginning of Development. This should be played: the movement is short, and the stress on its formal aspects is a positive æsthetic gain.

Allegro vivace : Sonata Form without Development : or Special Rondo Form.

First Group.
1–11.—Theme (A) in three 4-bar clauses containing figures

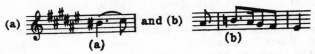

The 2nd clause goes to (IV.); the 3rd returns to tonic and overlaps the 1st bar of a new theme.
12–22.—New 4-bar theme (C) with semiquaver figure, closing into self-repetition. Two more bars lead to dominant with
22–31.—Ten-bar flight (F) on dominant, the semiquavers taking what proves to be the shape of figure (a), as appears from
32–42.—Repetition of theme (A), followed again by
43–56.—Theme (C), taking a new turn at 7th bar towards dominant of (vi.). Six bars on this new dominant lead to

Second Group : (VI.) and (vi.) (D♯).
57–64.—Eight bars (2+2 repeated) alternating chord of (VI.) with key of (vi.), using the prevalent semiquaver figure.
65–72.—Eight more tonic-and-dominant bars (twice 4). [The skip to the upper instead of lower D♯ in bass of bar 69 is not, as many editors suppose, the result of a misunderstood abbreviation : the autograph has no abbreviation, and is perfectly clear.]

73.—Extra bar, passing through B major to

74–88.—Sudden explosion on dominant 7th of C major, wherever that may be. Upon it the flight (F) arises, expanding to 14 bars. Remote as the chord seems, the underlying fact is that the main theme itself began with a chord of the augmented 6th. Hence this strange dominant 7th can turn enharmonically into an augmented 6th.

First Group in (IV.).

89–109.—The augmented 6th proves to be that of our sub-dominant B major, in which key bars 1-18, or 32-48, are recapitulated; the main theme being distributed in different octaves.

At bar 106 (=49) the harmony is diverted so as to lead to the home dominant through (iv.) and (i.).

110–115 ⸗ bars 51-56 on the home dominant, leading to

Recapitulation of Second Group in (I.) and (i.).

116–132.—Exact recapitulation of bars 57-73.

133–149.—The bass having reached D, the explosion and flight (F) now take place on that 7th. It is now not so foreign a chord as that of bar 74, but is manifestly ready to become our initial augmented 6th. The flight is expanded to 16 bars and leads to

Final Return and Coda.

150–161.—Main theme distributed in different octaves. Instead of overlapping with the semiquaver theme, the 3rd clause is completed.

160–178.—Figure (b), with an inversion in bass arising from the last clause, is developed in a paragraph of 19 bars overlapping the end of the previous theme, and consisting of four 2-bar steps (reckoning from bar 160), six 1-bar steps (making a climax), and 3 chords about dominant with pauses. (The free arpeggios are the 3rd chord.)

179–183.—Close; in three 2-bar phrases, with (a) in lower part (C♮ = B♯) twice, and the semiquavers of theme (C) above.

25

SONATA IN G MAJOR, Op. 79.
(Sonatina.)

It is not certain that Beethoven ever called this work a Sonatina;
but the title is appropriate at all events to the slow movement
and finale, which are not only on a small scale, but easy enough
for young players. The first movement is decidedly more difficult
—as difficult as some much bigger things. It is also by no means
sketchy. The inspiration that produced that marvel of concentration, Beethoven's own favourite Sonata in F♯ major, is still
reverberating in a faint echo; as happens once or twice when
Shakespeare follows a great tragedy by a weaker one on a similar
theme—*Lear* by *Timon of Athens* for instance. The first movement of Op. 79 is a brilliant and witty piece in a pianoforte style
which, if not full-dress, is certainly well turned out. The Andante
is like the first Bagatelles of Op. 111: it is a beautiful piece which
a child can learn. The finale has a delicious theme, with episodes
ostentatiously perfunctory. The strokes are bold and efficient,
but schematic, as if the artist had neither time nor inclination for
finished work. The work is finished in another sense: it is done
with.

To see in Op. 79 " a reversion to the style of an earlier generation " is to misconvenience earlier styles and its own style. You
might as well say the same of the drawings in Edward Lear's
Book of Nonsense. They show an obvious *adversion* to the style
of the very latest generation as long as Time shall run ! Slight
and careless as Op. 79 is, its idioms are utterly unlike either
Mozart's or Haydn's. The only thing they resemble is the style
of Beethoven's third period, not ready to dawn for some years
yet. Take, for instance, Beethoven's later method of ousting the
dominant by a proleptic tonic.: In the first movement of Op. 78,
bar 39 (5th bar of the Development), we have a serious use of
the device in the premature entry of the key of G♯ minor; and
in the 5th bar of Op. 79 we have a witty example made *almost*
unintentionally comic by Beethoven's inability to reproduce it
twice in the same way. The player is not to blame if he fails to
memorize these variants or the order in which they occur. Why
should his memory in playing be better than Beethoven's in the
very act of composition ? But all three versions are characteristic

in themselves and in their discrepancy. To any person, pupil, teacher or editor, who thinks it a matter of conscience to level them up, we, who take Beethoven's style seriously, can only say, " Why throw away upon music talents intended by Nature so plainly and so exclusively for the more perfectible art of book-keeping by double entry ? "

Presto alla tedesca: G major. Sonata form.

[The *alla tedesca* is more significant to the modern student than the *presto*. The *tedesca* is the *Ländler*, the German or Austrian waltz. If experts can distinguish it from the *austriaca* of Beethoven's exquisite early variations on *La stessa, la stessissima*, let them do so. At all events you can waltz in a leisurely way to an ordinary *tedesca*, and you can still waltz, though very energetically, to this *Presto alla tedesca*. The dance takes glorious shape in the Development and Coda. In one of his last works, the Quartet, Op. 131, Beethoven turned the first figure of the Sonatina upside down and wrote another *tedesca* on it.]

First Group.

  Bars 1–7.—Eight-bar melody (A) on tonic pedal: 4+4, with the 2nd pair allied to the 3rd, the 8th bar overlapping into new theme.

The initial figure (a)  is used,

with and without its 4th note or its 1st note, in other contexts. The other figures never leave the whole theme.

  8–11.—New 4-bar theme (B) in rising sequence closing into

  12–23 *Transition.*—Three steps of new 4-bar arpeggio figure winding upwards in groups of 4 quavers across the ¾ time, representing chords of (V.), (iii.) =(VI.) of dominant, and G♯ closing into dominant of (V.).

Second Group in Dominant.

  24–31.—Twice 4 bars on dominant of (V.) (*not* A major), with new scale-figure (c) rising and falling in bass. [A faint reverberation of a passage similarly placed on enhanced dominant of (V.), in the second group of the first movement of the D major Trio, Op. 70, No. 1.]

  32–35.—The scale-figure (c) is taken up in treble in two 2-bar steps in rising sequence over dominant pedal.

  36–45.—Twice 4 new bars of dominant-to-tonic (same type of

theme as in second group of Scherzo of Op. 31, No. 3), with 2 extra cadential bars completing the geography of D by touching its subdominant, closing into

46–47.—Cadence-group; 2 bars of ('a') on tonic pedal. (Such is the terseness of this movement !)

48–49.—Two steps of ('a') in bare octaves, falling in sequence back, in the first instance, to repeat.

Development.

50–51.—The sequence of ('a') is continued 2 steps further, in E major (VI.).

52–58.—Theme (A) in E major. [Perhaps it is the abrupt change to this foreign key that makes Beethoven here simplify the harmony of his 5th and 6th bars.]

59–66.—Figure ('a'), with its first note relegated to the purpose of marking the bass, becomes a Waltz in E major, on the 8-bar scheme of Tonic, T, T, Dominant ; D, D, D, T. The last bar is minor and suddenly *piano*, the rest having been *f*, with *sf* on every second beat.

67–73.—The Waltz, *piano* and *dolce* without *sforzandos*, in C major. Its 8th bar remains major.

75–82.—Theme (B) in C major. Its last 2 bars are echoed in a higher octave, and then carried to a close into C minor.

83–90.—The Waltz, *forte* in C minor, its 8th bar leading with sudden *piano* towards E♭.

91–98.—The Waltz, *p* dolce, in E♭ throughout.

99–110.—Theme (B) in E♭. Its last 2 bars echoed, as before, in higher octave, and then carried into G minor. In another 4-bar group, the figure gathers into a run down towards the home dominant.

111–122.—The Waltz, *piano* and *dolce*, apparently transposed to D, but in this context evidently on the home dominant. Figure ('a') is preserved in 8th bar, and in the next 4 bars ('a') flits from octave to octave in crotchet pairs across the ¾ time in the bass, while the harmony adds a decisive 7th in the last 2 bars, closing into

Recapitulation.

First Group.

123–129 = 1–7.—The discrepancy in the 5th bar is again by no means pointless, any more than the new ornament in the 7th bar.

130–133.—The 4th bar of theme (B) is now in sequence with the other 3, leading to a new starting-point for the transition.

134–145.—The chords of the transition are now $\overset{6}{\text{B}}$, (IV.),

7
and #
A.

Second Group in Tonic.

146–167 = 24–45 in tonic.

168–169.—The 2-bar cadence-group is followed in the first instance by bars 47–51, leading to repeat of the Development. This should certainly be played: the whole movement will hardly take five minutes even then, and the Schubertian breadth of its development will be enhanced.

Coda.

167–175.—In the event the Coda shows itself to have begun with the cadence-group 167–168; for this is continued as part of two 4-bar groups made by echoing it in lower octave *piano*, and repeating the whole 4. This tonic-and-dominant swing closes into

176–190.—Theme (A) turned into a regular 8-bar tune, its original first 4 bars given by bass and answered sequentially a step higher by treble moving from (ii.) to close in tonic. The 8 bars are repeated an octave higher with grace-notes (acciaccaturas of the snappiest kind), the last bar over-lapping with

191–201.—The Waltz, summarized in twice 4 bars below treble arpeggios in two positions, closing into final upward tonic arpeggio (2 bars+end).

Andante: G minor (i.) A B A, the middle part in (VI.) E♭.

1–8.—Symmetrical 8-bar melody: 4 bars, 1+half-close, answered by repeat with full close in (III.); then 4 bars, 1 moving from (III.) through (iv.) to a medial tonic close, linked with repeat ending in final close. All the closes fall on the 3rd main beat.

8/9.—The last two notes of *L.H.* in bar 8 are the beginning of a link-passage, modulating to (VI.). One complete bar suffices, this close being the first that falls on to the beginning of a bar.

Middle Episode in (VI.).

10–16.—New melody in (VI.), beginning with 3-bar phrase (2 bars, +sequential answer to the second bar). It is continued in a 4-bar clause, which repeats its first bar in an upper octave with a 3rd bar forming a medial close (vi.); and this 3rd bar is repeated in lower octave and broadened into a full close into next period.

17–21.—New 2-bar clause, emphasizing (IV.), and closing into ornamental repetition, in which the 2nd bar contains an augmented 6th which resolves on to the home dominant in next bar.

The bass rises in the figure with which it accompanies the main theme.

Return of Main Theme.

22–29 = 1–8.

Coda.

30–34.—At the end of the 8th bar the bass rises into the figure with which it accompanied the middle episode; while the treble gives 2 bars of the main theme followed by a third, which carries bar 2 sequentially downward, the bass substituting (VI.) for (i.). Then this new bar is expanded, with broken rhythm, to 2 final bars.

Vivace: G major. Rondo.

Main Theme.

1–8.—First strain: 4 with weak medial tonic close, answered by 4 with strong close in dominant; the whole built on a 3-note figure (a). Repeat.

9–16.—Second strain: 2 dominant bars (a)+new tag, answered by tonic close, a new figure (b) (in bar 11)+the tag. Four bars answer with soft harmony in contrast to the *forte* bare octaves (15ths) of the previous 4; the close (approached through IV.) being strong. In the first instance the bass leads to a repeat of the strain. In the second instance it mentions figure (a).

First Episode : E minor (iii.).

17–24.—The mention of (a) causes it to be discussed as the starting-point of a peevish new theme in (iii.). In spite of the belated entry of a bass accompaniment in bar 18, the period has really begun at 17, and duly finishes with a half-close at 24. And that concludes the First Episode.

²⁴/25–34.—Figure (a), arising out of 24, asks three questions, with measured pauses for a reply. Each question, with its pause, lies across 2 bars. The first, recalling bar 17, implies dominant of (iii.); the next tries A minor; the third, starting from F♯ is, satisfied that it is on the home dominant, and, without pause, continues for 6 bars, reducing its compass until it reaches the position from which it can drop into the main theme.

First Return.

35–50 = 1–16, with new triplet accompaniment throughout, except at bars 43–46, which remain bare.

Second Episode in Subdominant.

⁵⁰/51/52–65 (66).—New 8-bar theme in C (IV.); 4 bars consisting of 3 on tonic closing into 1 on subdominant, answering by 3 on (IV.), closing into bare octave on 1. The whole is then repeated in a variation. Rhythmically, as the sequel and the accentuation show, there was a change of step at the outset, so that the whole semiquaver run is in anacrusis. Beethoven has not troubled to show this by his double bars, which record merely the changes of key.

66–71.—Entering on 2nd bar of a period, figure (a) over triplet accompaniment finds its way back in 4 more bars through (ii.) to its place in the main theme.

Second Return.

72–79 = 1–8, with semiquaver accompaniment.

80–87 = Repeat, with new variation.

88–95 = 9–16, the first 4 bars, as usual, left bare, the other 4 given according to the new variation. The bass runs down to link up with the repeat.

Coda.

96–102.—The Coda is grafted on to the repeat of the 2nd strain, by the device of echoing each pair of bars, from 9 to 12, *piano* in a higher octave, with semiquaver accompaniment.

103–117.—The last echo is repeated in the normal octave, leading to a new 4-bar phrase on (a), twice 2 with sub-dominant colour; closing into repetition in the mode of variation used at 80 foll.; closing into 4 bars with (a) rising on the tonic chord, which gives way at the last moment to a final full close.

26

SONATA IN E FLAT MAJOR, Op. 81a.

(Les Adieux, L'Absence, et le Retour.)

THE emotions represented by this sonata are not those of a love-story. The music is a monument to the friendship of two men, deep as any friendship formed in schooldays or in the full stress of life, and manly as Beethoven's ripest art. The Archduke Rudolf was a musician who might have made a reputation as such if he had been cast adrift upon the world. At the age of sixteen he became a pupil of Beethoven; and it is impossible not to recognize a special quality in the numerous important works that Beethoven dedicated to him—the present Sonata, the E♭ Concerto, the last Violin Sonata, Op. 96, the last Trio, Op. 97, the Seventh Symphony, and the Missa Solemnis in D. These do not exhaust the list of works dedicated to the Archduke Rudolf; and they have in common a magnificence of scale, a gorgeous wealth of invention, and, almost more conspicuously than any other quality, a beauty at once majestic and energetic that may indeed be found wherever Beethoven has much to say, but here more obviously than in other works. One might almost assign dedications to this particular patron on internal evidence, though not without risk of mistake—*e.g.*, there is something very Rudolfian in the first Rasumovsky quartet.

We need harbour no doubts as to the sincerity of Beethoven's emotion in the present sonata. Court etiquette was no more to Beethoven than the mace to Cromwell. The published dedication to the Archduke was formal; but in Beethoven's sketches, which he showed to nobody, the sonata is described as " written from the heart and dedicated to H.R.H." In the lower orders of sentimental journalism persons may be found to whom the true circumstances of this sonata are not romantic enough. But sane and manly friendships formed in schooldays and in the full stress of life are very fine subjects for Beethoven's music.

It is with the emotions of parting, absence, and reunion of such friends, and with no external circumstances, that this sonata deals. Nothing in it would lead us to guess that while Beethoven's friend was absent (with the rest of the royal family) Vienna was being attacked by Napoleon's forces, and that Beethoven's chief anxiety during the bombardment was to spare the last remains of his rapidly failing hearing. For this reason alone he spent long hours in the cellar, taking refuge from the noise, though otherwise he expressed great contempt for the inefficient gunnery on both sides. All that he chose to tell of these terrible days in his music was that he had said farewell to a dear friend and that he was longing for the friend's return. For that return he waited, and wrote not a note of the music for it until the happy time had really come.

There is any amount of minute psychological accuracy in the form and style of each movement of the sonata; and its external story, in revealing Beethoven's capacity for friendship, helps us to understand the depth and subtlety of the music. To look for more pictorial details is to miss all that matters. Commentators who see in the end of the first movement the departure of the Archduke's (or some more acceptably romantic person's) coach may happen to be nearer the mark than the lady who congratulated Berlioz on his realistic representation of Romeo *arrivant dans son cabriolet;* but they are in no position to laugh at her. Like the Pastoral Symphony, this sonata is *mehr Ausdruck der Empfindung als Malerei;* indeed, as it has neither bird-songs nor thunderstorms wherewith to shock those who disapprove of *Malerei* in music, we may profitably regard it as wholly concerned with *Empfindung.* " Not painting, but the expression of feeling " is an excellent description of all Beethoven's music, whether absolute or associated with things that can be explained in words.

Les Adieux.

Introduction: Adagio. E♭ major.

Bars 1–4.—Four-bar phrase (2: ½, ½: 1), the first 2 embodying

a figure inscribed *Lebewohl !*

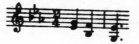

and hereafter referred to as *L.*

At the 2nd bar the bass enters below the horn-like pair of upper voices, starting a downward drift from (vi.) to its dominant chord, while a new melodic figure (b) in rising sequence leads to a half-close on that chord.

⁴/5–6.—Repetition of the half-close (bar 4) in higher octave. The G major chord then changes to minor, and so leads, with further descending steps of bass, back to tonic.

7–12.—Bars 1-2, with chromatic harmony resolving on (♭VI.) instead of (vi.); figure (b) following so as to reproduce bars ²/3-4 in a progression from the key of (♭VI.) to the home dominant, from which another bar in descending sequence passes through subdominant minor to another position of the home dominant, the bass still maintaining its downward drift with slight inflections.

12–16.—A new 1-bar figure repeats itself in a broken rhythm, with the bass in contrary motion continuing its descent. First repeated in a dominant position, the figure proceeds (upwards in treble, downwards in bass) to the subdominant minor.   On repetition this becomes major.   Its chord ($^6_4$) is insisted on with syncopation, and leads to the Allegro.

Allegro : Sonata Form.

First Group.
    1–4.—Theme (B): a 4-bar phrase (1+1+2) on bass, descending (first chromatically, then diatonically) from C ($^6_4$) towards home dominant; containing 2 figures, of which one (b)

is (perhaps accidentally) reminiscent of (b) in the Introduction.

The second figure is not developed outside its original context. (Caution is necessary in imputing remote derivations throughout this movement. Beethoven must have known that the ubiquitous descending basses would often remind us of the *Lebewohl* figure if we listened to them instead of to the main themes ; but he does not build upon accidental foundations. The function of these descending basses is not to allude to themes, but to produce the effect of depressed spirits at the time of parting, while on the surface the music is full of impatient energy.)

5–12.—New 8-bar theme (C) consisting of a 4-bar phrase (2+2) on a bass *rising* from (I.) to (V.), and closing into self-repetition modified so as to close into dominant.

Transition.
    13–18.—New 2-bar phrase on dominant. Its 2nd bar is echoed and suddenly developed into 2 more bars of rapidly modulating quaver chords, in which the bass runs down for 2 octaves while the treble rises.   In the next bar, 2 chords reach dominant of (V.).

19–33.—The next 15 bars, being all in the nature of " dominant preparation," may still be grouped with the Transition, though they contain a variety of new figures and are unquestionably in the new key. The extreme terseness of this sonata makes the borderline between its groups hard to fix ; especially as one of the best ways of getting an effect of breadth in a short time is by devoting ample space to dominant preparation. Beethoven had already shown this in the first two movements of the D minor Sonata and the Scherzo and Finale of Op. 31, No. 3; and the present sonata is the last of five almost consecutive works in which, while the main key-relations are established with the utmost clearness, there is little point in classifying the transitions apart from the themes to which they lead.

Bars 19-22 consist of a self-repeating 2-bar phrase, with bass in contrary motion to treble, and with play upon the contrast between the flat 6th and major 6th of the scale. Arising out of an inner part, a 4-bar phrase (1+1+four half-bars) repeats itself on a dominant bass. Its last bar merges into a new dominant bar (rising scale in bass), which, repeated in an upper octave, is then augmented a 3rd higher (still on dominant harmony), closing into the next phrase. Meanwhile the melodic figure has become subtly suggestive of the *Lebewohl* theme, already latent in the bass of bars 19-20. If this point seems as yet remote, it becomes immediately clear in the sequel.

Second Group : (V.).

34–41.—The *Lebewohl* theme *L* is worked into a new 4-bar phrase (*Lx*) richly harmonized, accompanied by quaver details from bars 20-24, and closing into self-repetition in lower octave, closing into

42–45.—New 2-bar cadence-theme playing with flat 6th and closing into repetition in upper octave; closing into

46–49.—Imitative figure suggestive of *L* in double diminution, and descending through 2 octaves in 4 bars.

49/50–53.—Figure *L* in full size intervenes on home-dominant 7th, answered, after 2 bars, by treble in contrary motion, the bass descending so that in 4 bars the progression closes into bar 1. Exposition repeated.

Development.

54–56.—The last bar (53) of the Exposition being altered by substituting a diatonic step (C^2) for the semitone $D\flat$, the Development begins on dominant of C minor with 3 bars of (b), the bass descending as usual. Suddenly figure *L* interrupts and begins the following subtle process.

57–74.—Two notes (2 bars) of *L* entirely unharmonized alternate with 2 bars of (b) in the bass below remote modulations for 4 steps. The modulations are chosen with regard to the fact that as the 2 notes of *L* are unharmonized there is nothing but custom to prevent their changing their meaning as they proceed, and no means of guessing in what direction they will change. In bars

57-58 the notes F, E♭ originate in C minor. In that key tneir meaning is not very obvious, and the next 2 bars seem to clear it up by resolving into B♭ minor. In B♭ minor accordingly figure *L* continues. But, while it sings unaccompanied, miracles happen, and the dominant of G shines out from halfway round the harmonic universe ! It is idle to ask whether this is an enharmonic modulation: the whole point is that we do not know what happened while bars 61-62 were proceeding unharmonized. There are any number of ways in which the modulation might have been explained, and many of them are better than the diminished 7ths which any fool could have put there. The stroke of genius is self-evident by its very mystery. And the mystery is made chiefly by our own expectations. We instinctively try to harmonize figure *L*; and we find first that it is difficult to guess any plausible harmony for it, and secondly that whatever we guess is wrong. Thus in bars 65-66 we naturally continue to think of the dominant of G major; and then we find that the 2nd note of *L* is not B♮ but C♭. As a matter of fact, the sequence of chords, though far-reaching, is by no means incoherent. If we eliminate *L* and put the chords into conjunct positions, bars 59-71 will fall into the following quite intelligible scheme,

from which it is evident that figure *L*, though it mystifies us while it is unharmonized, is really tracing the main line of the process. Beethoven's art of using unaccompanied notes in this way has remained unimitated by later composers. It is not Wagnerian, and it is quite impossible in atonal and polytonal schemes. Upon the 4th step, at bars 71-72, figure (b), finding itself on the home dominant, becomes insistent in 2 extra bars. But for the tendency of the bass to descend, we might now be about to begin the Recapitulation.

75-77.—The bass, however, subsides by a semitone, and a 3-bar version of bars 1-4 passes from dominant of A♭ into G♭, leading to

78-93.—Slow descent of *L*, with (b) in bass. Bars 78-85 are an 8-bar phrase closing into another 8 bars, which close into the Recapitulation. At the 2nd bar (79) an enharmonic change brings us instantly from G♭ to C minor (again half round the universe). and the key of C minor now remains. At the 5th bar the bass reaches C and remains there, with only one inflection at bar 89. At the 10th bar (87) it becomes evident that the chord reached (C with ⁶₃ of A♭) is significant. It is dwelt upon with dramatic tension, and the rhythm of (b) becomes agitated till it breaks into stretto in both hands and the chord reveals itself as that of bar 1.

Recapitulation.

First Group.

94–105 = 1–12.—At bars 102-103 the strange discrepancy in the bass is no mistake, though Bülow thought fit to correct it without comment, while he scolded other editors for disregarding Beethoven's intentions. But Beethoven's autograph* shows the present discrepancy as an alteration, written after he had crossed out the original version. There is no possible doubt of his intention; his writing, though untidy, is so widely spaced that he has always room for any amount of interlineation, and the alteration here is as legible as if no disturbance had occurred.

There is no difficulty in seeing the point of a new speeding-up of this vehement self-repeating theme at bar 101. The difficulty lies in the fact that it results in a decidedly awkward stagnation in the bass during bars 102-103. And yet this very awkwardness has its psychological fitness: for why should a man not stammer when indignation has tripped up his words? This explanation would be too subtle if its object were to defend a text of disputable authority, but it is the only possible explanation of what Beethoven unquestionably went out of his way to write. We may think as we please on the question whether what Beethoven wrote here is convincing; but his autograph teaches us a most necessary lesson.

* See facsimile in edition of the Associated Board.

106–110 = 13–18 shortened by omission of the 3rd bar, and with the sequel shifted so as to return to a tonic position.

Transition and Second Group.

111–141 = 19–49 in tonic, unaltered except for change of octave at 119 = 27.

Coda.

142–145.—Following the course of bars 50-53b, figure *L* modulates through (IV.) towards (ii.).

146–150.—Five bars (3 – 2) of theme (B) about dominant of (ii.) lead to

151–164.—Theme (C) in (ii.), returning to tonic at 8th bar and continuing in tonic minor as if for another 8; but with the 5th bar the bass presses upwards to the subdominant minor, which it reaches at the end of the 6th bar. (This dramatic detail, perfectly clear in its own right, may possibly have suggested to Beethoven that strange abortive rise in bar 102: at all events, what was frustrated there comes to fulfilment here.) The use of the supertonic at the beginning of this coda has a powerful effect, for the whole movement is so terse that the appearance of the main theme in the supertonic now sounds like a thing that might have happened sequentially at the outset. The whole coda is considerably longer than the Exposition and Development together, and is thus, in its proportion to the rest of the movement, by far the most important coda in all Beethoven's works. Yet its total effect is, by such devices as this use of the supertonic, to weld the whole movement together like a single melody. What now follows is all *Lebewohl*, and its length is partly expressive of the nature of affectionate farewells and partly the result of the slowness of the *Lebewohl* theme.

165–180.—Dialogue on *L* for 16 bars (4 groups of twice 2, coalescing into 8), starting in (iv.), changing to dominant of dominant, and thence to home dominant. The harmonic drift is faintly sketched in two-part dialogue, until at the 11th bar the harmony fills out and the characteristic descent of the bass reaches the home dominant with a penultimate chromatic step and closes into

181–192.—Theme *L* as in Second Group, with new quaver counterpoint in bass. Its 4 bars are answered by the theme in the bass with the counterpoint in the treble, but the answer reaches only the 2nd bar, and the 2 bars are twice insisted on in higher octaves and concluded with a drift down again in 2 more bars, making 8 as the total answer to the previous 4, and closing into

193–211.—Repetition of 181-192 slightly varied, and expanded by 2 more bars falling another octave and closing into

207–226.—Dialogue on figure *L* for 20 bars: 4 (twice 2)+4, +twice 2, +4 times 1, +4 times 1 in quicker rhythm closing into next period. At first *L* is represented by its horn-like inner part, then in its two-part horn-harmony. Then its accent is reversed in a kind of diminution ♩ | 𝅝 | ♩ , and the tonic and dominant harmonies overlap impulsively. (Early editors corrected this. If you wish to laugh at them, you must not correct bars 102-103 !) With the further diminution in bars 219-222 the overlapping is cleared away; and a more normal overlap appears in the final stage of compression (with the last vestiges of *L* in the inner part of the *R.H.*) at bars 223-227. These close into

227–239.—Final descent of the *Lebewohl* figure in the extreme bass below interior tonic pedal, with running counterpoint rising to extreme height in treble. The bass, having reached the mediant, hovers about that region in echoing bars, and pauses there until a loud full close ends the movement abruptly. Count from bar 227 in 4-bar groups; this will make 235 a main bar and will bring the last chord into place as the 1st of its period.

L'Absence.

Andante expressivo : C minor.

Intermezzo, dealing with a series of short themes in rotation, recapitulating them in another group of keys, and making as if to recapitulate again, but interrupted by change leading to finale.

This form, musically very simple, admirably solves the problem of expressing the sorrow of absence without inflicting its tedium on the listener. The cycle of thoughts, at first wistful, then yielding to a mood of affectionate reminiscence, which is interrupted by a passionate protest against the present solitude—this cycle must recur for ever unless miracles happen. Beethoven allows us to witness one recurrence, which suffices to show that there is no prospect of escape. But the wistful first theme rises for a third time with a new, if forlorn, hope, and the miracle happens—for Beethoven's enharmonic modulations do succeed in being miracles instead of bad puns or duodecuple theorems.

1–4.—Theme (A), a 4-bar phrase (twice 1,+2) about dominant of C minor. [The resemblance of its second figure to (b) of the Introduction to the first movement is perhaps accidental, but is very apposite.]

⁴/5–8.—Modified repetition of 1-4 in C minor about tonic.

⁸/9–14.—A new 2-bar phrase modulates from VI. to (iv.). Then the main figure of (A) enters on dominant of (v.), and is compressed into an urgent rising sequence in its 2nd bar, followed by 2 bars of unharmonized dominant preparation in demisemi-quavers (sequences of 2-quaver steps ending in four 1-quaver steps).

15–18.—New 2-bar theme in major dominant closing into ornamented self-repetition, leading to

19–20.—Two bars of agitated sequence passing from (v.) to home tonic.

21–36.—Recapitulation of 5-20 in (iv.) and (IV.). [The sudden irruption of F minor at 21 is quite unexpected; and at ²⁶/27 there is a change of direction which keeps the whole recapitulation in F minor, whereas an exact recapitulation of bar ⁸/9 would have brought us back to C minor. Notice also that it is not until the 3rd bar (23) that Beethoven is found to be recapitulating from bar 5 and not from bar 1. Great composers are never more subtle than when their forms seem most rectangular and schematic.]

At bar 32 the ornamentation is slightly enhanced.

37–42.—Sudden irruption of figure (A) in tonic. Its 1st bar is developed in a new rising sequence. The pair of bars so formed (37-38) is repeated a step higher up the dominant chord. Then the diminished 7th resolves on to dominant of E♭ (B♮ =C♭), on which 2 more bars arise from figure (A) and lead to the finale.

Le Retour. Das Wiedersehen. (Meeting again.)
Vivacissimamente : Sonata form.
1–10.—Themeless dominant preparation, from which rhythm gradually emerges: 4 bars +4 times 1 (twice 2), + 2, closing into

First Group : E♭.
11–16.—Six-bar theme (A): twice 2 in sequence rising to (ii.), · with 2 bars closing into tonic.
17–22.—Repetition of theme in bass with breathless exclamatory counterpoint in treble; *crescendo,* closing into
23–28.—Third statement of theme in extreme bass, *fortissimo* with tremolo accompaniment, closing into

Transition.
29–36.—New 4-bar theme, tonic and dominant over tonic pedal, closing into self-repetition, which is diverted towards key of dominant, closing into
37–44.—Four bars of grotesque simplicity on ♭VI. of B♭, repeated (a semitone lower) on dominant of B♭.
45–52.—Delicate and sparkling variation of 37-44, closing into

Second Group : B♭ (V.).
53–60.—New 8-bar theme (B) in double counterpoint, twice 2+4, closing into
61–68.—Repetition of 53-60 in higher octave, with last 4 bars transferred to *L.H.,* closing into
69–76.—New 2-bar figure in sequence falling from supertonic, repeated in lower octave, and followed by twice 2 cadence-bars closing into
77–81.—Cadential scale, a single bar repeated in 3 octaves and ending in 3 descending tonic chords (x). Exposition repeated from start of main theme (bar 11).

Development.
81/82–93.—The 3 descending tonics (x) are whimsically combined with quavers so as to allude to the figure of theme (A). The 2 bars of tonic minor thus produced are answered by a new melodic figure (y) rising towards G♭ (♭III.). The whole 4-bar process is then repeated on G♭ = F♯ as dominant of C♭ =B♮.

and the new figure (y) is expanded by 4 more bars closing into

94–99.—Theme (B) in alternating positions of double counterpoint, in B♮ (=C♭) for 4 bars, followed by 2 that modulate to G by descent of bass from D♯ through D♭ and down the scale to G.

100–103.—New positions of theme (B) in G major closing into

104–109.—Three-part imitations of figure (a) passing in 2-bar steps from G to C, which, by momentary change to minor, leads to A♭. After 2 bars of this the whole main theme casually returns in the home tonic without any warning that the development is over. A still bolder abrupt return may be found in the first movement of the Trio in E♭, Op. 70, No. 2, where the same conditions occur—viz., a terse development that has moved through an enharmonic circle without calling attention to the fact.

Recapitulation.

First Group and Transition.

110–121.—Two statements (treble and bass) of theme (A) in new scorings.

122–129 = 29–36, diverted at end (with subdominant colour) so as to lead to

Rest of Transition and Second Group in Tonic.

130–176 = 37–81 in tonic.

Coda.

176/177–184.—Theme (A), announced by an emphatic sforzando, is treated in a slow tempo (Poco Andante) as a quiet 8-bar cantabile: 4 bars of sequence in rising modulation leading to 4 of tonic chord, yielding to dominant at last half-bar.

185–190.—The last 4 bars repeated with ornamental variation, and the last 2 again with further variation, coming to a pause.

191–196.—The last 2 bars at full speed in broken octaves, closing into final 4 bars.

27

SONATA IN E MINOR, Op. 90.

IN dedicating this sonata to Count Lichnowsky, Beethoven rallied that nobleman on the occasion of his engagement. Qualms were alleged to be represented in the vehemently pathetic first movement. It was with no intention of throwing light on that movement that Beethoven called it " a contest between head and heart." Even a patron with the most august lack of humour would have seen that this title was a joke; and, in fact, Beethoven's patrons cheerfully endured gibes from him in far worse taste. The gibe in this case is a classically charming piece of raillery; for the whole point of the sonata lies in the contrast between a movement full of passionate and lonely energy and a movement devoted to the utmost luxuriance of lyric melodies developed in Rondo form. The passion and energy are noble; and in the Rondo the toil is rewarded and the loneliness becomes a tale of long ago. " Happy Conversation with the Beloved " was Beethoven's unofficial title for the Rondo, and in this title Beethoven turns from raillery to modestly smiling congratulation.

The German marks of tempo, already presented as alternatives in Op. 81a, and here used exclusively, represent a wave of Chauvinism that affected other musicians besides Beethoven and other matters besides music. Italian was a Bonapartist language, and Napoleon's day was over. The German language has always had a tendency to reject foreign elements, and has generally ousted them by literal translation or by descriptive compounds. Two years later the very word Pianoforte is replaced by *Hammerklavier*.

Mit Lebhaftigkeit und durchaus mit Empfindung und Ausdruck : E minor. Sonata form.

First Group.
Bars ⅓/1–8.—Theme (AB), a sequence of pairs of 2-bar steps, rising in melody and falling in bass; starting on tonic and immediately modulating through (III.) to (v.): containing rhythmic figure (a), overlapping with melodic figure (b), which alternates with another form (b'). [In the first sketch the sequence was a plain series of (b'), and the variety is an improvement probably also associated with the present alternations between *forte* and *piano*.]

⁸/9–16.—Theme (C), answering theme (A) by a contrasted 8-bar cantabile, beginning with a new 4-bar (2+2) figure in (III.), continued in 1-bar steps leading down by thirds to pause on home dominant:

¹⁶/17–24.—Self-repeating cadential derivative of (b'), with new continuation, on rising bass, answering interrupted close of 4th bar by full close (with *ritardando* and pause) at 8th, and, by its formal emphasis and firm tonality, consolidating the key of E minor.

The whole First Group is a *locus classicus* for the handling of modulation in such a way as to define the tonic. It is the most subtle of the three cases of this kind in Beethoven's works. The other two are also pianoforte sonatas—viz., Op. 31, No. 1, and Op. 53. The student should know these three openings intimately, and be able to see their contrast with the drifting modulations at the outset of the Development in each case.

Transition.

²⁴/25–36.—New theme derived from rhythm (a), answering 4 bars of T and D in bare octaves in that rhythm by 4 in which it breaks out in full harmony on dominant of C, with a descending scale and a close into that key (VI.). These 4 bars are repeated in A minor (iv.).

³⁶/37–44.—The ♭II. of A minor is now represented unharmonized, with rhythm (a) and its new scale. The scale having fallen for 2 octaves, the isolated B♭, in rhythm (a), becomes the bass of an ambiguous chord built up note by note—always in rhythm (a)—until it is manifestly a diminished 7th. The B♭ becomes A♯ so that the chord resolves as dominant of (v.), into which key it closes in next period, having taken 8 bars since the start of the B♭ scale.

45–54.—New phrase in B minor (v.): 2 bars followed by 4 in rising sequence on rising bass, and a modified echo of the last bar dwelling for 2 bars on enhanced dominant of (v.), followed by 2 similar dominant bars closing into

Second Group in Dominant Minor.

55–60.—New 6-bar theme, 4+2 on bass, which, trying to rise
in each of the first 4 bars, succeeds in reaching its dominant in the
last 2. The phrase closes into

61–66.—Varied repetition of 55-60, closing into

67–81.—Cadence-theme, a 4-bar phrase (1 in bass answered by
3 of Neapolitan cadence-harmony) closing into self-repetition
expanded with pauses and 2 echoes (T and D) of its last bar;
closing into 3 final tonic chords (x).

Development.

82-91.—An unharmonized echo of the 3 chords (x) initiates an
interior dominant quaver-rhythm over which theme (AB) rises
in a new sequence over slowly falling bass, drifting in 4 bars from
home dominant to (iv.); from which point it proceeds in 3 more
bars through an enharmonic modulation to the extremely remote
key of Eb, into which it closes with rhythmic overlap.

92–99.—Starting in Eb, figure (b′) moves in twice 4 bars through
Eb minor, from which the bass descends in 1-bar steps through a
diminished 7th, which changes enharmonically so as finally to
resolve on dominant of G, which closes into dominant of C in
next period.

100–109.—Over the dominant of C the rhythm of (b′) is broken
up in a chromatic descending scale in *R.H.*, after 4 bars of which
the bass rises chromatically to meet it, all inner harmony being
eliminated. The scales meet on their dominant, and there is a
pause of 2 bars. Harmony is built up in the 2nd of these bars,
closing into

[109]/110–117.—Theme (C) in 2-part harmony in C major for
4 bars, answered in F major by 2 lower parts, while semiquaver
arpeggios arise above.

[117]/118–132.—A bass voice enters with (c) in D minor, ousting
the other voices, while the arpeggios continue above. Figure (c′),
starting on G♯ as dominant of A minor, rises for ten 1-bar steps
in the bass, soon passing into the home tonic, and culminating in
the home ♮ at bars 130-131.

132–143.—Over the ♮ the arpeggios have coalesced into a new

conjunct figure (y)  This is suddenly left

unsupported except for an echo in a lower octave. As if in
bewilderment, this figure (y) is then developed in imitative 2-part
dialogue, transformed by augmentations in a kind of geometrical

progression, in the course of which it is reduced to the 3 notes G, F♯, E. The meaning of these seems to attract attention. The 3 notes speed up their rhythm again in various ways: the 2 voices, shifting among 3 octaves, collide and rebound, until the figure, now in quavers, proves to be a version of (b'), into which it finally closes. And so the Development is finished, and the home $^6_4$ chord has never resolved on to the dominant at all. And this is the most important point in the whole process. If the main point lay in the ingenious thematic transformation, those critics would be justified who find it far-fetched. Nothing is easier than to derive anything whatever from anything else whatever on such lines. Again, if Beethoven had not carried out the whole process in our actual hearing, it would have been mere lunacy to impute any connexion between the main theme and the casual figure (y) in bar 132. Nor would it be less foolish if that figure had been clearly related to some other theme. Indeed, an essential point of the passage is that the figure (y) is the most casual of accidents. The main theme is made to emerge dramatically from something as nearly nothing as can be embodied in sounds at all. The $^6_4$ chord is evaporating while awaiting its resolution; the anxious voices ask, Where? Where? When? and How?—and all the time the answer is " Here and now "; and the answer is at last given without troubling to remind us that the $^6_4$ has not been resolved. This *locus classicus* thus introduces us to what becomes a prominent feature of Beethoven's third manner—viz., the avoidance of the dominant chord in cadential positions. All such avoidances are expressive of the dramatic discovery that the questions " When and where " are to be answered by " Already here and now."

Recapitulation.
First Group.
   ^{143}/144–167 = $\frac{1}{2}$/1–24.

Transition.
   ^{167}/168–179 = ^{24}/25–36, but the key of C major is substituted for the tonic in the first 4 bars. The next bars remain in C (a root-bass being no longer necessary at 29 = 172), followed by the modulaton to A minor.
   ^{179}/180–197 = ^{36}/37–54, but the unharmonized ♭II. is replaced by a full chord of ♭VII., to which is added what proves to be not a 7th but an augmented 6th, from which the bass, rising by a semitone, brings the rest of the transition over the home dominant.

Second Group in Tonic.
   198–221 = 55–78, the repetitions being in lower octaves.

Coda.

222–231.—The cadence-paragraph, instead of closing into final tonic chords, closes into a further echo of its last 6 bars in a higher octave. The beginning of a still higher echo is answered by a lower voice and leads to

232–237.—Quiet version of theme (AB) compressed into 6 bars leading to pause about dominant.

²³⁷/238–245 = ¹⁶/17–24 used as a final close.

Nicht zu geschwind und sehr singbar vorgetragen : E major. Rondo with recapitulated First Episode and a development by way of Second Episode.

Main Theme.

¼/1–8.—First strain, a self-repeating 4+4 melody, answering medial close in 4th bar by full close in 8th, containing figures (a), (b), (b′+c) used in later developments.

⁸/9–16.—Second strain, a single 8-bar phrase, 2+2 in sequence falling from key of (V.) to key of (IV.), with a 4-bar close moving from (IV.) through dominant to tonic, ending with a new figure (d)

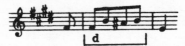

¹⁶/17–24.—Second strain repeated in higher octave.

²⁴/25–32.—First strain da capo, with ornamental variation in its third and fourth bars, and with *forte* close instead of the original sudden *piano*.

Transition-theme.

³²/33–40.—Figure (c) is detached as a rhythmic figure, and built into a new theme in C♯ minor (vi.) over a bass detached from the end of the previous accompaniment. After 4 bars T and D (alternately *forte* and *piano*) the bass moves in 4 steps down to dominant of B.

First Episode in Dominant.

41–48.—New 8-bar theme (twice 2+4) hovering around interior dominant, on which it comes to a half-close.

49–59.—Continuation of the new theme melodically a 3rd higher around the dominant (illustrating the empiric " added-third " theory of dominant chords). From the 5th bar it trails away in 3 bars leading towards its supertonic, from the dominant

of which 4 imitative bars on a casual semiquaver figure return to
B, closing into the next period. (The resemblance of the casual
semiquaver figure to the ornaments in bars 28-29 is accidental.)

60-69.—New 4-bar cadence-theme (E) on a rising bass in
triplets, closing into self-repetition with semiquaver bass and
with subdominant inflection which turns it into a preparation on
the home dominant for return. Two extra bars accordingly lead
to

First Return.
70-101 = 1-32.

Second Episode, a widely modulating Development.

[101]/102-113.—Figure (b'+c) is echoed in lower octave, whereupon the tonic suddenly becomes minor. The figure is again given
in each octave in the minor, and its bass is used as the beginning
of a scale descending through 2 octaves till it reaches dominant of
C (♭VI.). Four bars on this dominant close into

114-129.—Theme (E) developed in four 4-bar steps (the bass
alternately in triplets and semiquavers as before). Starting in C,
the change is first to C minor; thence to D♭ minor =C♯ minor;
and thence to C♯ major, which is suddenly diverted towards the
home dominant into which it closes. (The development has thus
passed through an enharmonic circle.)

130-139.—Ten bars (thrice 2, +twice 1, +2) of dominant
preparation for return: a new 2-bar figure in bass being, after
6 bars, taken up in 1-bar repetitions by treble.

Second Return.
140-171 = 1-32.

Transition and Recapitulation of First Episode.

172-180.—The transition theme is diverted at its 3rd bar by a
downward step of the bass towards the home subdominant, by
which step the whole bass becomes a steady descent in 9 bars
(instead of 8) to the home dominant.

181-207 =41-67 in tonic. (Change to lower octave at 9th bar.)

Digression before Final Return.

208-211.—The subdominant tendency in the second clause of
theme (E) leads, by enharmonic change of the diminished 7th, to
dominant of C major (♭VI.).

212-221.—An imitative development of figure (b) leads in
4 bars of falling sequence from C (with a flat 6th) to D minor.
Thence the sequence proceeds, compressed into half-bar steps,
round the enharmonic circle D minor, B♭ minor, G♭ major =F♯
major (the bass effecting all this by moving down in whole tones).

The F♯ major chord, thus reached, remains for 2 bars, then becomes minor, and so leads by a further descent of the bass to a position about the home dominant.

221/222–229.—Eight bars (thrice 2+a final 2) on a figure imitated in upper octave at a bar's distance. The figure, at first apparently new, proves to include (a) into which it finally drifts as the entry of the main theme in the tenor.

Final Return.

229/230–251 = 1–22, with the melody distributed in dialogue between a tenor and treble, bars 1-4 and 8/9-16 being in the tenor, and their answers in the treble.

Coda.

252–261.—At the bar corresponding to 23, figure (d) develops into a tonic-and-dominant swing; 2 bars in treble, answered by 2 in bass, and developed in 6 more bars in treble passing through (ii.) to half-close on dominant.

262–265.—A hurried allusion to theme (E) in two lower voices leads towards (ii.) and pauses on its dominant.

265/266–275.—A new imitative development of (b) returns to a home dominant pedal, over which it descends sequentially in tapering rhythm for 10 bars (thrice 2, +twice 1, +4 half-bars), closing into

275/276–288.—Final epitome of main theme, represented by bars 1-4, with an echo of 3-4, followed by 7-8 with a *ritardando* (the only one in the whole movement).

288–290.—Overlapping the last bar, a new development of b′ is begun by four imitative voices, the last two crowding in at half-bars. Suddenly the *ritardando* yields to an *accelerando* as the treble breaks into semiquavers. Regard bar 286 as the 4th of its period. After this the sonata closes at the last beat of another 4-bar period, the last bar being a diminution of (b′+c) in bare 2-part counterpoint.

28

SONATA IN A MAJOR, Op. 101.

Etwas lebhaft, und mit der innigsten Empfindung : A major. Highly concentrated Sonata-form.

First Group : A major.

Bars 1–4.—A 4-bar theme (A), containing figures (a) and (b),

starts with 2 bars on dominant, answered by 2 in which the tonic is represented with a subdominant ($\natural$) colouring, and only for the purpose of closing on to the dominant again, leading back to the first 2 bars. (Actually nothing more is heard of the tonic until the Recapitulation; yet the sub-dominant tinge of bars 3-4 suffices to make the balance of key perfectly true. Thus the whole movement powerfully illustrates the vital difference between being *on* the dominant and *in* the dominant.)

5–6.—Bars 1–2, resumed, swerve to (vi.), with a pause.

Transition and Second Group, in Dominant.

(It is not worth while discussing where the Second Group begins. The Recapitulation reproduces the dominant material in the tonic from bar 9; the dominant key becomes firmly fixed at bar 12; and a definite new theme first appears at bar 16. All this might, as far as outward form can show, be merely a single stream of lyric melody; but it is dramatic in every subtle detail.)

7–15.—Two bars of (a) rise towards dominant of (iii.) and lead to a new 3-bar group; moving thence by rising bass to dominant of (V.), where a somewhat similar 4-bar phrase establishes that key and is about to close therein.

16–24.—A mediant chord interrupts the cadence and introduces a new theme (C), beginning a figure (A), answered by its inversion (ᗄ). (The whole figure is not comprised in the first 4 notes, but includes the next 2 or 3.)

A bass voice, entering with 3 notes of (A), rises to the bass of a ⁶₄, on which a 2-bar cadence interlocks three times with enhanced repetitions, achieving its purpose the third time and closing into

25–32.—Cadence-themes: first, a 2-bar tonic-and-dominant dialogue between bass and treble closing into self-repetition; secondly, a 4-bar phrase (twice 1, +2) of syncopated chords, hereinafter called (f), closing into

Development.

33–40.—The syncopated chords (f) linger on their tonic (E) for 2 bars, after which figures (a+b) enter in the tenor in a tonic position. In an interpolated bar the chords of (f) receive an addition which construes them as dominant of F♯ minor, on which footing (a+b) answers in the tenor again. The chords of (f) then confirm the modulation to F♯ minor, into which they close.

41–52.—Figures (a+b) enter in treble above (f) in bass, in F♯ minor. Figure (b) is echoed, and then developed alone. A downward step of the bass brings the harmony over dominant of D, where it lingers for 2 bars. Passing more quickly through D and B minor, figure (b) at last breaks into half-bars, leading towards C♯ minor. Meanwhile the underlying rhythm (f) has been agitated out of existence; and figure (b) itself is merged into 3 bars of new matter, descending against a rising bass over dominant of C♯ minor, with pause on its ⁶₄ chord.

52½–54.—New imitative sequence, rising in 3 compound steps to home dominant.

55–57.—Entry of theme (A) in A, but it is A minor. The bass answers figure (a) in a minor scale, that rises from E and reaches the upper octave (via D♯) in an extra bar.

Recapitulation.

58–60.—Theme (A), restored to the major mode, is again represented by 2 bars, with a 3rd bar leading with rising bass to

61–84.—Exact recapitulation, in tonic, of bars 9–32. Change of octave at 68 = 16, and an alteration at 75 = 44; which must not be ascribed to the compass of the pianoforte, since Beethoven uses the top E in the finale.

Coda.

85–91.—The syncopated chords move downward over their tonic pedal in two discords, pausing, *fortissimo*, at joint of 3rd bar of this period.   Through the 4th bar figure (c) emerges in the bass, while the treble descends.   An alto, followed by a crowd of other parts, imitates the figure; and 2 more bars close into the next period.

92–102.—Theme (C) built into another 4-bar phrase leading to 3 bars of broken allusion to (f).   Theme (C) again intervenes in its original imitative form, and in 5 bars brings the movement to an end.

Lebhaft.   Marschmassig: F major (♭VI.).   March, in elaborate melodic binary form; with canonic Trio in subdominant.

1–8.—First strain, of which the 8 bars are not square, but have an overlap at bar 4, which proves to be the 1st of a new 2-bar group closing into modified self-repetition, which leads to a final close in dominant.   From this the bass leads back to the opening.   The following features are important.   First, the steady descent of the bass by semi-tones from tonic in bar 1 to dominant in bar 4; secondly, the continued and much quicker descent after bar 6; further, the following thematic figures, viz.

the ubiquitous rhythm (a) 𝄇 | 𝄇 and the melodic figures (b), (c), (d), and (e).

8a–11.—After the repeat a surprising new construction is given to the whole strain.   The bass figure (e), instead of leading back to F, is left " in the air," and the whole cadence-bar, figure (d), repeated an octave higher, with (e) as part of it.   Then these 2 bars (8a+9) are reproduced in the tonic, first with (d) in the left hand, and (e) in the right.   This tonic close changes the aspect of the 1st strain from " binary " to " ternary "; that is to say, we now have a completed section instead of an open-ended strain.

Middle Strain.

12–18.—With an explosion of the rhythm (a) on A, treated

as an A major chord, 3 bars of imitative dialogue on (b) lead to
D minor. On the dominant of this a new figure is carried
downward in imitative sequence for 4 bars, leading through C
(with minor 6th) towards dominant of A minor. The new figure
ends in a group (f)

which becomes combined with (b) in the following passage.

19–29.—New sequences on (f) answered by (b), descending
in couples of bars. The first couple, (f) over (b), descends from
dominant of A towards D minor. The second couple, (b) over
(f) doubled in thirds, confirms D minor. The third couple, (f)
in deep bass under (b) in two imitative parts, descends from
dominant of G minor. An extra bar leads in two half-bar steps
to a Neapolitan aspect of F minor, through which (marking
its ♭II.) a fourth couple continues the descent, which is completed
by 2 more bars moving in half-bar steps, closing into D♭ (♭VI.).

30–35.—New rising imitative sequence of (b) in D♭ over
tonic pedal (sustained by raised dampers), 3 bars, followed by
3 with bass hovering between D♭ and home dominant.

36–43.—Eight bars of dominant preparation, consisting first
of bars 4-5 twice, descending by octaves; and secondly of 4 bars
imitative development of (c), rising to climax on subdominant and
closing into

Third Strain.

44–46.—New 3-bar cadential phrase of scales in contrary
motion, the top part meeting and coalescing with the middle
parts. Scheme:

47–49.—Varied repetition of 44–46.

50–54.—Emphatic halt before subdominant, from which the
steps are resumed in their dotted rhythm, leading to 3 final bars
with the cadence-figures (d+e).

Trio: B♭ (IV.).

First Strain.

55–64.—A new half-bar figure builds up the chord of B♭ during

2 bars, by way of introduction to a theme which, beginning in 3rds, turns into a quizzical dialogue between treble and bass, which interchange the figures of the 2nd bar (58). This interchange having produced a 3rd bar, the dialogue proceeds for another 5 bars (4+echo) in the dominant, in canon at the ½-bar in the lower octave. This reaches an echoing close. Nottebohm found reason to believe that at this point Beethoven wished to repeat the whole 10 bars from bar 55, and Mandyczewski in his edition puts double bars and a repeat-mark accordingly. This has an excellent effect in clearing up the grotesque structure of the Trio, and it accounts for the F in the bass at the end of bar 64, which many editions replace by E♮ in conformity with bar 83. At all events these 10 bars constitute a 1st strain closing in the dominant.

Middle Strain.

65–75.—The canon is continued at 1 bar in the upper octave, beginning with the figures of bar 58, replacing one of them with a new figure in the 3rd bar, and passing in sequence from F to G minor. At the 6th bar the bass, after a half-bar rest, introduces a figure in an entirely different rhythm. The treble, omitting the minim rest, answers at the distance of half a bar, and the canon proceeds in rising sequence for 2 more bars with drastically logical " false relations " whereby the top outline rises chromatically till it reaches the slopes of the dominant 9th of B♭. Here 3 more bars of catch-as-catch-can close into the tonic.

76–83.—Bars 57–59 recapitulated in *L.H.* below a trill; after which bars 60–64 are recapitulated in tonic, inverted in double counterpoint so that the bass leads.

84–90.—The introductory figure of bars 55–56 proceeds to build around B♭ the dominant 7th of F minor. At the 4th bar the entry of the figure in a deep bass produces an overlap with another 4-bar group, which leads to the reappearance of bars 36–39, modified at the last beat so as to lead to bar 1 instead of to another dominant chord. The Da Capo of the March completes the movement without any coda.

Langsam und sehnsuchtsvoll: A minor. Introduction.

1–8.—First strain of a lyric melody in 4 pairs of bars; the first 2 couples about dominant of A minor with half-close, and the rest closing in C major (III.). (Note the method, now permanently established in Beethoven's style, of starting the modulations by changing the dominant chord in bar 4 from major to minor.) The first 2 bars contain 2 figures, (a) in the melody and (b) in the bass, the melody duplicating (b) in an

ornamental version not used later.   The figures of the other bars
are different.   The bass, when not occupied by (b), descends
regularly on its way to its cadential dominants.

9–20.—Figures (a+b) enter in C major in unaccompanied
bass, answered in the next bar in the treble; and developed in a
sequence of imitations at the half-bar over a bass descending by
semitones.   At the 3rd step the lower voice abandons the figure,
and the upper voice works it out in a new line while the bass
moves 2 steps in each bar.   At bar 17 the dominant is reached
and held for 4 bars, while the melody abandons figure (a) and
slowly descends to a half-close with pause.   A themeless and
timeless cadenza rises over the dominant chord in 4 quintoles,
followed by 5 triplets (carefully *not* marked as such) coalescing
into a plain arpeggio and leading into

21–24.—First 4 bars of the first movement, broken by pauses
in 2nd and 4th bar.

25–28.—The last half-bar echoed as a question and then
carried upwards in three half-bar steps of rising sequence,
stringendo, culminating in dominant cadenza, with trill rising
from 7th through ♯7th to 8ve and leading to finale.

Geschwind, doch nicht zu sehr ; und mit Entschlossenheit : A major.
      Sonata form.

1–4.—Introduction, a rhythmic figure (a) joining each pair of
bars below the dominant trill and anticipating the main theme.

First Group : A major.

⁴/5–12.—Theme (AB), an 8-bar phrase (2+2+4) in imitative
double counterpoint in tonic, with close on (or in) dominant
marked by pause.   The following figures are used throughout
the movement except in some 20 bars of the Second Group.

The counterpoint to the second 4 bars is new.

[12]/13–20.—Theme (AB) inverted in double counterpoint and made to close in tonic.

[20]/21–28.—New phrase (AD) on the dominant, like a middle strain; 8 bars $(2+2+1, 1, \frac{1}{2}+\frac{1}{2}+1)$ working (a) into a new

context (ad) 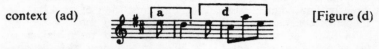 [Figure (d)

is obviously a reduplication of (a), though it has its own character.] The dialogue remains imitative, 2 bars in treble being answered by 2 in tenor, and the bass participating in the speeding-up of (a) as the phrase develops. Notice the anticipated tonic sketched in bar 28 as the phrase closes into a 3rd strain.

[28]/29–36.—Da Capo of bars [12]/13–20 led by deep bass; a close imitation replacing the counterpoint of the 2nd quatrain, the close of which is delayed so as to arrive in the next period.

Transition.

37–52.—Above imitations of (b) a new sustained melody moves in a tonic-and-dominant scheme for 4 bars, closing into self-repetition. This merges into a rising sequence of three 2-bar steps, the bass ascending the scale by a step in each bar and the harmony moving into (V.). The bass having reached the upper A as 7th of dominant of (V.), that harmony is retained for 4 more bars, with a halt.

53–62.—The long paragraph is at last finished by an entirely new imitative theme (with 3 voices entering at 2-bar intervals) moving to B as enhanced dominant, the 6th bar closing into 4 more $(2+1+1)$, which end in the now established key of E. Note that the abrupt " feminine end " is characteristic of the whole movement, being already manifested in bar 20.*

* Distinguish between superficial feminine rhythm imposed upon the

cadence by an appoggiatura, such as  and a

feminine cadence inveterate in the harmony, as

Even this could be regarded as superficial ; but such a close as

 manifestly cannot.

Second Group in **Dominant.**

⁶²/63–69.—New 4-bar imitative offspring of (ab) over tonic pedal, followed by varied repetition, the 4th bar of which overlaps with next phrase.

70–77.—Tonic-and-dominant dialogue between bass and treble in 2-bar steps on a running sequence of (b), accompanied by a new rhythmic figure, and closing into repetition of its 4 bars in higher octave, closing, with interrupted cadence, into

78–85.—Cadence-theme (E). Its rhythmic resemblance to (a) is probably accidental. In effect it is a new melody, consisting of 4 bars (1+1+2) moving from (vi.) through (ii.) to dominant, and answered by 4 similar bars coming to full close. The final figure (e) is developed later.

Exposition repeated.

Development.

⁸⁵/86–93.—New 8-bar phrase on home dominant, rising slowly from (a), accompanied by (e) in the tenor. [It would be far-fetched to regard the rising minims as an enormous augmentation of (b), though a genuine double augmentation does occur at the end of the Development.]

The phrase is coming to a deliberate half-close with pauses, when the ⁶₄ chord, instead of resolving, becomes minor, and is thus left in the air.

⁹³/94–95.—Figure (a), in A minor, asks an angry question and pauses for a reply.

Fugue, with modulating exposition, but centred on home-tonic minor.

⁹⁵/96–102.—Theme (AB) in low bass joins with a new figure (x) so as to form a 7-bar fugue-subject, consisting of 2 sequential pairs of bars on (ab), overlapping with 2 sequential pairs on (x).

¹⁰²/103–109.—A tenor answers in C major, modulating through F to D minor, and accompanied by a counter-subject consisting first of (b) inverted on 1st beat of bar, and then of (x) in imitation.

¹⁰⁹/110–117.—Alto enters, with subject in D minor modulating to A minor, the lower voices giving the countersubject in 3rds and 6ths. An extra bar is added (in sequence) before the next entry.

¹¹⁷/118–126.—Soprano enters with subject in A minor, the inner voices giving the countersubject in 6ths: 2½ extra bars lead to

128–140.—Entry of subject in C major in bass with reversed accents (through displacement by one beat). Figure (x) is compressed into a new sequence, which occupies 8 bars (2+2+4) ranging around F major and D minor.

^{140}/141–144.—The tenor initiates 4 bars of (ab) imitated inversely above and directly below, moving from dominant of A minor towards C.

^{144}/145–153.—Entry of subject in C major in upper part (presumably alto, though there is nothing but a later entry of the soprano to show that the alto has taken office after its rest at the end of bar 40). Figure (x) is doubled in 10ths, with answering imitation in bass. Two extra bars (during which the soprano reappears as such) lead to a new process.

154–165.—New series of rising sequences of (ab), with reversed accents in quatrains rising from F in scale of C. The 1st quatrain gives (ab) in dialogue between the upper voices; in the 2nd quatrain the bass behaves like 2 voices, and becomes 2 real voices at the end of the 3rd quatrain, which has moved into A minor below a chain of suspensions.

166–180.—Development of (b) in continuous running sequence (as in bars 70–77) in pairs of bars, 2 lower voices rising in 3rds over dominant of E minor, being answered by 2 upper voices descending in 6ths with inverted figure. The process is repeated in G major. Thereupon a closer sequence fills 2½ bars, leading to a 2-bar close in E minor. This is interrupted by 2 answering bars which invert it in double counterpoint and close in A minor, with characteristic feminine rhythm.

^{180}/181–189.—Four-part stretto on (ab) in A minor, led by bass and merging after 2 bars into the whole theme (ABX) in alto, with direct imitation by soprano and tenor in 6ths. Figure (x) is in 6ths in upper parts, imitated with 6ths in lower parts, the bass having previously added a new imitation of (ab).

190–195.—Compressed sequences of (x), first in 2 single bars with imitations at half-bar, then in half-bar steps in contrary motion, reaching home dominant in 4th bar.

^{195}/196–203.—Over home-dominant pedal, figure (ab) is thundered out in double augmentation in deep bass, while upper parts fall headlong with the ordinary figure (b) for 2 bars, followed by 2 on (x). Then 4 bars of dominant arpeggio lead to the Recapitulation.

Recapitulation.
First Group.
204–211 = 5–12.
^{211}/212–215 = ^{12}/13–16 led by extreme bass under dominant pedal, with new contrary imitations in 2 upper parts.

215/216–223.—Figure (bc), starting in bass alone, is answered at 2 bars in the upper octave, and joined after another 2 bars by a 3rd voice in the next octave. The 3 parts go on rising in 6ths for 2 more bars, closing into (IV.).

Transition and Second Group.

224–241 = 37–52 transposed to (IV.) leading to tonic, with an additional bar (232) completing the repetition of the first 4; the subsequent rising sequence being simplified and another bar added before the 4 on 7th of dominant.
242–274 = 53–85.

Coda.

275–285.—Figure (e) is repeated 5 times in bass, making a tonic-and-dominant swing; while a new and leisurely derivative of (b), entering at 3rd bar, fills 8 bars with a self-repeating 4-bar phrase. This leads to a pause on A as dominant 7th of (IV.).

285/286–289.—On the threshold of (IV.) figure (a) asks the same angry question as at bars 93/94, with the same pause for reply. Two bars later the question is quietly repeated in the minor, with the same pause.

289/290–296.—The bass answers with (ab) in D minor, but the figure refuses to form a fugue. After 2 bars a tenor joins in 3rds (10ths), closing into F major. A soprano follows a step higher in the next octave, leading to home dominant, on which the 2 upper voices in 3rds, with major harmony, drift into

297–310.—The 2nd strain (AD), omitted in the Recapitulation, reappears. It is compressed into a 7-bar phrase (2+2+3), closing into varied repetition, leading to

310/311–319.—New tonic-and-dominant swing; a 2-bar version of (bc) in 3rds punctuated by (a) at middle of 2nd bar, first above, then below. After third couple the figure (a) descends 5 octaves in 4 bars, the bottom note, A, at 319 being disguised by the G♯ which helps it to imitate a measured drum-roll.

320–330. = New 4-bar derivative of (ab) with reversed accent and an appearance of being distributed among 3 voices. The drum-roll continues, but the G♯ is essential at the 3rd bar, where the dominant appears in an outlying bass. The 4th bar is again tonic. The phrase is repeated, and its last 2 bars are twice echoed, *ritardando*, closing into 3 bars of final tonic, representing a 4-bar group.

29

SONATA IN B FLAT MAJOR, Op. 106.

THE title " Hammerklavier," commonly given to this Sonata, might just as well be given to Op. 101, which was also published as " für das Hammerklavier." The idiomatic English translation of " Hammerklavier " is " pianoforte." If the Italian language should ever become as unpopular in England as it was in Vienna in 1820 we should presumably translate " pianoforte " into Saxon as " softloud."

Allegro : B♭ major. Sonata form.

First Group.

Bars ⅛/1–4.—Theme (A), a 2-bar figure on tonic chord, repeated higher up the chord with pause. It contains three elements (a), (b), (c), which for purposes of analysis may be projected onto one plane thus—

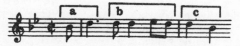

⁴/5–8.—Contrasted theme (D), a 4-bar phrase (1+1+2, the 2 in tapering rhythm with pause), making half-close on dominant.

⁸/9–16.—Counterstatement of theme (D) an octave higher, the bass rapidly drifting down 4 octaves. The 3rd and 4th bars interlock into a varied repetition, leading to a further rise to a climax in the next 2 bars, which close into

17–34.—New theme (E) on a tonic pedal, over which a 2-bar figure rises for 4 steps. Its 2nd bar is then carried 2 steps further, reaching the octave (plus appoggiatura) in the next bar; whereupon it descends in 4 bars through 3 octaves of tonic chord, closing into a 4-bar building-up of dominant chord. Pause.

Transition.

³⁴/35–38.—Theme (A) resumed. Its 2nd couple of bars does not move higher, but remains about D. For one moment the D is left unharmonized, whereupon the B♭ chord is instantly replaced by a D major chord. Pause.

[This dramatic stroke is a *locus classicus* for the characteristic avoidance of explanatory dominants in Beethoven's later works.

In so large a movement the key of (VI.) must not be established without dominant preparation, but its dominant may be introduced without enhancement or explanation.   A comparison with the transition of the first movement of the *Waldstein* Sonata will show how necessary the augmented 6th is at bar 22 at that movement, and how out of place anything of the kind would be here.]

³⁸/39–66.—Dominant preparation for (VI.). Six bars (3 couples) of (a) in bass, followed by 2 of a quaver-figure resembling part of (b), lead to 16 bars of a new running figure in 4-bar groups, alternately dominant 7th and ⁶₄, the last 8 bars being a transference of the first 8 to the *L.H.*, the whole passage being essentially an imitative duet.

Second Group : G major (VI.).

⁶²/63–66.—The last 2 quavers of the *L.H.* begin a new 4-bar theme $(1+1+2)$,

the treble taking over the melody at the 3rd bar and closing (*ritardando*) in (or on) the dominant.

⁶⁶/67–74.—Counterstatement of the new theme, with the 3rd bar now diverted to dominant of (vi.) (reckoned locally $=$ E minor).   The 4th bar overlaps with a sequence descending the dominants for four 1-bar steps and two half-bar steps, leading to

75–90.—Another new theme, 6 bars, consisting of 2 (Dominant to tonic) repeated and 2 forming a half-close.   The whole 6-bar phrase is repeated in a higher octave, and the last 2 bars carried further in 3 steps of sequence, rising through subdominant to enhanced subdominant, and leading to

91–99.—Three bars (thrice 1) on subdominant with a figure, in dialogue, reminiscent of (c).   The bass rising a semitone, 2 bars of syncopated chords lead to 4 of cadential ⁶₄ resolving at last crotchet and closing into

100–119.—Cadence-group consisting first of a new 6-bar theme (F) (2 allied couples and a 3rd couple) tinged with minor subdominant, and closing into varied repetition *crescendo*, closing more excitedly into a final theme (G), a 4-bar cadence-phrase tinged with major subdominant, and echoed in a figure (g)

 which is repeated 4 times, with

variation by broken octaves, closing into

120ª–125ª. Three bare octaves (x)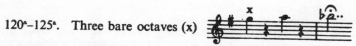

rise in 2 bars to the home tonic, whereupon, after a pause, figure
(ab), in two efforts separated by whole bars, builds up the tonic
chord and so leads to the repeat.

Development.
120ᵇ–123ᵇ.—Figure (x) reaches B♮ instead of B♭. Having
thus failed to change the key, it mounts further and pauses on
the 5th.
124–129.—Theme (G) resumed in 3 rising sequential steps:
dominant and ⁶₄ of C minor, followed by dominant of E♭, and
leading to
130–137.—Figure (x) in 3rds with bass in contrary motion in
E♭, pausing on complete chord. Gentle echo in lower octave
with pause. The procedure of bars ¹²¹/122ª–125ª now builds
up the chord of E♭ by means of figure (ab).

Fugato in E♭.
¹³⁷/138–146.—Canonic development of (abc) with a new
figure (y).

[All pairs of conjunctly descending quavers must be reminiscent
of those in figure (b); but they deserve a special name when they
are part of a phrase with a character of its own. Figure (y) is
not a pair of quavers, but a 2-bar matter beginning at the slurred
minim.] The subject (abcy) is propounded in a low tenor,
answered by a bass in canon at 1 bar in the lower 5th, which becomes the lower 7th by contracting the upward stretch at the
beginning of figure (y). This figure rises in three 2-bar steps of
sequence (reckoning from the upper voice). After the 3rd step,
2 more bars lead to
¹⁴⁶/147–155.—Answer by 2 upper voices in the local dominant.
(Notice how this is entirely without any effect of a return to the
home tonic.). The answer returns to E♭ in 9 bars equivalent to
138–146, leading to
¹⁵⁵/156–166.—Treatment of the canon in 4 parts produced
by doubling in interlocking 10ths. After 7 bars a rising sequence
of four 1-bar steps leads to the next entry. (In these last 4 bars
Beethoven uses Bach's method of endlessly changing the surface

of a straight sequence by means of triple or quadruple counter-point.)

167–176.—Fourth and last entry of the canon, in close 3rds. The local supertonic, present in the former entries, becomes part of a drift away from E♭, and after the 6th bar the sequences press on in four half-bar steps, bringing the fugato to an end on dominant of C minor.

Modulations resumed.

176/177–200.—Development of (ab) together with a new use of the conjunctly falling couples of quavers. A sequence of 4-bar groups (2 of (ab)+2 of the quavers) rises in 3 steps (dominant of C minor; C minor, dominant of E♭), and is continued by 2 bars of (ab) alone on E♭, followed by 3 more pairs of bars rising melodically over dominant of G.

The sequence having reached the octave of that dominant, there are 4 bars of preparation, with (a) as in the bass of bars 39–40, the harmony disappearing.

200/201–212.—Instead of the expected G, major or minor, the remote key of B major suddenly appears; and theme (F) enters. Its last 2 bars are echoed by a lower voice, and then repeated in a variation which the lower voice again echoes, with a change that prevents it from resolving its 7th into the next bar.

212/213–226.—Theme (ABC) enters loudly in extreme bass on dominant, and is answered bar by bar in 3 upper voices (or 2 acting as 3). Figure (ab), without (c), is then discussed by the 4 (or 3) voices, rising in two 2-bar groups up the dominant chord of B. A further rise, in 2 single bars, reaches its minor 9th (G♮). Upon this the bass rises chromatically, and the figure doubles its pace.

Whether the 3rd step of the bass is A♮ or A♯ we shall never be able to prove. An advanced sketch, with figures indicating the implied or projected harmony, proves that Beethoven originally intended A♮, first supporting its own (implied major) chord, then as 3rd of the home dominant. On this showing the progression is chromatic and regular, passing down the dominants from B to A. Bulow condemned it as trivial until the evidence of the sketch induced him to recant.

On the other hand, if A♯ is right, the only chromatic note is the G♮, which becomes *merely* chromatic, effecting no modulation at all. With E above it the A♯ is still leading-note to B major. With F♮ above it there arises a double enharmonic quibble, for the first meaning of the F♮ is E♯, a merely chromatic note that should lead to F♯ above the A♯ as a penultimate dominant of B; but it is treated as a perfect 5th and identified with the chord of the home tonic. All this is so cogently in keeping with Beethoven's later style, especially in the matter of avoiding explanatory dominants, that only very hard facts can induce us to reject it.   But the adverse facts are very hard indeed. The sketch shows that Beethoven meant A♮, not merely at some early stage of his plans, but when every bar was approximately in place.   Beethoven is always liable to forget accidentals, and this danger increases in his later works when he takes to changing his key-signature, often to fewer sharps or flats than the main key of the passage, and then forgets that he has made the change. In this very instance he left an unquestionable blunder standing within a few bars of this place; thereby showing that his attention was not drawn to possible subtleties of notation here.   And, inconveniently subtle as Beethoven's notation sometimes is, the writing of B♭+F as A♯+F♮ is more perversely unpractical than any of Beethoven's authenticated perversities.   Precautionary accidentals would be necessary to prove the intention, and Beethoven supplies precautionary accidentals more often than he forgets necessary ones.   This weighs heavily against the only plausible theory as to how Beethoven might have finally intended A♯—viz., that when he noticed the omission of the natural he might have said, " Ha ! das ist aber genial ! " and so let it stand.   The evidence is totally against his having reviewed the accidentals at all.   Still, we cannot dismiss the case without thus laying the alternatives before the student; and Beethoven might still agree that A♯ is a stroke of genius worthy of him.

Recapitulation.

First Group.
    226/227–234 = 1–8.—The main theme in the home tonic bursts out over a bass counterpoint on (b²).   This counterpoint continues under theme (D), there being no pause in the 4th bar.
    234/235–240.—Theme (D), having paused at bar 234 = 8, is now continued in a new way.   Its last 2 bars are repeated *in situ*— viz., on dominant—then, melodically a step higher, on tonic. (Bülow shrewdly points out that the A♭ in bar 237 does *not* give the character of a dominant of E♭.)   The sequence continues to rise, compressed into 1-bar steps.   Two of these pass through (iv.) into ♭VI., and drift into bar 11 in that key (G♭).
    241–266 = 11–34 in G♭ (♭VI.) with the following changes. The bass does not roam, but remains high and fixed on its dominant of G♭.   The couple 11–12 is reiterated in two variations instead of one.   Lastly, at the extreme end of the 4-bar dominant arpeggio (bar 34) an unexpected added bass-note changes it from dominant of G♭ to dominant of C♭.   This is written as dominant of B♮, and there is a pause on the unexpected bare 5th.

Transition.—(In these circumstances the term is obviously overdue, though it could not have been applied to 11–34.)

[266]/267–276.—Theme (A) bursts out in B♮ minor, pausing in 2nd bar. Eight bars on the material of [38]/39–44 proceed in 4 couples—B minor to G, G as dominant to C minor, C minor to home dominant, and the last couple on home dominant. The key of B♮ has thus lost its identity with C♭, and we have come round an enharmonic circle.

277–294 = 45–62 on the home dominant, closing into

Second Group.

[294]/295–351 = [62]/63–119 in tonic.

Coda.

352–361.—Figure (g) continued in a sequence, rising bar by bar and step by step from B♭ through C minor and D minor to E♭ minor, where, avoiding further modulation, it rises to the home-dominant chord, down which it descends, with minor inflexions, for 4 bars. The rhythm of the whole passage dates from bar 350 = 118; and the result amounts to three 4-bar groups, closing into

362–376.—Theme (F) in darker scoring for 4 bars, which are repeated, over an inner trill and a flowing crotchet bass, with major instead of minor 6th; followed by 2 bars leading to a ⁶₄ chord with pause and trill. The trill debouches into 4 bars of scales, 2 in 3rds and 2 in contrary motion, which, characteristically avoiding the effect of a dominant chord, close into

[376]/377–385.—New sequential treatment of (ab) rising in 2-bar steps (each a *piano* answered by *forte*), with bass moving in semitones from (i.) through (ii.) and (iii.) to (IV.). Here the sequence halts, resting for the next bar. The figure makes its final demand on the dominant, and pauses again (through a measured bar) for a reply.

[385]/386–405.—A deep bass provides a foundation of distant thunder for a tonic harmony, chiefly in ⁶₄ position, with a G♭ auxiliary vibration, over which figures (bc) rise and fall, *pianissimo*, with (c) repeated *forte* in lower octave at the end of each 2nd bar. 2+2 bars are thus occupied, corresponding to bars 1–4. Then figure (c), with its *forte* answers, makes a 4-bar group, ending with a stationary dominant bar over a tonic pedal. This group is repeated in a lower octave. Four bars are then occupied by a new 1-bar vestige of the theme, resolving the minor dominant 9th on to the tonic (over the vibrating tonic pedal). In the next 4 bars these vestiges die away wholly on tonic chord, at first ⁶₄ in the bass, which then takes root position. In the

middle of the 3rd bar a *fortissimo* chord crashes down into a final bare octave.

Before discussing the Scherzo it is necessary to deal with a new issue that arises from it. The movements of this Sonata, and of Op. 110, show a subtle and elusive relation in their main themes. Such subtleties ought not to be imputed to classical sonatas without very cogent evidence; when people see more than is there they will be very unlikely to see all that is there. But the evidence, both internal and external, is quite adequate here. While this Sonata was in the press Beethoven added an introductory bar to the Adagio, and explained to the publisher that his object was to echo the end of the Scherzo. This being so, we can hardly regard as accidental the fact that the theme of the Scherzo is like that of the first movement in consisting of a third which rises and falls back again; while the upward 10th, with which the fugue-subject of the Finale begins, is reminiscent of the upward leap at the beginning of the first movement. Here, then, is the scheme of these relations:

These resemblances are purposely vague, and are in a wholly different category from such phenomena as the resurrection of the openings of previous movements in the introduction to the Finales of Op. 101, the Violoncello Sonata, Op. 102, No. 1, and the Ninth Symphony. In those resurrections obvious identity is essential. In the present resemblances it is no less essential that the themes should stand entirely on their own individual characters. Thus the added 1st bar of the Adagio remains outside the theme; it happens to be present in the counterpoint at the beginning of the Development, but is absent from Recapitulation and Coda. Juxtaposition is another essential point; and also similarity of function. There is not much point in a resemblance between a main theme in one movement and a transitional figure in another.

In these matters Beethoven does not, as is often supposed, foreshadow modern developments. The separate movements of a sonata lose their own momentum and achieve but a flaccid and precarious unity if they try to live by taking in each other's thematic washing. The modern works of symphonic size that have achieved thematic unity have done so by abandoning the sonata style and adopting the Wagnerian time-scale. Strange to say, the pioneer work in this line is contemporary with Beethoven's later works, being the Wanderer-Fantasia of Schubert. This, in spite of its external resemblance to a four-movement sonata and its formal tonic-and-dominant opening, is maturely Wagnerian in its methods. Mozart's C minor Fantasia, published by his request with the C minor Sonata, is an earlier and very great work that raises these issues. We must not suppose that Beethoven's contemporaries were unaware of such possibilities. Beethoven wrote fewer fantasias and quasi-fantasias than Hummel or Clementi; indeed, the " orthodox convention of sonata form " rather deserves to be called a modern generalization than an orthodoxy of Beethoven's day.

Scherzo : Assai vivace.   B♭ with Trio in tonic minor.
⅜/1–7.—First Strain, of 7 bars, on a figure (a)

falling in sequence of 3rds for 3 bars, followed by a medial close which, modifying the figure, initiates a rise over a falling bass, terminated by dominant close into 7th bar, with a new rhythmic

figure (b),   The general proportions of the First Strain will probably be heard as 1+1+2, interlocking with 1+1, answered by 1.   But the construction 3+3+1 is also possible.

⁷/8–14.—Repetition of First Strain an octave higher, the close being melodically more final.

¹⁴/15–30.—Second Strain, beginning with (a) in falling sequence of 2 couples over dominant, with colouring of (ii.), followed by tonic.   In the next 4 bars the bass rises semi-chromatically from F to C, closing on to dominant of C minor ; the melody meanwhile abandoning figure (a) and descending in contrary motion.   After a bar's pause, figure (a) is resumed, dispersed in different octaves, and hovering in C minor for 4 bars.   With a 5th bar it treats C minor as the normal antepenultimate (ii.), and closes in tonic with (b) as a bare octave.   The general proportions of the Second

Strain are 4+4: pause of 1 bar; then 7 bars in the proportions of the First Strain. These 7 bars are easiest to construe as pairs with a truncated end; the 8 bars of 16–22 cannot be construed except in pairs; and thus the main tendency is against a 3-bar basis for the First Strain.

³⁰/31–46.—Repetition of Second Strain an octave higher.

Trio in tonic minor

⁴⁶/47–54.—Over (b) in the bass, figure (a) is melted down into the opening of a grotesque 8-bar melody, which goes round and round in the chord of B♭ minor till in the 7th bar it finds its way out to a close in D♭ (♭III.). Meanwhile the bass, after first tapping out figure (b), has been rumbling in the tonic chord, which at the end of the 6th bar has, by subsidence of the bass-note, become the ⁶₄ of D♭. This chord refuses to resolve, and so the bass closes by merely moving up to its root.

⁵⁴/55–62 = ⁴⁶/47–54, the bass taking the melody, and the treble tapping out figure (b), and then proceeding to imitate the bass in the octave at 1 bar with triplet vibration.

⁶²/63–71.—While the treble finishes its imitation, the bass taps out figure (b) on D♭ and resumes its rumbling. The treble then starts its melody, a bar late, in D♭. At the end of the 3rd (delayed) bar the bass moves down to the ⁶₄ position. At the beginning of the 5th bar the bass changes to B♭, enabling the melody to return to the tonic in 8 bars from its delayed start. At the 7th bar (70) the bass drops to the ⁶₄ position (in B♭ minor) and, as before, returns to root-position without resolving.

⁷¹/72–80.—Repetition of ⁶²/63–71, with same changes as in ⁵⁴/55–62. The bass adds another echo-bar to the overhanging treble bar, and leads to

Presto ²₄: still in tonic minor.

81–88.—Entirely new melody in duple time and trochaic metre, beginning with unharmonized 8-bar phrase in 4 pairs, the last with end-stop in dominant minor.

89–96.—Eight-bar answer in bass below syncopated chords. The first 6 bars are in minor dominant; the last pair returns to minor tonic, into which it closes without end-stop.

97–112.—Third 8-bar clause in tonic minor, with melody above independent bass, and stopping on half-close. This half-close is repeated and its last chord carried down 5 octaves to the bottom of the pianoforte. Pause ending in 6 octaves of *prestissimo* rising dominant scale, with silent pause afterwards.

¹¹²/113–114.—A home-dominant minor 9th shakes itself in the tempo of the Scherzo, adumbrating (as Bülow points out) the rhythm of figure (a), and so leading, after a bar's pause,

to the Da Capo. Bülow suggests that we might at this point repeat from the beginning, Trio and all, before going on to the varied Da Capo, thus making the movement like one of the greater scherzos in the symphonies and chamber-music.

This is a very interesting idea. But the double Da Capo belongs to scherzos of a much greater and steadier momentum than can be found in any scherzo in the pianoforte sonatas. It is not clear why the pianoforte scherzos should be so limited while other movements can develop on the largest symphonic scale; but such is the case. The great doubly-rotating scherzos seize us in a whirlwind which nothing can stop; the present scherzo trips us up in dialogue by quips, and in dance-movement by booby-traps. Behind its humour lies a formidable power. But we are not invited to go through booby-traps twice.

Da Capo of Scherzo.

$^{114}/115-160 = \frac{1}{1}/1-46$, varied, on repeating the First Strain, by rhythmic click in an inner part or in bass.

Coda

160-172.—The odd bar at the end of the strain is very ready to behave as the 1st of a new group; and so the body of the Scherzo overlaps its Coda by one bar. From this point (160) there issues the following process of 8 bars. Figure (b) on its final tonic is softly answered by the impertinent suggestion, " I think you mean B♮." The B♭ indignantly reasserts itself. The B♮ says, " Oh, very well; but I suppose you are really A♯, so figure (a) will kindly turn itself into B minor, and I shall stay where I am." A *ritardando* during these last 4 bars indicates some hesitation; and in another 4 bars of *Presto* in ₵ time the B♮ breaks out in panic, losing its rhythm and rising by octaves, and finally collapsing on B♭ after all. So it was not the B♭ that was really A♯, but the B♮ which was really C♭; in other words, the perfectly respectable ♭II. (But figure (a) had certainly gone into B♮ minor, not major.)

$^{171}/172-175.$—B♭ and triple time being restored, figure (a) concludes the whole matter, rising through 3 octaves and accompanied by the rhythmic click in an inner part. This inner part descends below the bass, making the final tonic a ⁶⁄₄ chord; but the progression of the true bass leaves the ear perfectly satisfied.

Adagio sostenuto : F♯ minor [G♭ minor =(♭vi.)]. Sonata form.

The doubly indirect key-relation of this movement is not

without earlier precedent.   A nearly converse relation is used by Haydn in his G minor Quartet, Op. 72, No. 3, where the slow movement is in E major.   Beethoven uses the exact converse relation in his C minor Concerto, where the slow movement is in E.   A year after Beethoven's death, Schubert (whose mature tonality closely resembles that of Beethoven and Brahms) uses the similar relation (♭iii.) in his B♭ sonata where the slow movement is in C♯ minor (=D♭ minor).

Such remote keys are felt to be related if and when they are left in bare juxtaposition.   Even an explanatory dominant is apt to be apologetic rather than fortifying; and further explanation simply destroys all conviction of relationship.

The wonderful 2 introductory notes of this Adagio break the shock of the first F♯ minor chord, but do not weaken its meaning, for they offer no explanation or apology for it, but are themselves parts of it—viz., the 3rd and 5th.   They leave it to the full chord to reveal what they mean.   Until its arrival their meaning varies. After B♭, A sounds like its leading-note.   After A, C♯ sounds like the leading-note of D.   These implications are indeed too obvious for the listener to take notice of them; but his mind moves by their direction, and the F♯ minor chord utterly transforms everything. These 2 notes constitute one of the profoundest thoughts in all music.

1.   *Introduction*, discussed above. Call its figure (A).

First Group.   F♯ minor.

2–26.—Main theme, a melody in two 8-bar strains, the 1st coming to feminine half-close and the 2nd coming to a full close, which swings back into a repeat expanded by an extra bar closing into next period.   Only the fact that the 2nd strain is repeated induces the listener to separate it from the 1st strain; for the whole melody is one of those enormously wise utterances which, moving with apparent caution and hesitation, allow nothing to interrupt and nothing to escape their infinitely patient attention. Where the movement of harmony seems to be held up, as when the dominant reached at the end of the 1st strain persists through 2 bars of the 2nd, it is poised ready for such a surprise as the 2 Neapolitan bars (G major) before the full close.   In its first statement that close is medial, falling on the 2nd half of the bar. In swinging back to the repeat it takes the opportunity of reproducing the opening figure of the melody (bar 2 of the movement); an incident which greatly enhances the subtlety and continuity of the whole.   The total proportions of the theme, then, come to this: 1st strain in 2 interlocking with 2,+1+1+2: 2nd strain in 1+1 (rising by 3rds on dominant chord)+2 in (♭II.)+2, leading to repeat; the repeat substituting a new 8th bar, of which the 1st beat is a quasi-final tonic, immediately passing through (♭II.) to a close into the next bar, which constitutes a coda of two half-bars of interlocking full closes, the 2nd of which is left unresolved on the dominant. The figures used in later developments are those of the first 3 bars (2-4). They are as follows:

Transition.

27–38.—New theme beginning with interlocking 2-bar groups. In the slow tempo of this Adagio a bar is too big an item to invite any interest in distinctions between strong and weak bars. The ear dwells upon what most impresses it; the memory holds together what it is stimulated to grasp, and accepts changes of meaning without either noticing them or misunderstanding them. Thus, bar 27 is too evidently a new beginning to be taken as a completion of a pair begun by 26. But in the next bar the entry of the melody makes what went before seem introductory. On the other hand, the melody enters about the half-bar, and thus throws extra stress on the 1st beat of the next bar. The stress is increased by the fact that the harmony shifts at that moment from tonic to dominant, and remains dominant for a couple of bars. In the retrospect this dominant couple therefore answers to the previous tonic couple (27-28). By this time the melody, which only accidentally resembles bar 16 or figure (c) of the main theme, is closing into a varied self-repetition (bars 31-33). If you like to call the result a 3-bar period your arithmetic is correct, there being no doubt that it is 3 bars that are repeated. But you might as well claim to identify by ear the rhythm ♩ ♩ ♩ with the rhythm of two half-hours plus one hour as claim to recognize such slow 3-bar periods across an alternation of tonic and dominant that is mainly in couples.

The varied repetition closes into a new single bar, which closes into varied self-repetition. The bass, which has swung conjunctly within the tonic and dominant chords, is here swinging about the 3rd of the tonic. With the next bar it rises modulating in half-bar steps through subdominant. Having risen for 4 such steps, it crowds 6 steps into the next bar, the last step being dominant of D (VI.).

39–44.—Six bars of dominant preparation for (VI.). A new 1-bar figure is imitated at the half-bar, descending over a dominant pedal for 2 bars, after which it moves for six half-bars with locally modulating bass below a more sustained melody. A whole bar on the plain dominant finally closes into

Second Group : D major (VI.).

45–53.—Theme (D), a new tonic-and-dominant figure of 2 bars, announced in deep bass and repeated in treble, accompanied by a figure derived from the previous passage. The 4 bars close into a varied repetition, the accompaniment changing from duple semi-quavers to triplets.

54–56.—Flowing continuation on new melodic lines: 4 bars rising through four half-bar steps, and 2 of accelerated rise reaching dominant in higher octave, but evading it chromatically; leading to

57–62.—Six bars of new material: (2:1+1:2) 2 making cadence from dominant of (ii.) (reckoned locally) to the local dominant; the impending cadence is then interrupted by a sequence in which the melody glides chromatically against rising bass, through (iv.) towards dominant, which is again diverted to dominant of (ii.), which fills three half-bars before leading to final close into next period.

63–68.—Cadence-theme: a 2-bar phrase (1+1), starting on 3rd quaver and closing into repetition in which the 2nd bar is inverted in double counterpoint. Two more bars, arising out of the final chord, lead through dominant chord to the

Development.

69–72.—Four bars of main theme in D major, with a new bass counterpoint in contrary motion. (A further happy result of the added introductory bar (A) is that it forms the beginning of this counterpoint.) At 3rd bar the theme moves into B minor, and thence to dominant of C♯ major, closing into

73–76.—Bars 69–72 inverted in double counterpoint, starting in C♯ major with minor 6th. The 3rd bar does not modulate, but leads to the 4th bar on dominant of D♯, written as E♭. (There is no real enharmonic modulation.)

77–87.—The treble resumes the melody in E♭ major (the bass outlining the harmony in semiquaver arpeggios). In the 2nd bas it takes figure (b) a step higher, compressing it into three noter

thus:  These 3 notes are carried

upwards for 9 modulating steps. As these steps lie athwart the ⁶⁄₈ time, their aspect is always changing; and further variety is given by alternations of octave and of *una corda* and *forte* every 2 steps. The notation is changed back to sharps at the 3rd step. But there are none but the most diatonic modulations throughout the whole of this development. The harmonic boldnesses consist mainly in the Bach-like conflicts between the various inflections of the minor mode and at the frequent points where a minor tonic becomes a major dominant. These conflicts give extraordinary power to the drastically plain series of modulations down the dominants. The 9th step is a half-step, for it has landed on the home tonic. A big platform of home dominant will be needed if our return is not to sound accidental. The note B represents a moment of subdominant, and from it the figure descends through 2 bars of home-dominant 9th. In a 3rd bar the figure breaks into demisemiquavers (their first appearance in this Adagio). Note the anticipated tonic with which the last quaver leads to the

Recapitulation.

First Group.
88–112 = 2–26.—Both strains are elaborately ornamented with demisemiquavers, which cease only when they reach the repetition of the 2nd strain. This repetition gives the plain melody while the bass moves in semiquavers, contrapuntally for 4 bars, in broken chords for the rest.

Transition.
113–129.—Here Beethoven does not scruple to begin his transition in the key of the Second Group; such is his conviction (and power to convince us) that a key prepared by organized transition is quite different from a key introduced sectionally. Bars 113-116 are 27-30 transposed, with enhanced detail, to D major. The self-repetition (116½-119 = 30½-33) is shifted into B minor (iv.), where the next 2 bars (120-121 = 34-35) remain. After this the bass falls instead of rising. In 2 bars it descends the scale from D, impinging on the home dominant in the lower octave at the beginning of next period. The 6 bars of dominant preparation (39-44) accordingly follow on home dominant in 124-129.

Second Group in Tonic Major.
130–152 = 45–67 transposed to tonic major. (Beethoven's curious dislike of double sharps induces him to spend thirty-one accidentals in changing the chord of D♯ major to that of E♭ in bars 145-147, merely in order to avoid Fx !).
153.—A full close is substituted for the continued dominant of bar 68. The tonic chord then proceeds as dominant of (iv.) and leads to

Coda.

154–157.—Two bars of main theme (b) over its counter-point (A) in B minor (iv.); breaking off at beginning of 2nd bar. Bass completes the bar by a move down chord of ♭II., and the 2 bars are inverted in double counterpoint in that key, the 2nd bar being filled by an echo in an inner part, and a close into next bar.

158–165.—Theme (D) in its varied form (as in 49-52) enters in (♭II.). After 4 bars the bass rises chromatically, the treble persisting in inflected and syncopated monotone until forced up a 3rd by the harmony. After 2 bars the bass reaches B♯, and remains there for another 2 bars, while the treble monotone is passionately accelerated.

166–173.—With a sudden collapse upon C♯, implying the home ⁶₄, the main theme returns. It is summarized in the selection of bars 2, 3 (slightly enhanced), leading to 10-16, with the second version (25) of the last bar closing into

174–180.—Plagal cadence (with major tonic 7th and minor subdominant) dramatically interrupting the previous close, and filling a 2-bar phrase in the style of the transition-theme. This closes into varied repetition, which closes into 3 bars of dying tonic major chord (root, ⁶₄, and root).

181–187.—Final farewell of main theme, its first 2 bars fading, through (iv.), into a bar of hesitating close into 4 of major tonic chord (1+1; ½, ½, end).

Largo: Modulating Introduction.

The purport of this Largo is simply to find its way down a series of descending 3rds until the right key for the finale has been reached. (For purposes of analysis Beethoven's groups of 4 semiquavers may be treated as bars. The only short measure comes at a pause.)

The process starts with a 5-octave F. After the key of the slow movement (G♭) this is a leading-note, which will presumably turn into a dominant. From it mysteriously syncopated triads descend in 3rds. Halts are called at 4 significant places, and the situation debated at each. At "bar" 5 the descending 3rds have reached G♭. This was the key of the slow movement. Three voices, with a hesitating little subject for imitation, explore that key in 4 "bars", but see no way out. The steps are resumed. Two of them arrive at C♭. Whether this be C♭ or (as written) B♮, it is a semitone above the required mark, and 2 voices discuss it canonically in running figures with some animation. In their 7th "bar" they move to its dominant chord, and pause there. It closes on to B again, and another step is taken. Bother ! This lands us in G♯ minor (A♭ minor), which is absolutely contrary to our purpose.

The debating voices brace themselves up into strict common time, and explore the key with a new theme. After 3 common-time bars of 2-part discussion 2 other voices crowd in, to bring the question to a head in 2 more bars, the key having been thoroughly explored with its subdominant and even its ♭II. A pause cuts the debate short on the dominant. The steps are resumed from G♯. In 3 steps we reach A. This is promising. It is a semitone below the mark; but that means a leading-note, or, at worst, the dominant of the mediant. The A fills 5 octaves (like the F at the beginning), and a leisurely recitative descends over a dominant chord on tonic pedal bass, filling 2 bars of irregular slow common time, with sustained pause. Now let us continue. The steps proceed without interruption in pairs at the end of every second 4-semiquaver "bar", upward 6ths counting as falling 3rds. After 8 steps why are we not in sight of the goal? We must have taken a wrong turning! Hurry up! Here is D; let us break the circle and jump down a 4th to A again. (*Prestissimo*.) Ah! there was our mistake; from A we must drop a *major* 3rd, not a minor. Here we are on F, knowing at last that it is the required dominant.

Allegro risoluto: B♭ major. Fugue for 3 voices ("*con alcune licenze*"). The "*licenze*" are the remarkably rare deviations from strict 3-part writing.

1–5.—Four bars of dominant preparation close into tonic. They anticipate two features of the fugue-subject, viz. its trill (in the Treble) and its initial upward leap, which is twice given in bars 1–2, and compressed twice across the rhythm in bars 3–4. The Treble breaks into the semiquaver motion that pervades the fugue, and an echoing run in a lower voice overlaps with the entry of the Subject and anticipates its 3rd figure (c).

Exposition.

6–15.—The Middle voice announces the Subject, which contains 4 figures used in development.

So long as we can recognize them it does not matter how we articulate the running figures.   They run into each other with logical connexions quite independent of the way in which they happen to break up in development.   The 5th and 6th bars close into self-repetition, a feature frowned on by theorists, but, just because of its formality, very useful to a fugue that is to come to terms with the inveterately dramatic style of the Sonata.   (Compare the opening of the finale of the C major Quartet, Op. 59, No. 3.)   It gives the present fugue occasion for effective turns in the dialogue.   What is unusual, though not unnatural, in the present opening, is that, even after this repetition, there is a delay of 2 more bars before the Answer enters.   The reason for this is interesting.   Beethoven finds it vitally necessary to have an orthodox tonal answer.   Its initial tonic Bb (corresponding to the initial dominant F) will urgently need resolution when the rest of the Subject proceeds in the dominant.   That resolution must be supplied by the other voice, and the 2 extra bars of descending sequence bring it into such a position that the resolution is reached by finishing the sequence in a 3rd bar as the Answer begins.

16–24.—Tonal Answer by Treble in dominant, accompanied, from its 2nd bar, by a Countersubject containing the following figures.

The self-repetition is welded into three 1-bar steps of rising sequence leading to

25–30.—Entry of subject in bass in tonic.   The Treble has the Countersubject, and the Middle adumbrates a second Countersubject with the following figures, rhythmically imitating those of the first.

31–41.—Episode.   (In the terminology of fugue the word episode does not mean a definite or contrasted section, but refers simply to all passages that intervene between definite entries of the more or less complete Subject.   Highly organized episodes may recapitulate each other, and so it may be convenient to number them for reference.   But in any case a different term is required for episodes that consist of new matter. The ordinary episodes of the present fugue do not allude to each other, and serve merely to separate the entries of the Subject. But the fugue contains an important recurring episode based on new matter. This will be distinguished as the Independent Episode.)

The present Episode arises during the repetition of the end of the Subject, and proceeds in irregularly rising sequences on (f′) combined with (i), interchanged in the upper voices over the rolling Bass (a tangle of (c), (d), and arpeggio), culminating in a speeding-up of the steps in cross-rhythm. At bar $^{37}/38$ the Middle gives figure (a) in dominant a beat ahead of its time, the Bass answering likewise in tonic at the turn into 39. The process being repeated a step higher, landing in C minor (ii.), the Bass plunges into

Subject treated by Reversal Accents : D♭ (♭III.).

$^{41}/42$–48.—Subject in Bass in D♭ (♭III.) advanced by a beat. The Middle eventually represents the Countersubject from (f+g) onwards. The repetition of the last 2 bars is transferred to other parts, the Treble taking (d) and the Bass taking (f+g). [Beethoven, who could himself stretch 10ths easily, mutilates (g) in order to avoid them.]

$^{50}/51$–55.—Episode. Arising from bar 48, figure (f′) in Treble, greatly changed by its reversal of accent, ascends in 2-bar sequence of 3rds, answered in lower 5th by Bass. The Middle accompanies with (c). The 3rd step breaks into a quicker descent across the rhythm.

$^{55}/61$.—Answer. In the middle of the bar the Treble gives the tonal Answer in A♭, *delayed* by a beat. The first Countersubject is completely represented in the Bass, and the Middle represents figure (h).

$^{61}/77$.—Episode. As before, the voices exchange at the repetition of the end of the Subject; and an episode arises consisting of sequences in double counterpoint of (d) with (g) in the 6ths or 3rds, the new accentuation again producing a novel effect. After two interchanges (starting from end of Subject and rising from A♭ to B♭ minor), the sequences continue for 2 bars, Middle and Bass (d) uppermost, without interchange; then for 2 more, with (g) in upper 3rds, rising from G♭ to A♭ minor. An extra bar on the dominant of this last key leads to the re-appearance of (a) in Bass with the forward reversal of accent, accompanied by (g) in 3rds. This is another novelty, for (g) had not been represented when the Subject was thus accented. With this combination the 2-bar group descends in sequence from A♭ minor to G♭ major, and an extra bar in that key closes into

Independent Episode in G♭ (♭III.).

75–83.—A double counterpoint of entirely new figures (x y), (z), is developed in interlocking bars—

[Notice that the 1st note of the bar, though liable to change, really belongs to figure (x).]

The Bass, taking a short run, answers (x y) in the lower octave, while the Treble answers (z) in the upper octave, checking on the last note. The next 2. bars gives 2 permutations in D♭, the Middle changing (z) into a descending scale (w).—

A new sequence arises, bringing (y) forward to the main beat without (x), and in combination with (w), also advanced by a beat. This combination, in several positions, occupies 5 bars of E♭ minor (iv.).

Treatment by Augmentation : E♭ minor (iv.).

84–100.—The Subject enters by augmentation in the Middle. As this augmentation makes the notes twice as slow, while the time remains unaltered as ¾, the result gives a completely new rhythmic sense. Ordinary augmentations and other fugal devices lack this kind of transforming effect, which is essentially dramatic.

This is a convenient point on which to base a discussion of Beethoven's fugues in their dramatic aspect, as related to the sonata style. Many prejudices are current, not only as to Beethoven's fugues, but as to the general subject of contrapuntal forms " imported " into sonata works. The subject will never be understood so long as we regard fugue as an " academic " device inherently foreign to forms of later origin. A Hyde Park orator once asked rhetorically, " Did Paul know Greek ? " He was not wider of his mark than the critic who regards Beethoven as anxiously displaying unsuccessful learned devices in his fugues.

Beethoven's counterpoint is not classical. Neither is St. Paul's Greek. But both are languages in their own right, and in a right too divine to need our patronage.

Two things are manifest about the fugues in Beethoven's later works : first, that a dramatic force at white heat underlies them : secondly, that their polyphony stands out only by an aggressive harshness from the polyphony that pervades the rest of the works. The analysis of Op. 101, even more than that of the previous movements of the present work, has been possible only by considering almost every line as having a contrapuntal aspect; and an unprejudiced listener would notice nothing unusual in the fact that the development of the sonata-form finale of Op. 101 is entirely fugal. With that material, no other line of development would have been either adequate or relevant. But it is not every kind of fugue that will answer the purpose.

The sonata style is essentially dramatic, and fugue is related to it as debate is related to drama. A sonata-fugue is like a trial scene. A good dramatist would hardly attempt a trial scene if he were not sure of making it the most exciting passage in his play. At less high pressure we find that Cabinet councils and other debates are very effective in chronicle plays.

A condition common to all such scenes is that they immobilize the actors. No doubt, any fool could fire a pistol on any occasion. But violence ends the scene instead of developing it. Now the forms of fugue have exactly the same effect in sonata-music as the forms of trial or debate have in drama. While they proceed nothing else can happen, and nothing else matters. Thus, not only is the fugal development of Op. 101 confined to one key, but we hardly notice that that key is the home tonic minor until the debate is ended by the triumphant dawn of the recapitulation in the major.

This being so, we cannot expect the modulations of a fugue either to let new keys flash upon us in sudden contrast or to establish them by long preparation. In the present work neither the explosion in bars 37–38 of the first movement nor the calm expanse of its following 24 bars would be conceivable in the fugue. Keys can drift during a fugue, but it is normal for them to drift merely to and fro between " natural " limits (i.e., along the top line of our Table of Key-relationships). A drift slightly beyond these limits will not attract much attention; and if an entry of the Subject is in one of the related keys, its answer in the dominant thereof will not appreciably change the outlook. How, then, does Beethoven contrive to produce in the present fugue, as Parry pointed out, a scheme of key-contrasts, enormous in range and " ideally balanced " ? This is the heart of the problem.

The analysis has already shown that after the Exposition the first two lines of development have started from keys related to the tonic minor, the development by reversed accents starting in (♭III.) and the independent episode starting in (♭VI.).

These keys, though outside the direct relations, are the easiest to bring into touch with the tonic, as Mozart often shows. And by associating them with definite lines of development Beethoven has drawn attention to them so that their colour is not without its proper effect. The analogy of a trial may again help us to appreciate the problem of a widely modulating fugue. A trial is confined to its place. For convenience of legal form the " venue " may be changed, so that a mutiny on a ship in the South Seas may be alleged to have happened in Cheapside. This legal fiction is not calculated to dispel the London fogs by South Sea winds. The only kind of trial that can itself be an incident of travel is that in which the explorer has earned a right to powers of summary jurisdiction. Beethoven, in the finale of Op. 106, is Sir Francis Drake on the Golden Hind.

One question more is apposite here. Could Beethoven have achieved his present purpose better with a smoother counterpoint ? There is no doubt that he would gladly have achieved a smoother counterpoint, and that with it he might have done some quite different things. But Mozart and Brahms have shown us exactly what can be done by smooth counterpoint in sonata forms, and it has not the slightest bearing on Beethoven's object. When Mozart in the " Jupiter " Symphony puts the oldest contrapuntal tags into sonata form before making them into quintuple counterpoint, he is enjoying himself like Portia in cap and gown. When Brahms, in his E minor Violoncello Sonata, Op. 38, and his F major Quintet, Op. 88, writes finales in close fugue texture, his results, in spite of their bristling Brahmsishness, are of Mozartean compactness and symmetry. This is what smooth counterpoint does achieve: it is a language of urbanity and wit; like the language of Dr. Johnson, even when used as a bludgeon. But what have such things to do with the prophet Elijah on Mount Carmel ? Even Mozart became harsh when he took instrumental fugues seriously, as in the C major Fantasia and the C minor Fugue for 2 pianofortes or string-quartet. His harshness is a disciplined logic, like that shown by Beethoven in the " false relations " in the development of the Adagio of this Sonata; and we should not suspect the harshness of Beethoven's fugue-counterpoint to be less logical if we did not happen to know that he found academic counterpoint difficult.

Let us now return to this fugue, knowing ourselves to be on holy ground.

In bars 87-102 not only the Subject but the Countersubject, including even the figures (h) (i) of the third part, is augmented.

One of the few " licences " for which Beethoven's title apologizes is to be seen in the fact that if the *R.H.* is really representing the Bass with figure (e) and the Treble with figure (i) taking over figure (f) with a change of octave, then the Middle has become a double voice as the Subject is doubled in 6ths. As usual the parts are interchanged when the end of the Subject repeats itself. Now comes the Earthquake.

100/101–106.—Stretto by Augmentation and Inversion: the Tonal Answer in Treble combining with the Inverted Subject in Bass, both being augmented. The combination extends nearly to the 4th bar of the original Subject, making 7 bars by augmentation, and merging into

106/107–119.—Figure (a) in augmentation discussed directly and by inversion in three 3-bar steps through F minor and B♭ minor to dominant of A♭; on which figure (g) led by the Bass is quietly discussed for 4 bars, closing into

Recurrence of the Independent Episode, starting in A♭.

120–142.—The previous 4 bars have prepared this key with a deliberation that puts it into another category from that of an answer to D♭. It stands here in its own right, definitely associated with an independent theme, and its relation to the tonic is one of flat contradiction. Thus it is a fit starting-point for travels into remote regions.

The figures (xyz), in new permutations, spend 4 bars in A♭ before modulating. Then, with a turn into F minor, the combination breaks into a long sequence of (w), with (y) advanced a beat (as in bars 79–83). The bass descends with (w) in four 1-bar steps; then rises for another 4 with (y). Hereupon the 4th step develops into a 2-bar limb of a further sequence, which, starting from A♭, moves in three 2-bar steps down the dominants to C♭. This becomes minor and is then written as B minor. Two extra bars in a ⁶⁄₄ position, with a 2-part carefully noncommittal suggestion of cadential dominant resolution, lead to *Cancrizans Development* in B minor, combined with New Subject.

143–151.—In the indefinitely remote key now reached, the Middle is running in a winding figure, reminiscent, as all such runs will be, of figure (d). The run breaks off into a figure of peculiar rhythm ♩♩♩♩ ♩♩ 𝄾 ♩ which rises by 3rds in sequence and leads to a trill beginning on the 1st of the bar and dropping a 10th on the last beat. It is hardly possible that the listener can fail to be reminded of the leap and trill, the broken rhythm, and the winding run of the original Subject; though there is no reason to suppose that the ear, unaided by the eye, would ever detect that Beethoven is here turning his Subject backwards note by note. Still, it is a mistake to suppose that this *cancrizans* (*sc.* " crabwise ") treatment is a mere trick for the eye, used by Beethoven to complete his display of classical lore. On the contrary, it is unique among such specimens in that it does interest the ear, and that Beethoven takes special measures to show its relevance.   It is the older and later classical examples that are addressed only to the eye.   It amuses Mozart in the " Jupiter " Symphony to answer

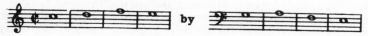

just as it amuses Brahms in his A minor Quartet to answer

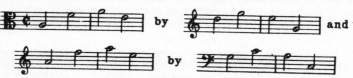

These devices depend on the clefs used ; and the listener knows no more of them than of the watermark on the paper.   The composers would never have indulged in them if better harmony and melody could have been produced without them.   Beethoven appealing to the ear, is not concerned with clefs, and is not exact at the cost of sense.   He would no more think of putting the turn before instead of after his trill than Samuel Butler would think of spelling his Utopia *Erehwon* instead of *Erewhon*.   But, though the cancrizans Subject is not the pedantic triviality which Bülow took it for, it is, as Bülow rightly urges, less important than the beautiful new cantabile which the Treble combines with it. Definite counterpoints thus established in the mid-course of a fugue, whether in present or destined combination with the Subject, deserve the title of Second or Third Subject, to distinguish them from the ordinary countersubjects of the Exposition.

This Second Subject has 2 figures, (k), (l) :

The last note of (l) becomes the 1st of (a) proceeding forwards. This is answered by the Middle, and then in D major by the Bass, thus calling attention to the relevance of the cancrizans Subject.

152–158.—Answer in D major, the cancrizans Subject in the Treble, and the Second Subject in the Bass.   The last bar is deflected back to B minor.   The Middle again answers the backwards trill forwards, while the Treble anticipates figure (l).

159–164.—Entry of cancrizans Subject in Bass (in B minor) with Second Subject in Middle.

165–185.—Episode arising from cancrizans (a) with echo (in

Middle) of (l). Swinging for 2 bars on tonic and dominant of **B** minor, this combination moves to D major, which key is deliberately established in 6 bars of cancrizans (b), rising for 4 bars, and inverted for 2 more, an echo in Middle filling out the bar. Now this filling out happens to produce the original rhythm of (b), and the inversion produces the very notes. On the tonic of D major figure (b) is developed forwards by inversion and backwards by simultaneous combination. The second 4 bars are in an opposite permutation, ending with a speeding-up across the beats and leading to 4 more bars, preparing emphatically for

Re-entry of Normal Subject : D major (III.).
186–190.—The Bass plunges into the Subject, forwards and direct, in Answer-position in D major. The upper parts are fused in an instrumentalized accompaniment, which only in the 5th bar recovers the style of the original Counter-subject, without the actual notes.
191–197.—Episode. Instead of repeating itself, figure (d) rises for 4 degrees, reaching G major. There the Middle takes it up, continuing the rise for 4 more steps, establishing that key.

Development of Inverted Subject : G major (VI.).
198–205.—Entry of Inverted Subject in Treble, in G major, accompanied by inversions of (e) in Bass and (b) in Middle. The 6th bar is not quite exact and drifts into a 2-bar preparation for the next entry.
206–212.—Inverted Answer, delayed by a beat, in Middle, with inverted (e) ornamented in Treble, and inverted (h) in Bass. The 5th is answered in the octave by the Treble, and leads in 1 more bar to
213–218.—Episode: a modulating falling sequence of twice 3 bars, Trills in the Treble, runs arising from (d) in Middle, suggestions of (f) in Bass; permuted in the second 3 bars, which lead down the dominants through C into
219–224.—Third entry of Inverted Subject in E♭ (IV.), on the beat, in the Bass. The counterpoints imitate (b). The 6th bar is diverted into a scale, leading to
225–239.—Episode: falling sequence in two 2-bar steps of dialogue on inverted (a), accompanied by rising scale, answered by rising sequence of direct (a), leading to 4 bars in which (a), direct and inverted, is diminished to quavers and hurled upwards towards dominant of D minor; whereupon, with a momentary burst into octaves and orchestral chords, there is a measured pause on dominant.
All this was the Fire. Now comes the Still, Small Voice.

Exposition and Development of a Short Third Subject (or *Attacco*)
    in D major (III.).

240-268.—The Treble announces a new Subject in D major,
which the Middle answers in the Subdominant at the 3rd bar, the
Bass entering in the tonic 2 bars later.

The whole Subject is as follows:

but the Middle and Bass carry it no further than the first 2 bars.
After the Bass has carried it thus far, 2 more bars lead to a 3-part
stretto of the whole subject at 1 bar in successive lower 5ths.
This merges into sequences on the first 3 notes. At bar 255 the
Bass leads with 2 rising steps. The Treble answers with 2 more.
Then the figure is passed from voice to voice in 3 single bars, till
the Bass, with the 2 bars of (m), leads to a full close in the
dominant. From this, 4 bars of rapid modulation (none the less
rapid for the *ritardando*) obliterate D major and return to the
home tonic.

Combination of First and Third Subjects in tonic; which key now
    remains, varied by merely local drifts, till the end of the
    movement, *i.e.*, for 121 bars, or nearly a third of the whole
    design.

269-284.—Three bars of First Subject in Middle, with Third
Subject in Treble. A supertonic bias leads to entry of Bass in C,
as dominant of dominant, with First Subject, while the Middle
has the Third Subject, which the Treble, after 2 bars, answers in
F. One more bar returns to the tonic and to figure (a) in Treble
as if to begin the First Subject. The Bass thunders out the Third
Subject and turns its 2nd bar into a rising sequence of 6 steps,
while the Treble, leaving the trill of (a) unresolved, brings (b) a
beat ahead of time, likewise leaving it in the air. The Middle
echoes (b) a beat behind time, and the Treble and Middle thus
proceed in cross-rhythm dialogue at various intervals till the Bass
joins in a general zigzag run, leading to

Stretto.

284-298.—Inverted Subject in dominant in Bass a beat behind
time, immediately answered by Direct tonal Answer in Middle
2 beats behind time (= 1 beat ahead of time). This Stretto is thus
the converse of that by Augmentation, in which the Direct
Subject led. The 5th bar is so turned as to lead to an answer to
this Stretto in the tonic at the same rhythmic phase, the Treble
leading and the Bass answering. The parts interchange in repeating figure (d), which drifts into

²⁹⁷/298–307.—Episode on the lines of bars 213–218, in three 3-bar groups: first rising, with the trills in Middle, then falling, with trills in Treble, then rising, with trills in Bass, and with a 4th bar leading to

Formal Peroration.

308–322.—Four bars on dominant pedal, consisting of 2+2 in sequence falling from (ii.), over dominant, to tonic ⁶₄. This is equivalent to a tonic-and-dominant swing such as befits a big coda of a sonata-form movement; and it does not lose that equivalence when it is repeated with complications and speeded up. Its material is an explicit quotation of the combination of (fg) over (d), as in the Subject and Countersubject. In the first 2 bars a " licence " is taken for an extra part, not for the purpose of supplying the all-important dominant pedal, but for the luxury of doubling the Middle in 6ths. The whole 4 bars are turned round, the bass leading with (fg), which the treble imitates before taking over (c) from the Middle. The drop from (ii). to tonic is then compressed into 2 bars, upon which a still quicker sequence rises across the rhythm in pairs of beats. The bass joins, imitated at one beat, soon reducing the sequence to single crotchets. We are, in short, in full stress of the dramatic tapering rhythms of a sonata movement.

323–328.—Sudden irruption of (a), up in Treble and down in Bass, on a diminished 7th in dominant. The Treble resolves the trill a note too high, from which it continues with (b), which, however, is checked. Meanwhile, the Middle is making a genuine entry of the whole Subject (in the position of Tonal Answer). The Treble drifts into the Countersubject, the Bass giving figure (h). (If the lower stave has rests, these do not refer to the Bass voice, but are merely to confirm the fact that the *R.H.* is to play the Bass notes.)

328–334.—The 5th bar, combining (d) with (f), is worked into a new rising sequence of 3 double steps (in double counterpoint). An extra bar descends in 3 crotchet-steps to

335–338.—Simultaneous combination of Direct Subject in Bass with Inversion in Treble, for 4 bars, with (f) in Middle; leading to

339–344.—Three short entries of (a+b) only, delayed by a beat: first on dominant in Middle, the Bass interposing on tonic at 2nd bar with (a) diminished; next in Treble in a distorted position (beginning on B♮), the Bass again interpolating (a) diminished; thirdly, in Bass in dominant, with the following energetic turn to (b) in rising sequence.—

etc.

This clinches the whole argument of the Fugue. Figure (b), thus enhanced, spreads out in all 3 voices, and in 4 bars from its inception debouches into

349–356.—Final Entry of Subject. The Treble gives the Subject as Tonal Answer in the tonic. Figure (a) reverberates in the other voices for 2 bars, after which they proceed with the Countersubject. The voices interchange at the repetition of (d); and on the last quaver of its 2nd bar the Fugue ends. Yes, ends ! One-and-two-and-three-and——

Coda.

357–358.—In the subdominant, after one silent beat, the frightened voices ask four almost simultaneous questions as to (a) inverted and direct. A trill on F♯ intends to resolve on G. But this becomes G♭. Notice that this is not an enharmonic *change*; it is a genuine enharmonic *interval*; the F♯ *goes to* G♭. The intended expression

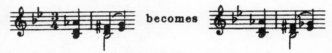

becomes

The trill, besides being thematic, removes any difficulty the ear might have in reconciling the implied subtle sense with the crude facts of the tempered scale.

359–370.—Inverted (a) crashes down in (iv.) to a thunderous E♭ trill, which supports a diminished 7th for 4 bars. Beethoven clings to the suggestion of 3 voices in his notation of the arpeggio above; and indeed 3 voices soon enter in whispers above the thunder.

The E♭ moves up to F, and a trill now mutters at a 4th above it. Over this, and as if about minor dominant 9th of subdominant, the Subject reappears with (f) below and (h) above. The subdominant colour yields to that of minor 9th in major tonic; and an 8-bar phrase is completed by the voices drifting into imitations of (f+g), welded into tapering sequence, *ritardando*. All these 8 bars are over the double pedal of tonic trill with dominant below.

371–374.—At last the Bass rises in 2 semitones, and in 4 bars of *poco adagio*. A dialogue of the trills, with resolutions, proceeds harmoniously to a pause on the dominant 7th.

374½, 375–378.—Debouching at its normal speed into a 4-bar group, figure (b) asks a question twice, implying dominant 9th with tinge of supertonic. It turns its 3rd query into a downward run, leading to

379–390.—Final sequence of (a) rising in cross-rhythm (each step taking 4 crotchets) by 2nds for 6 modulating steps. A 7th step, landing in (IV.), is forced up to (V.), which becomes cadential dominant, whereupon the melody, without trill, reaches the tonic plumb on the beat. This cadence is repeated a beat ahead, and the last chord held indefinitely. Even up to the 4 last chords, which are complete handfuls, the suggestion of 3 parts survives in Beethoven's not allowing the *L.H.* to play in octaves during the sequence. It is three voices, not two fists, that unite in that last ascent.

30

SONATA IN E MAJOR, Op. 109.

Vivace ma non troppo, alternating with ADAGIO ESPRESSIVO.
Two ideas in contrasted tempi, worked out in terse but free sonata form.

Fantastic as this first movement is, its form is not unprecedented. But the precedents have no such rhapsodic or mysterious character, and they are all on the opposite basis, beginning in the slow tempo, with their 2nd group in the quick tempo.

Domenico Scarlatti produced several movements of this kind; and Mozart's violin sonata in C major, (Köchel No. 303,) begins with a delightful example.

In three points Beethoven's form in the present movement is unprecedented. First, there is this reversal of the order of the two tempi. Already this fact implies that the purport of the movement is much graver than in the earlier cases. It is a light-hearted thing to break from a slow tempo to a lively one—unless, of course, the quicker music is loaded with tragic passion. But nothing short of a serious dramatic event can suddenly check the course of a quick movement and then proceed in a slow tempo, nor can the slow music be less than solemn in such a position.

But, in the second place, Beethoven has give the quick tempo only the minimum of time to assert itself at all. In it we hear just two 4-bar phrases of short bars. Only the 1st of these asserts the tonic; the 2nd modulates straight into the dominant. As to the rhythm, the word " bar " is not so meaningless here as we often find it in classical rhythms; the $\frac{2}{4}$ bars are here a genuine accentual frame for a uniform series of iambic feet; and we have 8 such feet without disturbance. This is certainly enough to establish a sense of tempo, if the player is not careless. In the same way, the tonality is clear; the tonic is unmistakable at the outset, and so is the deliberate modulation to the dominant. Here is no occasion for such devices as the avoidance of all accent on the tonic throughout two-thirds of the first movement of Op. 101.

But this uniform rhythm and this clear tonality are destined to receive a shock. The *Adagio cantabile* interrupts with a chord that casts a deep shadow on the dominant key that had been so quickly established. One bar of this *Adagio* takes considerably more time than 4 of the *Vivace*; and until we have heard at least

243

2 *adagio* bars we shall not know what the new pattern of rhythm is to be. Meanwhile this cloudy harmony takes the greater part of the huge new bar to show that it is impinging on the supertonic of our dominant key. The 2nd bar brings things into shape by imitating the 1st sequentially a step lower; and the 3rd bar rounds off the period by a cadence which closes into what is evidently going to be a repetition of the whole. This repetition begins quite clearly with the cloudy diminished 7th. But the cloud does not evaporate in time, and the supertonic drift does not show itself in that bar at all. On the contrary, a chromatic appoggiatura that adorned the melody in the 2nd bar now attracts attention and claims harmonic rights of its own; misleading the bass into supplying it with the root of the quite remote chord of which it is the major 3rd. This strange chord fills almost the whole 2nd bar; but at the end of the bar the major 3rd flattens and becomes, as if nothing had happened, part of the tonic chord; so that the cadential 3rd bar follows in due course and is greatly expanded, closing into a 4th bar on the tonic (*i.e.*, of the present key). Thus, although the supertonic has entirely disappeared, giving place to an utterly remote modulation, bars 12, 13, and 14 have preserved the form of the 3 which they purport to repeat—viz., 2 bars in falling sequence and a 3rd cadence-bar.

With the return of the *Vivace* the third unique feature of this movement becomes evident—viz., that the *Vivace* is entirely uniform both as to its iambic rhythm and its arpeggio texture. In the finale of Op. 54 Beethoven had already written such a movement; but it was not exposed to shocks, though it already showed that in Beethoven's view the texture of Bach's arpeggio preludes could be steadily maintained in a fully mature sonata style. The ordinary notion of sonata-development does not quite meet such a contingency: a figure cannot be said to develop when it has been present unchanged all the time. Keys, however, may cover fresh (if not more extensive) ground; and the omnipresent figure may group itself into larger or differently proportioned phrases. In the present case Beethoven expects that the player and listener will have taken the opening seriously enough to appreciate the fact that, whereas bars $\frac{1}{2}$/1-2 were in falling sequence, bars ^{15}/16-17 are in rising sequence. This is typically a case of normal development; but after this point a new melodic process begins. To connect this with the descending scale of the bass of bars 1-8 would be to put inaudible resemblances that may well be accidental on a level with things that must be understood if the music is to make sense at all. The organizing of harmonies and modulations on a rising or falling bass is important; but such a bass is not in itself a theme and is not to be emphasized as if it were. But here we have a theme; necessarily a new one, because there is no other way in which the uniform figure of this *Vivace* can develop except by building new melodic sequences. These lead, by no means hurriedly, to a quite emphatic insistence on the home dominant; which makes the eventual return to the opening bars ([48]/49 foll.) give the unmistakable effect of a recapitulation. And nothing could, in retrospect, more thoroughly confirm the importance of the opening than the way in which bars [4]/5-6, after moving to the dominant as at first, are repeated in the tonic. And so the *Adagio* is recapitulated in due course; it is expected and can no longer startle us. But the harmonic surprise of bar 13 would also no longer be a surprise, and Beethoven will not reproduce it as it was then. It is an accessory, not a fundamental idea. The duly placed repetition of a fundamental idea is welcome: the repetition of an accessory, that loses thereby the power to surprise, is weak. And so Beethoven has, at bar 61, a new harmonic surprise, of a dark instead of a bright colour. Its results are just as faithful to the scheme as was the former device; and, besides the new colour, there is the gain that certain rhythmic matters have needed slight compression in order to resolve the new chords in time.

In the whole sonata this purple patch is the only passage in a key outside immediate relations, except its parallel passage (the mere chord at bar 12), and a few chords of D♯ minor on the way from G♯ minor (vi.) to the home dominant during the development. Such concentration of the full strength of a limitless resource upon a single spot is characteristic of a late phase in an artist's development; a phase in which immense experience has produced an ability to take much for granted that used to need explicit working out. But there is nothing in common between this and the false simplifications of the bored decadent. Everything is here that the decadent artist would have left out, such as the dominant preparation for the return, which preparation Beethoven even took pains to prolong by repeating bars 42-43 in bars 44-45, which some early editions, overlooking his repeat-mark, omitted.

After the *Adagio* has been recapitulated the *Vivace* returns, forming a Coda which alludes to points in the development and ventures to drop the semiquaver rhythm for 11 bars, resuming it with 12 bars of a final tonic pedal.

This explanation puts us in a position to work out a tabular analysis, which would have puzzled the student if he had not been prepared for its use of ordinary terms for so extraordinary a movement.

First Group : E major. Vivace.
    Bars ½/1–4.—Four-bar melody: 1 + 1 in falling sequence on a

figure (a)

followed by 2 with a rising medial close, the bass of the whole being a descending scale.

5–8.—Continuation (2+2); the melody rising in 2-bar steps, still over the descending scale, and modulating into the dominant.

Second Group : B major (V.).   Adagio espressivo.

9–11.—Three-bar phrase in slow ¾ time, consisting of 2 sequential steps reaching (ii.) of B major from the diminished 7th above it, and a cadential 3rd bar closing into

12–15.—Repetition of the 3-bar phrase, representing the first 2 bars by arpeggios depending from the 1st note of the melody. Each arpeggio nearly fills its bar, and the 2nd arpeggio takes the appoggiatura of the melody seriously as a harmony note, to which it gives the remote colour of (III.) (reckoning from the present B major). The note thus transformed returns to B major by merely flattening itself, thus making one of Beethoven's typical natural (or functional) modulations. The cadential ⁶₄ now resolves only at some late and purposely indefinite point in the triplets of bar 14. Bar 15 is on the present tonic, and the running demisemiquavers are prolonged by 2 extra crotchetfuls of rising scale, faintly suggesting another overlapping dominant and leading to.

Development : Vivace.

¹⁵/16–17.—Figure (a) in bass in rising sequence moving from B major to its supertonic.

¹⁷/18–21.—Melody continued in bass in C♯ minor, with a new figure (x):

²¹/22–35.—Figure (x) taken up in treble in G♯ minor, following the first 4 bars by 4 steps of 2-bar sequence rising by 3rds, and delivered (as Beethoven shows by slurs extending over whole lines and by repeated directions of *sempre legato*) without any analytical breaks. The sequence passes through D♯ minor to F♯ major, which explains itself away as an enhanced dominant of the home dominant. A 4th step of the sequence alters its figure (bars 32-33) and is followed by a similar upward step which reaches the home dominant itself.

36–48.—Dominant preparation for return: thrice 2 bars (rising sequence over dominant bass), and thrice 2 bars of repetitions, with dominant fixed in treble.

Recapitulation.

First Group.
⁴⁸/49–54 =½/1–6 rescored, the beginning of the 2nd clause being in an inner part.
⁵⁴/55–57 = ⁴/5–8 transferred to tonic (*i.e.*, beginning on subdominant) and compressed from 4 bars to 3, closing into

Second Group : Adagio espressivo.
58–60 =9–11, with additional ornament in inner part of 2nd bar and compression of detail in 3rd bar in order to prepare for new turn of harmony.
61–65.—The previous diminished 7th resolves enharmonically on to dominant of (♭VI.), through which key the varied repetition of the 3 bars runs its course: bar 61 on the dominant chord, 62 on the tonic chord, with a compression of detail towards the end of the bar so as to resolve (on the same principle as that of bar 13) on to the home tonic, where the cadence-bar follows. The resolution of the $_4^6$ is now delayed to the last quaver of a 4th bar, which closes into a bar of tonic chord.

Coda : Vivace.
⁶⁶/67–70.—Figure (a) moving from subdominant to tonic and answered in dialogue with inner part. The descending scale in the bass now takes shape as a definite legato figure (y):

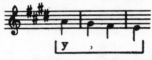

⁷⁰/71–78.—Dialogue continued with an inversion of (y) on tonic and dominant chords. This inversion, given a 3rd time, is broken short and repeated in syncopated crotchets (76-78), abandoning the semiquaver motion. A new turn of harmony leaves this tonic-and-dominant swing, and closes into
79–86.—Eight-bar cantabile reminiscent of (x), though Beethoven purposely puts it under one slur that begins before the resemblance appears. Moving from (vi.) through (ii.) back to the tonic, the phrase closes into
87–100.—Final tonic pedal, on which the semiquaver figures are resumed, coloured by minor subdominant, the minor 6th alternating with the major 6th over the tonic chord and the

rhythm tapering from 2-bar sequence to single bars. Bars 93-98 are on rising tonic chord with appoggiaturas; 99-100 contain the last chord as a syncopated note.

Beethoven's pedal mark shows that the next movement is to follow without break.

Prestissimo: E minor (i).   Sonata form.

First Group.   E minor.

1-8.—Eight-bar melody: 1+1+2 tonic to dominant, answered by similar phrase moving from subdominant to close in tonic. The bass is a counterpoint that becomes as important as the treble. The pair of themes contains 3 figures:

9-24.—New 8-bar melody (4 bars self-repeating) of tonic-and-dominant harmony on dominant bass, the rhythmic figures nearly the same as those of bars 1-4. The whole 8 bars are repeated with variation, the bass closing on to tonic in the middle of the last bar.

Transition.

25-32.—A new 4-bar theme, unharmonized in bass; answered in treble and clothed in 3-part harmony with new turn leading to dominant of (v.).

Second Group in Dominant minor.

(This is most conveniently dated from the moment where the new key is established, as Beethoven is not here concerned to differentiate the themes widely, while such contrast as there is becomes quite clear in the recapitulation.)

33-42.—Four-bar phrase on dominant of (v.), modelled on bars 9-12; closing into self-repetition, which takes an upward turn, expanding in 2 extra bars, and leading to

43-50.—New sequence, descending in three 2-bar steps from enhanced dominant of (v.), by tones, the bass gliding chromatically till it reaches the dominant of C (♭II.), from the present B minor.

51-56.—Neapolitan cadential phrase of thrice 2 bars; *i.e.*, 2 bars in C major, repeated, and repeated again with a turn into B minor.   The melodic figure

has a rhythmic member (d) which gives rise to the following

57–65.—Cadence-theme: a 4-bar phrase in bass, with expansion of figure (d), joined to new figure (e),

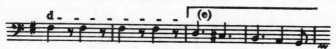

with counterpoint in treble; leading to repetition with inversion in double counterpoint; leading to final close by means of (d) in an extra bar, which closes into

Development.

66–69.—First theme, (a) over (c), compressed into a 4-bar phrase, closing into

70–82.—Figure (c) in sequences of 2-part canon in upper 4th at 2 bars, drifting downwards over a pedal. This pedal is at first the tonic of B minor; but after 6 bars it becomes the home dominant, from which, after another 3 bars, it moves up to C. At this point the sequence in the upper voice is broken. Beethoven's slurs are not beyond dispute here: but they tend to disprove the suggestion that if he had not scrupled to stretch 10ths and use pedal, he would have written a clear third answer to figure (c) by the upper part at bar 80, thus:

This suggestion should be considered, for it at first seems to throw light on an undoubtedly difficult passage. But it over-simplifies the rhythm; and the meaning of the passage lies elsewhere. It is the step of the bass up to C that breaks the 4-bar rhythm; and bars 81-82 are an echo of 79-80 in a higher position. At all events we have 13 bars from 70 to the following new paragraph; and we have no reason to look for regularity in the phrasing of the last 6 bars.

83–104.—Starting in C and passing through A minor to a position hovering between the home tonic and the dominant of (v.), figure (c) proceeds to develop by inversion in the bass; answered by the tenor in the upper 5th after 2 bars (bar 85). A third voice answers the tenor on dominant of A minor. (Here an extra part takes over the bass.) Then, in a new position in A minor, figure (c) is given direct in the treble simultaneously with its inversion in the bass. This is followed by a compromise (also in contrary motion) between the two forms of (c); bars 93-96. This compromise lies in the home tonic, but lands on a dominant of (v.), upon which there is a pause. Is this chord chromatic ? We certainly do not expect its key, which was that of the Second Group, from which it was the purpose of the Development to get away. In bars 97-100 the question is put again, with the voices interchanged. Bars 101-102 reiterate the point; and the next 2 bars, still in a dramatic *pianissimo*, explicitly mention the forbidden topic, the $^6_4$-$^5_3$ of B minor. And this brings down the catastrophe.

Recapitulation.
First Group.

105-111 = 1-7.—Angrily ignoring the previous mention of B minor, the home tonic crashes in with the main theme, which closes, with overlap, into

112-119.—Inversion of bars 1-8 in double counterpoint, the 8th bar closing sequentially into

Transition.

120-131.—Transition-theme, at first harmonized in C major (VI.), then given unharmonized in bass; answered thrice at intervals of 2 bars by a succession of upper voices while bass descends in conjunct steps towards home dominant.

Second Group in Tonic.

132-166/[167]/ = 33-65/[66]/ in tonic, with the following differences· In the first place, as bars 9-24 have been omitted from the recapitulation of the First Group, the whole Second Group now stands out in clearer relief. Secondly, 2 bars (138-139) have been added between those corresponding to 38 and 39, with the result that the 4-bar phrase completes its self-repetition before rising. This is no inadvertence, but a calculated compensation, which might not have occurred if bars 9-24 had been represented at all. Thirdly, there are new high notes in the descending sequence 144-152. These amply account for the small discrepancy at bar 148, which some editors would like to bring into conformity with bar 46.

Bar 167 closes the Recapitulation.

Coda.
168–177.—Figure (d) echoed in á 2-bar cadence; followed by 8 bars in which the whole cadence-theme (d - - - +e), led by the bass and imitated by a gathering crowd of upper parts (without the quaver counterpoint), finishes the movement in a single phrase ending in its 8th bar.

Andante molto cantabile ed espressivo.   Binary melody with 6 variations.
Already in the playful little slow movement of Op. 14, No. 2, Beethoven had devised a theme which deliberately closed on the dominant 5 times in ways as little different as it was possible to keep distinct at all. The point of this subtle and dangerous game lies, of course, in the fact that the theme is meant for variations, and that these, if they are genuine variations, will make its subtleties clear by emphasis and repetition. Therefore the subtleties must not be weaknesses. This particular game of the delicately graded cadences fascinated Beethoven to the end of his life; and each time he played it his theme became more subtle and less of a joke. The theme of the variations in the A major Quartet, Op. 18, No. 5, is as witty as that in Op. 14, No. 2, but it aims primarily and successfully at being beautiful. The theme of the variations in the well-named Sonata Appassionata achieves the extreme *tour de force* of consisting entirely of tonic cadences; but that very fact is an element in its profound solemnity. There are heights and depths beyond that solemnity; and these are attained in melodies externally more normal and with greater liberty to move, in spite of their being built upon subtle. cadences. Such are the present theme, the Arietta in Op. 111, the themes of the slow movements of the Quartets Op. 127, 132 (the Lydian chorale), Op. 135 (the last quartet), and the Ninth Symphony. One direct result of the subtlety of these themes is that many people have no idea how strict the variations are. The slow movement of the last quartet has been seriously discussed as a curious bundle of detached episodes, though it sticks to its theme more closely than would have suited Mozart's convenience. The student and listener must not take a mistaken view of what a set of variations is supposed to convey to the ear. If the variations are mere embroidery, then we may be expected to trace the melody in them. But if the principle of the variation lies deeper, we are intended to appreciate the depths in the same way as we appreciate other depths: we attend to what reaches our senses, and we allow the sum of our experience to tell us more in its own good time. A painter shows his knowledge of anatomy by the skin-deep merits

of his work. His surface is so true that he must have produced it from a knowledge that penetrates beneath the surface. Accordingly, in the analysis, as in the performance of variations, we have no authority to prefer those points in which the variation resembles the theme to those points in which it differs from them. The naturalist knows that the bird of paradise is a crow, but he does not mistake either for the other.

Theme: Binary melody.

1–8.—First strain, (2+2+4): 2 bars tonic to dominant chord closing into self-repetition, with close into dominant key, swinging back to enhanced repetition, broadening into a close on to dominant *via* augmented 6th. Repeat.

The bass throughout the theme is in fluent note-against-note counterpoint with the melody.

9–16.—Second Strain: (1+1+2), sequential process through (ii.) and tonic to close in (iii.). This, falling on last beat of bar, passes on to (ii.), from which arises a 4-bar tonic full close. Repeat.

Variation 1: Melody mostly new; and bass simplified, moving at first only once a bar. The later part of the 2nd strain approaches more nearly to the melody of the theme.

Variation 2: A double variation on two contrasted ideas; in fact, two different variations dovetailed by means of the repeats.

33–40.—In the first case both melody and bass of the theme are clearly represented in the arpeggio formula.

41–48.—The repeat is represented by the second idea, in which 2 upper voices imitate (at the upper 2nd) a figure in rising sequence suggested by the first 2 notes of the theme, while the bass remains fixed on the dominant. After 4 bars this new idea is itself varied, the imitative two-part texture being lost. The bass moves up to C♮ for the augmented 6th. The whole 8 bars correspond to 1–8, though the actual dominant key of bar 4 is replaced by a home-dominant 9th.

49–56.—Second strain according to the first idea of this variation, and therefore easily recognizable as to melody, but not strict as to bass.

57–64.—Second strain according to the second idea, the original supertonic harmony surprisingly approached from its dominant 9th and spread over a larger area, crowding the assertion of (iii.) into the 4th bar; the bass controlling the harmony by conjunct descent as soon as it has to move at all. In the remaining 4 bars the melody is again recognizable.

Variation 3: Allegro vivace. A double variation by development, the repeats being variations of the variation.

65–72.—Melody traceable in semiquaver-figure of first 4 bars. The dominant cadence is clear in the 4th bar. The next 4 bars invert these 4 in double counterpoint; and a G♮ at the 8th bar gives an adumbration of the augmented 6th. Thus the whole corresponds bar by bar to bars 1-8, though at first it looks like a 4-bar phrase repeated.

73–80.—New version of the previous 8 bars; the augmented 6th in the 8th bar is now quite clear.

81–88.—Double counterpoint of the same kind as that of 73-80, the melody being clearly presented by the quaver-theme, 4 bars of which are in the treble, answered by 4 in the bass.

89–96 = 81–88 inverted in double counterpoint. The variation rushes into the next without break.

Variation 4: (A little slower than the theme.)

Single variation (with repeats) developing a pair of figures (x) and (y) in free imitative polyphony:

The distinction between the dominant chord of bar 2 and the dominant key of bar 4 is lost, but the augmented 6th of bar 8 is clear.

105–112.—In the first 4 bars of the 2nd strain the polyphony is dropped, except for the upper part on the 2nd beat of 105 and 106. The harmonies move more slowly than in the theme, but in the same sequence. In the last 4 bars the polyphony, with figure (x), is resumed, and a resemblance to the melody emerges.

Variation 5: Allegro ma non troppo. Double variation by development.

113–120.—Figure obtained from bars 1-2 of melody

imitated in upper 2nd at 1 bar by overlapping voice, with a sequentially rising bass. After 4 bars the figure enters the bass regions. As in Variation 2 at bar 44, the imitating voices cannot reproduce the dominant at the 4th bar, but the augmented 6th at the cadence is enhanced by strong accessories.

121-128.—Repetition, with a new quaver counterpoint, first below, then above; worked out in sequence rising with new harmonic colours, reaching the augmented 6th through (iv.) and (bIII.).

129-136.—The quaver counterpoint and the main figure represent, with some freedom, the general lines of the 2nd strain; the entries being distributed through widely separated octaves. As usual, the melody of the last 4 bars is clearly recognizable. (See especially the deep bass of 135-136.)

137-144.—Repeat, with the main figure in a tangle of upper parts and a rugged new quaver counterpoint in bass. An unexpected passing chord at the end of the last bar leads to

145-152.—Extra repeat, reproducing 137-144 *sempre piano*, and leading to

Variation 6: Double variation by continuous development.

Yet another kind of double variation, first found here and afterwards carried out on a larger scale in the slow movement of the C♯ minor Quartet. There is neither the alternation of two ideas nor the varied repetition of one; but the variation steadily increases its resources as it pursues its course, until the end of it has no resemblance to the beginning.

There was already a suggestion of this possibility in the second idea of Variation 2. There we found that the second idea itself produced a new idea after 4 bars. What happens here is that the radio-active break-up appears after every 2 bars.

153-160.—The original melody, in the original tempo, is heard below a dominant and above a bass in contrary motion. The dominant is at first in repeated crotchets; then, after 2 bars, in quavers; then, with an inflection, in triplets ($\frac{3}{}$) while the melody rises above. The triplets become sextole semiquavers, and, as the theme swings back to repeat itself, these become demisemiquavers.

160/161-168.—The melody, varied in quavers, returns to its position below the dominant demisemiquavers. After 4 bars these become a trill, and the melody, rising above them, is varied in triplet quavers.

169-176.—The 2nd strain is varied in demisemiquaver arpeggios over a dominant trill in the bass. The outline of the melody gradually becomes recognizable.

176-187.—On repetition the melody is given in syncopated quavers above a dominant trill, with a demisemiquaver counterpoint of wide compass in the bass. The suspension in the 8th bar does not resolve at once, but the syncopated quavers descend the dominant-over-tonic chord for 3 extra bars, which bring them into position to close into the opening theme. (Therein lies the beauty of the well-attested reading according to which bar 187 is *not* completed by the expected F$\sharp$, D$\sharp$, but the isolated A shares with the trill the honour of closing into the melody.)

188–203.—Da Capo of the original theme, which concludes the sonata. Thus the 3 bars 185-187 and the extra repetition of the 2nd strain in Variation 5 are the only points in this movement which are not comprised within eight exact lengths of a symmetrical binary melody with repeats.

31

SONATA IN A FLAT MAJOR, Op. 110.

Moderato cantabile molto espressivo: A♭ major.　Sonata form.

First Group.
　　Bars 1–4.—Four-bar theme (A) rising sequentially from tonic by varied steps, to pause on dominant, closing into next phrase. The first 2 bars comprise a figure (a)

　　5–11.—New 8-bar theme (B) (2+2+4), beginning with tonic-and-dominant symmetry and passing through (IV.) to close with overlap into

Transition.
　　12–19.—New theme (C) of demisemiquaver arpeggios, beginning with 2+2 of tonic and dominant closing into 3, with the 2nd of which the bass moves downwards by 8 accelerating steps from F to G, against rising treble, with modulation to (V.). (Already in bars 17-18 the semitone D♭-C is entirely subdominant in effect.)

Second Group in Dominant (V.).
　　20–27.—The previous passage resolves into a new theme (D), which initiates a broad 8-bar paragraph, beginning with 2 bars in sequence falling from subdominant to position over tonic, and leading to self·repetition with appoggiatura ornaments (d).
　　At the end of 2nd step the appoggiatura (d) expands into a new figure by reduplication, thus

which the bass proceeds to carry downwards, breaking into trills which, in contrary motion with rising treble, complete the 8-bar sentence with a close into
　　28–33.—New phrase, insistently upon tonic, the bass thrice delivering a figure descending from E♭ to G, while the treble rises in 3 interlocking steep sequential steps. These 3 bars close

on to subdominant, upon which an answering 3, with contrasted figures, come to full tonic close into next paragraph. The insistent bass G having resolved on the subdominant, the bass of these cadential bars is a rise up the scale (with interpolated semitone, A♮) to the dominant in the next octave. [The rhythm ♪♫♪♪|♪ is not intended to allude to theme (A).]

34–39.—Cadence-theme (E): a new 1-bar figure on tonic, closing into self-repetition; upon which an inner part, raised to the treble, rises in a figure (e)

and ascends for 2 bars of tonic chord. In the next bars, the top being reached, the harmony expires, and the bare octave descends to a flat 7th impinging on dominant of F minor.

Development.

40–55.—Sequence on figure (a) descending in 4 compound 4-bar steps, or 8 single 2-bar steps. Each 4-bar step is different, only the 2nd and 3rd being of the same general shape in contrasted modes and with altered counterpoints. The total effect is that of a straight sequence. The first 4 bars are in F minor on dominant bass with the homophonic accompaniment of theme (B). The rest is on a bass of flowing counterpoint, distributed bar by bar in different octaves as if in 2-part dialogue. The 2nd 4-bar step leads to D♭; the 3rd leads to B♭ minor; and the 4th closes into the home tonic. There is no need to seek a derivation for the figures in the bass. Only 3 separated bars have the same figure, and nothing is allowed to interfere with the unity of the wonderful melodic line which bridges the whole Development. Like the lines of the Parthenon, this sequence seems *wonderfully* straight just because it is not *mechanically* straight. We have not reached the end of it yet.

Recapitulation.

First Group.

56–59.—As if continuing the sequence, theme (A) enters in home tonic, while the bass breaks into the arpeggios of theme (C). The 4th bar proceeds without pause to

60–62.—The rising sequence of (A) carried upwards in 3rds by lower voices for 3 bars, moving to key of (IV.), while the *R.H.* turns the demisemiquaver figure into a tremolo and a downward coloratura, closing into

63–69.—Theme (B) in subdominant. After the 4th bar the chord of D♭ becomes minor; the melody hesitates and falls to dominant of F♭ (♭VI.), closing into that key in 2 more bars. (There is no enharmonic change. Beethoven merely prefers the 4 sharps of E major to the scale of F♭ with its B♭♭♭.)

Transition : F♭ major (♭VI.).

70–75.—Theme (C) in key of ♭VI. After the first 4 bars another 2 bars move through local subdominant to

76–78.—Entry of Theme (D) as if to recapitulate the Second Group in (♭VI.). But the end of the 2nd bar glides down to home dominant, from which an extra bar rises to

Recapitulation of Second Group in Tonic.

79–96 = 20–37 in tonic.

An additional ornamentation in bars 81-82 (= 22-23) has obliterated the " logical " derivation of the following bars. This does not matter, nor would Beethoven have thought the " logic " necessary in the first instance. His sketches often show a " logical " connexion which the finished version deliberately destroys.

Coda.

97–100.—The upward rise of figure (e) on the tonic chord does not reach the octave, but merges into twice 2 bars *in* the dominant. This is one of the boldest subtleties in all music. Beethoven has always been heroically ready to revisit a key that has already served its turn; but here he is using, in no merely decorative sense, the dominant, which was the key of his Second Group in a movement that had only one purple patch of (♭VI.) outside the immediate circle of direct relation. But just because that purple patch stood alone, the humble dominant can now shine like nothing else in music.

101–104.—The semiquaver figure had come to a halt in the previous bar, while the bass stepped down to D♭. This leads to 4 bars returning *via* (vi.) to tonic. These bars are in halting chords, avoiding the 1st beat. This avoidance maintains the sense of movement. It is at least probable that Beethoven at first conceived the whole 8 bars (from bar 97) in terms of figure (e), but, finding that 4 bars exhausted its power, stopped it when this wonderful dominant had made its point. The 4 bars of halting chords, having made theirs, close into

105–110.—Theme (C): 4 bars, +2 rising through subdominant and tonic 6th to

111–116.—Two-bar phrase in (IV.)+(ii.) impinging on tonic;

figure (a) appearing in inner parts as answer to the independent melody of the treble; closing into self-repetition, in which the 2nd bar is a mixture of plagal and dominant cadence over tonic pedal; closing, without alluding to (a), into final chords.

Allegro molto: F minor (vi.) Scherzo, with Trio in ♭VI.

Beethoven refuses to tell us if this Scherzo is in the rhythm of a Gavotte, thus—

The displaced double bar in the second part does not help us; for it is necessitated by the tied note at the joint of the repeat, and so cannot be treated as evidence like the displaced double bars in the Scherzo of Op. 27, No. 1.   At the end of the movement the Coda may support the Gavotte view; for the crotchet chord (bar 143ᵇ) would hardly have been filled out (instead of the bare octave of its previous occasions) unless it were to start a fresh sentence; and if the minim chords are not on " off " bars, there is no sense in the omission of a silent bar between the penultimate chord and the final 4-bar tonic chord. On the other hand, this is all quite compatible with the Coda starting (at the crotchet chord) on an overlap.   On the Gavotte view all the cadenzas of the Scherzo become strong, and the strain 27-32 becomes more graceful. Moreover, the ear is helped to take the Coda in that sense by the rests in the bass, which project the harmony into the next bars, an exact parallel to the shift of rhythm at bars 9-16 in the first movement of Op. 10, No. 1. But on the other hand, there is nothing to induce the ear to regard the whole movement as beginning off the beat; and the *forte* at the 5th bar would need a *sforzando* at the 6th as well as the one supplied at the 8th if the ear is to decide upon Gavotte rhythm in the 1st strain.   And whatever view we take, there will be an odd bar somewhere in the Trio.

And so in this movement we encounter, for the last time in Beethoven's Pianoforte Sonatas, but not for the last time in his works, a demonstration of his view of the meaning of short bars. He knew Bach's Gavottes, and could easily have used the proper notation if he had meant Gavotte rhythm. Why, then, not suppose that the elements of musical notation have been correctly applied by him; and that his short bars mean accents too frequent and too equal to tell us in what phase the larger groups stand as reckoned from the beginning?

This view, maintained throughout all these analyses, is no

abstruse theory. It is an account of what reaches the only kind of listener to whom Beethoven has anything to say;—the listener who believes his ears, waits for the end and accepts in due course the light which antecedents and sequels throw upon each other. It seems abstruse only because it has to contend with an abstruse modern prejudice. A modern cosmologist has finely observed that when Nature seems to conspire against the discovery of some expected principle, that conspiracy is in itself the obverse of a natural law. Thus the seeker for perpetual motion encounters the conspiracy known as the conservation of energy; and thus all attempts to measure the earth's absolute drift through the ether showed a systematic failure which gave an important line of approach to the theory of Relativity. And thus we may rest content with Beethoven's final refusal to tell us where the main accent would have come if the bars of this movement had been twice as long and there had been only half the number of accents. We do not need any external evidence, or we might unscrupulously make a case from a folk-song which Beethoven sent to his publisher at about the time when he would be planning Op. 110. The song begins undoubtedly on the main beat, thus

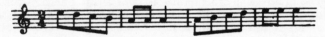

The hypnotic effect of that sacred term " folk-song " has induced some commentators to argue that we have here the origin of this Scherzo. The real importance of this folk-song to Beethoven is revealed in the covering letter (in the possession of Mr. Edward Speyer), which is a request for something involving some two-pence-ha'p'orth of postage. To defray this expenditure, Beethoven presents his publisher with all rights in two brand-new *Volkslieder-bearbeitungen*. These *Bearbeitungen* consist of the most ridiculous possible accompaniments expressed almost entirely by abbreviations; and their whole point is that they give the publisher exactly his money's worth.

The rhythmic ambiguity once accepted as an æsthetic value, the whole movement proves drastically simple.

Scherzo : F minor.

1-8.—First strain: 4 bars moving from tonic to half-close on dominant, answered by 4 *in* major dominant, as far as a major dominant can be more to a minor tonic than its dominant chord.

9-16.—Second strain: 8 bars of new material (2+2+4), modulating to (♭III.).

17-32.—8 bars (2+2+4) of another figure starting in (♭III.),

and moving at last crotchet back to tonic; closing into a similar
8 bars in tonic, moving to half-close on dominant. (In these 16
bars the ear readily suspects a change of phase. This is more
natural as well as more interesting than attempting to hear
Gavotte rhythm from the beginning.)

33–40.—Close in tonic: an 8-bar phrase with a *ritardando*,
which adds emphasis to the sour triad on (ii.) produced by the
rising melodic 6th (D♮); a sudden return to full tempo at 4th bar,
followed by silence in the next 2 bars (an integral part of the
rhythm), and ended with a full close and an immediate plunge
(with syncopation) back to repeat from bar 9. Reckoning on the
Gavotte view favoured by bars 17–32, the *ritardando* begins in
anacrusis, and the 2 silent bars lie across the joint of two 4-bar
groups.

Trio : D♭ major (♭VI.).

⁴⁰/41–72.—Arising from the end of the Scherzo, an 8-bar phrase
trickles down the main chords of D♭, 4 of tonic, 3 of dominant,
with close into tonic; the treble having a quaver sequence of 2-bar
limbs, each containing a 3-quaver sequence in cross-rhythm, and
the bass in hovering crotchets off the beat crossing over the treble
in the last 3 bars. In the *R.H.* the 1st note of the Trio follows the
last of the Scherzo in an upward leap, which is systematically
echoed by the bass at the joint of every 8-bar group, thus

This makes it more difficult than ever to settle the rhythmic
phase. The Gavotte view would make the Trio begin at bar 40;
and this is supported by the explosive accents every 8 bars with
these recurring pairs of figure (a). On the other hand, the new
material undoubtedly begins where Beethoven naturally puts his
D♭ key-signature—viz., at bar 41. Four 8-bar groups are given:
the one already described defining D♭; the second beginning by
repeating it, but moving with the second 4 bars into the subdominant G♭; the third recapitulating the 1st group in this
subdominant and the fourth modulating in its second 4 bars to
E♭ minor.

72–75.—The last possibility of holding to one interpretation
of the rhythm is destroyed by an odd 3 bars which, beginning as
though to continue the series in (ii.), break off into 2 of (a),
returning to D♭ and giving rise to

76–95.—The first 8 bars (41-48) closing into *piano* repetition an octave lower. The last left-hand crotchet is delayed. The treble figure (as a bar of 4 quavers) dies away in dialogue over the tonic and drifts, with a pause on its last note, into

Da Capo of Scherzo.

96–144^a/ = 1–41^a.—The repeat of the 1st strain is w.·itten out in order to enhance first 4 bars by a *ritardando*. Beethoven demands that the second part shall be repeated also. The repeat closes into a full final chord, followed by

Coda.

143^b/144–158.—Seven chords form a final cadence ending with major tonic (Tierce de Picardie). Until the last 2, the chords are each of 1 bar, separated from the next by a bar's rest. Beethoven puts the word " Coda " over bar 144; so that the eye, at all events, cannot date the Coda from the last bar of the Da Capo. For the eye, then, the Gavotte view has now been destroyed. But the ear will be more inclined to take the Coda as syncopated, especially when the dominant chord closes without pause into the final tonic.

The truth is that there is no real difficulty in enjoying the ambiguity as the acme of refinement in this apparently so drastically simple end.

Adagio ma non troppo: Modulating Introduction, with Recitative.

Introduction.

1–3.—Following the unexpected Tierce de Picardie of the Scherzo as if it had been a dominant, a melody begins in B♭ minor. For 2½ slow beats it defines that key over a tonic bass, then immediately moves, through its subdominant, to the key a semitone higher (C♭), and thence to the dominant of A♭ minor (the home tonic of the Sonata). Thus it is only for a moment that there seemed any intention of a slow movement in the supertonic of the whole work. These 3 bars are addressed solely to the end of the Scherzo in retrospect, and, in prospect, to the Finale, the key of which they have established in 3 apparently hesitating but really decisive steps.

Recitative.

4–6.—An arpeggio on the dominant 7th of A♭ minor proves to be the beginning of an unbarred Recitative. One phrase of this closes in A♭ minor, arising from which 4 chords of accompaniment move to dominant of F♭ (♭VI.); on which a second phrase, dwelling long upon the 7th of that key (written as E major) returns to tonic minor key, giving therein the usual form of recitative cadence.

It is instructive to note how enormously these two single clauses of recitative have bulked in the imagination of critics and composers. In musical histories they are the sermon-text of whole chapters on External Influences in the Disruption of Sonata Form. In the works of Mendelssohn's boyhood—the Sonata, Op. 6, and the A minor Quartet, Op. 13—they expand to pages and pages, in company with resurrections of previous movements on the instigation of 7 bars in Beethoven's Op. 101.

The total bulk of recitative in all Beethoven's sonata works would not overcrowd the slow movement of Haydn's G major Quartet, Op. 17, No. 5, a by no means immature work that was probably considered more old-fashioned in 1820 than it is now. It is not the only recitative movement in Haydn; and there is any amount of recitative in the sonatas of C. P. E. Bach, who was to Beethoven as much a classic as the Carracci were to Sir Joshua Reynolds. The total amount of recitative in Beethoven's sonata works is as follows: two clauses in the D minor Sonata, Op. 31, No. 2; the two clauses here; one clause (not on a vocal formula) in the C♯ minor Quartet, Op. 131; 2½ in the A minor Quartet, Op. 132; and five in the Ninth Symphony, two of which are eventually set to words, as all five were at first intended to be. In the Ninth Symphony the recitatives have two functions, first to prepare for the entry of human voices, and secondly to dramatize a review of the themes of previous movements. The 2nd topic, introduced by the Sonata, Op. 101, and the Violoncello Sonata, Op. 102, No. 1, has been discussed in its place.

A well-informed orthodoxy as to sonata style should rest on the following principles:

(a) The sonata is an essentially dramatic art-form, combining the emotional range and vivid presentation of a full-sized stage drama with the terseness of a short story.

(b) As the sonata forms accomplish their designs more quickly than they can satisfy their emotional issues, they retain the division into separate pieces inherited from the earlier suite forms which are their decorative prototypes.

(c) It was in the theatre that the sonata style differentiated itself from decorative music. Hence, as Spohr found when he wrote a Violin Concerto in the form of an operatic scena, an orthodoxy that regards the state as subversive of Absolute Music is liable to feel the distress of the hen whose supposititious clutch of ducklings takes to the water.

From (b) we may see, as has been already argued, that the risk in making sonata movements allude to each other's themes is that they may lose their own momentum and achieve only a flaccid and superficial unity instead of a deep and instinctive common impulse.

From (c) we may conclude that the risk of using stage-formulas in the sonata is exactly what it is in the short story. Staginess is hardly a fair term of abuse to apply to the stage itself. It is properly applied to things seen in daylight that were designed exclusively to be seen with footlights and the other apparatus of the lighting technician. But drama itself aims at convincing by truth to life. Staginess in speech means the use in real life of formulas appropriate to highly dramatic situations manifestly not present. The formulas are intrinsically sublime, but their abuse has made them unavailable even when they would be appropriate. Yet it is the mark of a great poet that he can use them without fear and without apology. He will not stop to explain or develop them, nor will he introduce them as quotations. They will come in their own right with no glamour of footlights, and their plain meaning will overawe.

Arioso dolente, A♮ minor (i.), alternating with **Fuga,** A♭ major (I.).

The Finale of this Sonata is best regarded as a single structure, beginning at this point. If the Fugue is taken as the starting-point of the design, and the recurrence of the Arioso regarded as an interruption, we shall set up a prejudice that will worry us when the second part of the Fugue crowds its events into less time than the first part. No such prejudice will worry the naïve listener, who cannot fail to see that the recitative leads to the Arioso, and that the Arioso has not the slightest suggestion of introductoriness in itself. Its recurrence in the middle of the Fugue is a recapitulation, not an allusion; and Bach does not end his F major organ toccata more punctually than Beethoven ends his Op. 110.

1–2.—After the vocal closing formula of the recitative, Beethoven, instead of the conventional cadence-chords, builds the tonic triad from the 5th downwards in repeated notes that define ¹²₈ time and become the form of accompaniment for the

3–20.—*Arioso dolente :* a continuous 16-bar melody, answering close in (III.) at 8th bar by tonic close at end. The bars are in pairs, with various degrees of interlock; otherwise the symmetry of the whole lies in balance of key, while the melody achieves its unity by avoiding symmetry altogether; using different figures as it proceeds, and reproducing its 1st bar quasi-accidentally towards the end of the 3rd quatrain, just where it cannot have a recapitulatory effect. The melodic rhythms are for the most part broken by syncopation, with some passages in long sustained notes.

Each 4-bar group asserts its key-centre straightforwardly: first, tonic, with half-close; secondly, (III.), with full close: thirdly, (iv.), with return to home dominant; finally, tonic, with full close.

¹⁸/19-20.—Two unison bars ($\frac{1}{2}$; $\frac{1}{4}$, , and final pause) form a codetta. It is important to realize the dimensions of this Arioso in relation to the whole. The semiquavers may reasonably be supposed not less than twice as slow as the quavers of the Fugue. (An exact ratio should be avoided.) This makes the length of the Arioso at least equal to either section of the Fugue. The mind, of course, moves at the pace of the music: we know all the time that the Arioso is taking us only round the four sides of a square melody, and that when the Fugue is in progress we are travelling fast and far. But the clock-time has its effect, all the more because Beethoven keeps the two *tempi* separate and does not anticipate the device of Berlioz's *Réunion des deux Thèmes* in Capulet's Feast.

Fuga, for Three Voices.
²⁰/21-24.—Fugue subject announced by Bass

and containing 2 figures, (a) and (b). (The sequence of rising 4ths and falling 3rds has a resemblance to the first movement of the Sonata; and, though in itself this would not be beyond the range of accident, it is too like the proved subtleties of Op. 106 to be ignored. The resemblance of the 1st bar of the Arioso to the 1st figure of the Scherzo is less likely to have a special meaning; if we stake our faith on that, we may as well go further and find cryptographic evidence that Beethoven's later works were written by Spohr.)

²⁴/25-30.—A Middle voice gives a Real Answer in the dominant. (According to the rules of Tonal Fugue a real, *i.e.* exact, answer, is the only kind possible with the present subject.) The Bass continues with a modulating counterpoint which, though not reproduced at the next entry, earns the name of Counter-subject by its important use later. It contains a figure (c)—

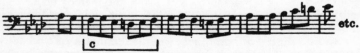

(To connect this with the first phrase of the Arioso would be to lose all sense of meaning.) Two extra bars, taking (b) in a downward sequence, lead through (IV.) to

³⁰/31-39.—Entry of Treble with Subject. The counterpoint is altered, and opportunity taken for some good suspensions. Figure (b) now descends in two 2-bar steps through (ii.), leading to three ½-bar steps closing into dominant.

³⁹/40-47.—Subject on dominant in Bass, with 2 bars of the Countersubject in Treble, crossing below Middle and inverted in double counterpoint at the 12th. This Counter-subject takes remarkable advantage of the fact that it is largely a decoration of the Subject in 3rds. Inversion of bars 24-26 in the octave would, of course, have produced 6ths. It would also have reproduced the modulations of those bars; whereas the present 3rds very firmly assert the home tonic. Figure (b) again descends a step, and an offshoot of the counterpoint, in 3rds (10ths) between Trelbe and Bass, descends for 2 more bars towards (IV.).

⁴⁷/48-56.—Subject in tonic in Middle, with Countersubject in original position in Bass doubled, as to the main 2 bars, in 6ths (13ths) in Treble. (This, whether Beethoven noticed the fact or not, is double counterpoint in the 13th, and is perhaps a more frequent by-product of counterpoint in 3rds than we generally realize.) The last 3 notes of (b) are carried down in four 1-bar steps of sequence in (iv.); and the Bass, which has joined in 6ths below (with semitones at the joints), carries the sequence a step further, reaching the home dominant in time for

⁵⁶/57-66.—Subject in Treble on dominant, with the Countersubject in Bass doubled by Middle (as to the important 2 bars) in 3rds (plus 2 octaves). This position is a still more curious by-product of added 3rds. It is not an " inversion " of the original position, for the Countersubject remains below the Subject. And if you compare it with the other positions (39-42 and 47-50), you can call it inversion in the 7th and 9th. Beethoven's calculations were not on these lines; for him this kind of omnibus double counterpoint is essentially a decoration of his Subject doubled in chords of the 6th,

 etc.,

and set at various angles in regard to its key. Figure (b) now rises instead of falling. Two rising steps bring it to C minor (iii.), where a 3rd step leaps higher (a 4th instead of a tone) and leads to

67-81.—Entry of bass *fortissimo* on dominant of (iii.) on the full bar, as if to begin the subject with a prolonged 1st note. Instead of proceeding to (b), the figure (a) strides upwards for

6 bars, covering a whole octave and merging into a further rise, reaching the 3rd of B♭ minor (ii.) at bar 75. Meanwhile the upper parts have been in dialogue, with figure (c) aided to rise by upward-resolving suspensions. Bars 74–75 are echoed *piano* in bars 75/76/77, the common element being the counterpoint arising (c). This suffices to establish a sequential model; and a similar pair of *forte* bars in the home tonic is answered with a similar interchange of parts above the continuous quaver bass.

81/82–85.—Entry of Subject in subdominant (IV.) in Middle Voice (rising above Treble). The counterpoint is free.

85/86–95.—The Treble answers, with the Subject in the tonic imitated, after 2 bars, by the Bass as far as (a) goes. The Treble carries (b) downwards for three 1-bar sequential steps, not cutting off the 1st note as in bars 51-54, but reducing it to a quaver. The Bass reaches a dominant pedal, whereupon the Middle takes up the sequence of accelerated (b) for another 3 bars. Then the Bass, echoing the quaver counterpoint, plunges down to

95/96–99.—Entry of Subject on dominant in Bass, harmonized in tonic and imitated in upper octave at 2 bars by Middle as far as (a), upon which

99/100–107.—Treble enters on tonic as if with Subject, but carries (a) upwards diminished in sequence, imitated in Bass, and reaching the octave; from which point a melodious cadence, suggested by (b), descends and expands in 4 bars of dominant 7th.

108–109.—The dominant 7th becomes an augmented 6th, resolving on to the ⁶₄ of G minor. And now we see the effect of dramatic sonata-like modulations in a fugue. They stop the Fugue altogether. There would be no more technical difficulty in carrying the Fugue through them than there is a grammatical difficulty in saying that " the soul tastes like the smell of half an hour." But composers are concerned with meanings, not with blank propositions in technique and grammar.

This dramatic stroke has come when the Fugue has, so far as we can yet tell, completed its course. Its short Subject has been developed simply, spaciously, and equally through all 3 voices. The episodes have been mere sequential continuations of figures of the Subject and Countersubject, securing a necessary freedom from stiff 4-bar phrasing; and it has not been advisable in analysis to draw a rigid distinction between normal entries of the Subject and expanded sequences like that of bars 67-75, or half-themes like the adumbrations of stretto in bars 87-89, 97-98, or even 101-102. The deep sorrow of the Arioso has found relief in the quiet discipline of a contemplative fugue on a noble and terse theme worked out in grand style and coming to its natural climax without disturbance. There are two signs that this cannot be

final. First, there is the external fact that the tone sometimes booms out suddenly and sometimes fades equally suddenly into mystery; as if we were listening in a vaulted building and had sudden doubts that the vault might be the night-sky itself. (This foreshadows a very prominent element in the *Missa Solemnis*.) Secondly, the speeding-up of the sequences has a sonata-like urgency which is a little discourteous to the forms of fugal debate, and is evidently under some restraint to keep it from becoming provocative.

As the dramatic modulation is enharmonic, it does not encourage us to recognize G minor as the ♯vii. to which the home-tonic A♭ is the Neapolitan ♭II. The purport here is to produce surprise and a break away into something remote from the key of the Fugue but near in pitch to the Arioso. Nothing could suit this purpose better than the drop of a semitone. The ⁶₄ chord settles into root position without resolving on the dominant.

110–130.—Complete recapitulation of the Arioso in G minor, its rhythm broken and details added, so that the whole is delivered as if through sobs. There is no 2nd voice in the last quatrain, but the accompaniment has details that replace it. The notes of the codetta are deferred to the ends of their beats; and instead of the bare final tonic a full major chord appears and grows during the off-beats of 2 whole bars, followed by 2 more in an arpeggio which suddenly vanishes into

Development of Fugue by Inversion and other Devices.

¹³⁰/131–145.—The top note of the previous arpeggio becomes the 1st note of the Inverted Subject in G major, announced by the Middle. The Treble answers and, descending a 5th instead of a 4th at the 3rd bar, modulates to the local dominant. Beethoven, who was anxious to make his fugues orthodox in all matters where classical precedent was relevant, afterwards wished that he had made this " tonal " alteration at the correct place—nearer the beginning of his answer; as G, D, E. With more reason he expressed a wish to correct his answer to the Subject of the Fugue in the D major Violoncello Sonata, Op. 102, No. 2, where it would certainly have been better to run the scale straight up to the octave before making the tonal change, instead of skipping at the beginning of the scale. Beethoven did not, however, execute these corrections; and they could not be executed without disturbing the counterpoint. This would be particularly undesirable here, where it is just its groping manner that is so dramatic, as the Fugue, *poi a poi di nuovo vivente*, feels its way back to life. The counterpoint becomes still more tentative as the Bass enters with the inverted Subject in tonic position, gliding away before

figure (b) and modulating towards C minor, the local sub-dominant. The Treble gives the inverted Subject once more in the tonic position of G with the outlook of C minor, again failing to give figure (b).

Stretto of Direct Subject by Diminution and Augmentation.

146–154.—Suddenly the Bass drifts into a diminution of the direct Subject in quavers—*i.e.*, 3 times as fast. As with the augmentation in Op. 106 (and in a more casual way in the Fugue in Op. 102, No. 2), this induces a change of accent that alters the theme far more than the ordinary classical diminution that merely accelerates it. The Middle overlaps the Bass with an answer reducing the 4ths to 3rds; the Bass gives a version in steeper steps leading to G minor, and so the Bass and Middle proceed in dialogue, breaking figure (b) off as the argument develops. Meanwhile the Treble bridges the whole passage by a syncopated augmentation of the Subject. Note, again, that this syncopation produces an utterly new type of rhythm; which is here the more significant since Beethoven has gone out of his way to secure it. The ordinary classical augmentation would have changed the dotted crotchets to dotted minims without any cross-rhythm. Beethoven thus shows that the cross-rhythm produced automatically by the augmentation in Op. 106, is necessary here even if special means have to be taken to obtain it.

154/155–162.—The Treble having brought the Augmented Subject into C minor, the Bass answers it in that key; and the other parts deal with the diminution, in 6ths and 3rds, breaking off (b) and smaller fragments in a syncopated rhythm, staggering down to E♭. The whole revival of the Fugue has so far been in twilight, as shown by the continual *una corda*, which is now lifted. (See notes to the pianoforte score of the Associated Board edition.)

Stretto by Double Diminution.

162½–168.—We are now on the home dominant, and the voices discuss the Subject in a double diminution further compressed by the omission of its 3rd and 4th notes. Apart from its dramatic value as expressing a breathless excitement, this double diminution is no mere scholastic device, but a very ingenious means of solving a problem which did not arise in the Fugue in Op. 106. The trill and running figure of that enormous movement enabled it to roam thunderously over the whole pianoforte with singularly little use of the *alcune licenze* mentioned in its title. But the present movement is on purely vocal counterpoint, which affords no prospect of developing into any climax characteristic of the pianoforte. Doublings in octaves, such as have already been applied to the Bass, might be applied to the other parts, and thus an organ-like climax contrived in normal fugue-style. But that solves the problem in a tone which would not satisfy Beethoven; a negation of the world, ascetic if sincere, and histrionic if " effective." But, like all Beethoven's visions, this Fugue absorbs and transcends the world. The double diminution is a means of bursting into flame. The vocal parts lose their identity as the angelic heads behind the Sistine Madonna become clouds. Note that if scholastic ingenuity had been Beethoven's motive he could have written and developed

just as easily, instead of puzzling the degree-examiner by omitting 2 notes.

The tempo has been retarded to make room for this compressed figure. The voices having established the key of E♭ in 2 bars, the Middle announces the normal-sized Inverted Subject with its intervals enlarged from 4ths to imperfect 5ths and from 3rds to 4ths. The other voices accompany with the double diminution, the Bass inverting it with grotesque inexactness, and the harmony passing through (ii.) to home tonic. The tempo revives.

Return of Normal Subject : Varied Recapitulation of Exposition.

[168]/169–182 = [20]/21–34.

[168]/169–172.—The Bass enters with the normal Subject (which has not been heard since the first part of the Fugue. The Middle bursts into flames arising from the double diminution. These flames outline two parts; so that though the Treble has just made its exit we now have a 3-part harmony in vibration, the counterpoint resembling those in the first part of the Fugue that do not use the regular Counter-subject.

[172]/173–178.—The Middle voice detaches itself in dominant answer to the Bass, while the upper flames continue to do the work of two other parts. By the same sequence as that after the answer at the beginning of the Fugue, 2 extra bars lead to

Peroration.

[178]/179–194.—Entry of Subject in Treble in full chords, the Bass breaking into the flame-figure. With the end of the Subject, the original Exposition has been recapitulated with a more than accidental exactness; and the following peroration avails itself of the rhetoric of bars 60-66 to bring figure (b) to a climax on the top

tonic note, with an exultant closing passage. The intention of the close at bar 194 is evidently to be like this

but a new idea crowds in and drives this into a single bar.

[194]/195-207.—Final tonic pedal over which the Subject mounts, carrying (a) a step further, bringing (b) on to the flat 7th, and finishing an 8-bar period by carrying (b) 2 steps higher (2 bars each); closing into 4 bars of final tonic arpeggio, ended at 5th bar by last chord.

32

SONATA IN C MINOR, Op. 111.

Maestoso: C minor. Introduction.

Bars ♩♩/1–2.—A 2-bar phrase defines the key of C minor by a diminished 7th on F♯, impinging on the G major chord as dominant.

²/3–4.—Beginning with the diminished 7th in C minor, the phrase moves to dominant of (iv.), defining that region with downward drift of bass.

⁴/5–10.—Starting a 3rd time, in (iv.), the diminished 7th resolves at once in B♭ minor; and the bass continues to move upwards in semitones for 5 bars, with treble making slow diatonic descent; the chords being in the rhythm of bar 1 without the trill. The drop of 2 octaves at bar 9 does not alter the harmonic value or rate of the rise, which amounts to 3 semitones in each bar. The various keys and dominants, near and remote, are a by-product of the rise which in bar 10 reaches its summit with an accelerated step on to A♭. This (with 6th and augmented 6th) impinges on home dominant. Some commentators have seen in these bars an anticipation of the Second Group of the *Allegro con brio*. There is a B in Both, and also in Bonnet.

11–16+*Allegro* 1–2.—Dominant preparation: a 2-bar phrase with interior dominant pedal, closing into self-repetition in lower octave, closing into 4 bars of dominant chord. These really equal 3 *Maestoso* bars, consisting of 1 marking the slow time, 1 with a vibration below, and a similar bar continuing the vibration and written in terms of a movement at double the pace. (The total period on the plain dominant chord is thus equivalent to 1 bar; +1+½+½.)

Allegro con brio ed appassionato: C minor. Sonata form.

First Group : C minor.

²/3–4.—The thunder in the bass gathers into a *Schleifer* (or short run) up to the tonic. The new length of rhythmic unit is defined by repeating this *Schleifer* at the end of the bar as a definite figure (a) at the beginning of a more important figure (b).

⁴/5–7.—Figures (a+b) are stated as part of a complete theme (ABC); a new figure (c) answering the implied dominant (B♮) by a tonic close with a sub-figure (d).

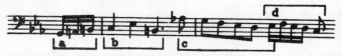

⁷/8–12.—Figure (cd) repeated, *ritardando*, leading to further repetition decorated in terms of (d) and carried upwards in half-bar steps of rising sequence, reaching (iv.); whereupon the semi-quavers proceed (without the figure) to dominant, and ascend the chord of minor 9th in cross-rhythm sequence of 3 semiquavers for 2½ bars, ending with run down closing into

13–19.—Counterstatement of theme (ABC) in harmony; repeating (cd) twice, the 2nd time in upper octave, carried downwards in four half-bar sequential steps leading to a 2-bar full close.

Transition.

19½–22.—The bass does not finish the close, but, leaving it in ♮ position, runs down into a new countersubject to the combination (BCD), with (c) in terms of (d), starting on the half-bar. (As in many common-time movements by Mozart, the difference between the half-bar and the full bar is negligible.) The compound figure (cd) rises bar by bar; the new counter-subject, with a quaver-figure, rising with it and leading to E♭.

23–27.—Answer to the 2-part combination in E♭ (III.), the quaver-figure of the countersubject being inverted in free double counterpoint in the 12th. This produces no mere transposition, but a new sequence of harmonies passing through (iv.) and B♭ minor to

27½–33.—Third statement of the 2-part combination, in VI., with (BCD) above and the countersubject below; 3½ steps of the sequence lead to chord of D♭; whereupon the counterpoint ceases, and the 2 steps D♭, D♮ (with diminished 7th) lead drama-tically to Second Group. From the outset (bar 22) of the 2-part combination the bottom notes of each step, whether in the countersubject or in figure (d), have traced a steady rise in the bass up a scale extending from C to these last semitones in the next octave. (This does not cease to be harmonically a rise when the right hand, imitating a superhuman 5-octave voice, dives below the bass.)

Second Group : A♭ major (VI.).

34–41.—New 2-bar theme on $^6_4$ and dominant of A♭, interlocking with slower ornamental self-repetition, which is harmonically diverted into local (vi.), and its interlocking cadence taken a 3rd up (Adagio) into medial position over tonic. Suddenly (in Tempo 1ᵐᵒ), a diminished 7th on D♮ impinges (after 5 beats) on the dominant, with close into

41–45.—Phrase of 3½ bars (BE) consisting of figure (b) in 3 steps of falling sequence, leading to a new cadential figure (e), stated in bass, and leaving the cadence unresolved.

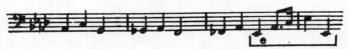

45½–53a.—The treble answers the bass at the half-bar and diverts (e) into a new cadence-figure, which is echoed twice in lower octaves, closing into 2 bars of final cadential uprush in groups of 4 semiquavers arising out of the more or less new running figure of the bass. The uprush ends in the A♭ tonic, descending in 2 crotchets. At the end of the bar, in the first instance, the *Schleifer* (a) leads to the repeat of the Exposition from bar 3.

Development.

53ᵇ–55.—Instead of returning to C minor, we have a soft echo of the 2nd crotchet a semitone lower (G) in the next bar, as a step down to a *forte* dominant chord of 6th on F♯, with (a) in treble.

56–59.—Dating from the silent 1st beat, the group (ABE) makes a 4-bar phrase in bare octaves in G minor, closing into

60–65.—Combination of (BC) with a new theme (x)

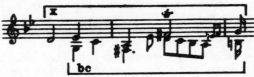

occupying 2 bars in G minor. It closes into answer in C minor, with (x) in an outlying bass voice, while the upper part proceeds with a running link to (BC), which it gives as (bcd), closing into 3rd entry in F minor. Here a new soprano enters with (x), and the previous upper voice proceeds with (BC), closing into

66–69.—A bar consisting of (d+c) in a new semiquaver variation over the cadential trill of (x), closing into repetition in lower octave; closing into 2 bars in which the new semiquaver figure boils up while the bass descends a partly chromatic octave of quavers to an F♯ impinging on home dominant.

70–75.—Four bars of (b) rising in steep steps over home dominant pedal. With a 5th step the figure reaches the tonic position and goes on to figure (c) in turns of (d), the bass joining it in octaves. Realizing that the development is over, the running figure (cd) joins the *Schleifer* (a) and bursts into the

Recapitulation.
First Group.

76–83 = the counterstatement, bars 13-19, substituting bare octaves for the harmony of the first 2 bars and rescoring and altering the course of bars [15]/16-19 (= [79]/80-83) so as to pass into (iv.), with emphasis on (♭II.) and close into key of (iv.) in next period.

Transition.

84–99.—The contrapuntal combination starts in F minor (iv.) on the full bar, with (BCD) in bass and countersubject in treble; answered, after 3½ bars, with the converse combination in B♭ minor. The double counterpoint is no longer in the 12th; for the present position is in the original phase, and the previous position inverts bars 19½-23 at the octave. The 3rd entry is in D♭ in an extremely high position; and now the countersubject disappears, the figure (cd) proceeding in 10ths or 3rds and rising for 5 steps, the last a steep one, leading to the 2-bar homophonic climax. This now rises through 4 semitone bass steps, E♭, E♮, F, F♯, ending in

Second Group in and about tonic.

100–105 = 34–39 in home tonic major.

[105]/106-107.—A new echo of the *Adagio* bar, in Tempo 1[mo], turns the chords, with falling bass, towards F minor (iv.), to the ♯ of which the next bar leads.

108–111.—Additional recapitulation of 100-104 in subdominant minor, the melody led by the bass, with the ornamental answer in treble.

112–115.—The close of the ornamental answer is carried up eight half-bar steps of rising sequence, the bass filling in the semitones of the rise, till the last step leads to the F♯ corresponding to the D♮ of bar [39]/40. The following crash is thus now reached as a climax, instead of bursting in as a surprise.

116–130 = 40–53[a], translated into the tonic minor (instead of major). An extra bar is interpolated at the outset, the crashing arpeggio consisting of 2 diminished 7ths; the enhanced dominant being followed by the ordinary dominant before the run leading to (BE).

Coda.

130–133.—The tonic crotchets give rise to a falling sequence of (b) in syncopated crotchets over tonic pedal, reaching (iv.).

134–142.—The bass begins rolling in generalized semiquaver figures in minor (iv.); and a series of plagal cadences interlocks in pairs of bars rising from the major tonic 3 times to successively higher notes, the 3rd time reaching the leading-note over $\frac{9}{6}$ and then closing into 2 bars of final major tonic. $\frac{}{4,}$

Arietta: Adagio molto semplice e cantabile. C major (I.). Theme with Four Variations, modulating Coda, Da Capo of Theme, and Epilogue.

Arietta : First Strain.

$\frac{1}{4}$/1–8.—Eight-bar sentence (1+1+2+4) beginning on tonic and closing, in the first instance, on dominant, swinging back to the repeat. But on the repeat the very delicately poised lower parts close on tonic before proceeding to the Second Strain. The initial figure (a) builds up the first 2 bars and recurs unsymmetrically at the join of 7-8. The further analysis of this melody would lead to subtleties difficult to control, and fortunately unnecessary for the purpose of following the extremely exact variations. It will be convenient to refer to the theme by bar-numbers rather than by its melodic figures.

Second Strain.

$\frac{8}{9}$/9–16.—Heaven help the composer or critic who thinks that such melody is built by " logical development " of figures ! The 2nd strain is also of 8 bars. Of these the first 4 define A minor (vi.) with half-close, and the remainder restores C major in 4 bars of the simplest and broadest possible arrangement of cardinal triads, closing with a medial position of (a) displaced to the 1st beat of the final bar. The strain is repeated, and on the repeat the bass leads into

$\frac{16}{18}$/18–32.—Variation 1. The 3 main beats are systematically divided into the 3 semiquavers of the $\frac{9}{16}$ time, the syncopated rhythm of the bass being complementary to the normal longs and shorts of the treble. At bar 8 the distinction between the dominant poise and tonic poise is kept clear.

$\frac{32}{33}$/33–48.—Variation 2. The 3 main beats are divided into 2 duple semiquavers (hence the incorrect time-signature $\frac{6}{16}$), and these are subdivided into 3 demisemiquavers. The true time-signature is thus ¹⁹₃₂, and all the quavers should be dotted, besides all those semiquavers that are half-beats. The prevalent rhythm is in longs and shorts of half the size and twice the number of those in Variation 2. The melody is opened by the bass and its figure answered in polyphonic dialogue by two upper parts, of which the treble carries out the melodic line from the 3rd bar onwards. The subtle alternate versions of bar 8 are again faithfully reproduced. In the Second Strain doublings and thickenings of harmony appear, and there is some 4-part writing also.

⁴⁸/49–64.—Variation 3. The 3 main beats are now divided into 4 demisemiquavers, and these subdivided into 3 semidemisemiquavers, in a rhythm of longs and shorts 4 times as fast and 4 times as numerous as those of the ⁹₁₆. The correct time-signature would be ³⁶₆₄, and the quarter-beat demisemiquavers should be dotted to distinguish them from the triplet ones. (The result would be no easier to read than the present notation is when correctly ranged.) At the 8th bar the distinction between tonic and dominant close is still present, but crowded into ₁₁₂ of a main beat.

⁶⁴/65–95.—Variation 4. The 3 main beats are divided into 9 demisemiquavers, which is, of course, a power of the original ⁹₁₆ time. The 9 demisemiquavers settle down in a steady vibration. They are nevertheless definitely rhythmic and are not a *tremolo*. The variation is double, the repeats of each strain being on a second pattern. The first statements (⁶⁴/65-72 and 81-88) give the melody in a lower octave syncopated chords over a vibrating bass. The repeats are 2 octaves higher, bringing the melody an octave above its original pitch, and stating it in terms of the demisemiquavers, preserving its main lines through an infinite variety of quivering ornament. At the penultimate bar (15=95) the bass has contrived to climb from the dominant to B♭, producing a harmony of modal solemnity on its way to the cadence.

Coda.

96–99.—The last bar (=16) merges into a 2-bar clause of tonic-and-dominant over tonic pedal, merging into repetition an octave lower, which closes into

100–102.—Three-bar cadence-clause (I., vi., V ⁶₄-⁵₃) closing into

103–105.—Varied repetition of 100-102.

Thus far Beethoven has begun a Coda on lines which were adequate in the variations of the Kreutzer Sonata. But they can in themselves give no finality to a movement on so static a theme, with neither change of mode in the variations nor any such changes of time as made the variations in Op. 109 seem to come full circle when they returned to the original ³₄ time and tempo. In spite of the novel kinds of subdivision, the progress of the present variations has been the merest straight line of *air et doubles* like the Andante of Op. 57 or *The Harmonious Blacksmith* itself. Hitherto Beethoven's static and ecstatic visions in this sublime mood have been aloof from action. In such variation movements as those in Op. 57, the B♭ Trio, Op. 97, and the Violin Concerto, the slightest intrusion of foreign chords can dispel the vision, the more roughly the better. But now in Op. 111, and afterwards in the Ninth Symphony, the E♭ Quartet, Op. 127, and the C♯ minor Quartet, Op. 131, Beethoven finds ways of modulating which bring action harmoniously into the contemplative vision. This kind of passage demonstrates the highest power of mastery of form. It is neither more nor less masterly than many passages we never notice; but the special problem makes it manifest.

106–117.—The expected close is indefinitely postponed by a cadential trill. Below this figure (a) enters in the bass, defining a ⁵₄ suspension. This is resolved by a modified answer in 6ths around the trill. The trill becomes minor, and the modified answer changes its mode also. The leading-note B, after hesitating for a bar, descends to B♭, while the treble rises from G to A♭. We are now on the dominant of E♭ (♭III.). Figure (a) in the bass defines this with its 5th, not its ⁵₄. The figure is echoed 2 octaves higher below the trill, which then becomes a triple trill on dominant 7th of E♭ for 2 bars. (Vast as the whole passage is, the autograph shows that it has been reduced by half.) The topmost trill mounts alone by semitones for 4 more bars; a dominant bass enters as at the bottom of an abyss, and the passage closes into

118–121.—Bars 5-8 of Arietta in E♭ (♭III.) in 2-part harmony 5 octaves apart, dropping an octave in the 2nd bar.

120–130.—Bars 7-8 become the first limb of a descending sequence, the bass answering each bar. The 1st step descends a 3rd, moving to C minor, and the next reaches A♭, closing into a more compressed sequence, the limb of which is ⅔ of a bar. This descends across the rhythm by tones; and in each alternate complete bar the left hand changes between positions below and above the right. Six bars on this plan have accomplished 8 steps in a straight line, but with perpetual change of surface, besides slight changes of detail. At the last step the bass is thrown into vibration (as in Variation 4), the harmony impinging upon the home dominant (through A♭-F♯).

¹³⁰/131–146.—Re-entry of the whole Arietta in home tonic, with unornamented melody, demisemiquaver bass, and no repeats.

Epilogue.

146–151.—The figure of bar 16 merges into a sequence with

limbs of $\frac{2}{4}$ of a bar, descending in 4 steps of 3rds (disregarding change of octave) across the bar-rhythm, through (vi.), (IV.), and (ii.); leading to a broad half-close, with which it forms a 6-bar clause. (This started at 146, and thus overlapped the end of Arietta). The half-close interlocks with

151/152–161.—Resumption of the cross-rhythm sequence, sounding like a repetition of 146-151, led by bass, but really beginning on 3rd beat. The 4th step is resumed by the treble and leads to a .much broader cadential sentence, filling 8 bars, and then not closing but leaving the dominant in the air and breaking into a trill.

161/162–169.—Final delivery of First Strain; 4 bars below trill, and 4 bars above trill, all in high octave, with high bass vibrating in demisemiquavers. The rhythmic progress has now reached its acme, the trill being used to provide indefinitely rapid vibration above the measured triplet demisemiquavers.

168–171.—Overlapping with bar 8 of theme, twice 2 bars are occupied with echoes of the cadence between 2 voices over tonic pedal. The 2nd pair is varied, leading, with abrupt cessation of bass, to

172–177.—Two bars of dominant 2-part run, in the style of the repeats of Variation 4, leading to a run in 6ths from tonic; closing into self-repetition in lower octave at each main beat and finally reaching figure (a), on 1st beat, in lower octave. This is answered by deep bass and worked into a subtle full close in 2 more bars; a suggestion of inversion being given by the bass as it finally moves from dominant to tonic and reverberates in the last tonic chords.

CONCLUSION.

THE ink with which Beethoven wrote the ethereal end of Op. 111 was hardly dry before he was telling his publisher that "the pianoforte is, after all, an unsatisfactory instrument." The Ninth Symphony, the Missa Solemnis, and the not less gigantic last five string-quartets, occupied the remaining five years of his life. He was unexpectedly recalled to the keyboard by the very prosaic waltz which Diabelli sent round to fifty-one composers residing in Austria, in order to accumulate a volume of variations to be published for a patriotic charity. The excellently jointed skeleton of Diabelli's ridiculous theme inspired Beethoven to that Vision of Dry Bones, the Thirty-three Variations, Op. 120, the greatest variation work in all music, and even bulkier than the Sonata, Op. 106. Beethoven then bade the pianoforte a final farewell in the subtle and coherent group of Six Bagatelles, Op. 126, the last of which dissembles its love in an *Andante amabile*, but ends with something ominously like a kick downstairs.

The study of Beethoven's pianoforte sonatas is evidently incomplete unless it is at all points linked with the study of his other works, not omitting the opera *Fidelio* and the Mass in D. But the view obtainable from the pianoforte sonatas, though incomplete, is not one-sided. The sonatas cover all periods of Beethoven's development with important works, representing the first period very copiously, and marking the transitions of style by exceptionally clear evidence, such as the rejection of the Andante of Op. 53. The groups of movements are, as in Haydn's sonatas and trios, far more varied than in works for four and more instruments, where the rule appears to be that so many players should not be brought together without being given the full-sized symphonic scheme.

Though the present method of analysis is from phrase to phrase, it has been executed with careful avoidance of entering into minutiæ. In any other art such an analysis would be considered rather summary. The more generalized view of musical form usually cultivated is not so much general as fundamentally mistaken. It is not even as real as the "man in the moon," who disappears when you see the moon through a telescope. No musical composition exists at all in such distant views. Music exists in its own proper *tempo*, and is held together by vibrating in the memory. To read it backwards is not more nonsensical than to draw up a sort of formal ground-plan and try and explain the music by it. Small wonder, then, if a proper method of précis-writing results in the disappearance of most of the orthodoxies that have based themselves on attempts to see musical form like a naked-eye view of the moon. Musical précis-writing instantly shows that Mozart's mature phrasing is far more intricate than Beethoven's, and that Beethoven's transitions from First Group to Second acquire the breadth and organization of Mozart's only by the time that Beethoven's style has shed every vestige of early Mozartishness. On the other hand, Beethoven from the outset used resources that lay beyond Mozart's scope. The threading of a series of wide modulations on a conjunctly falling or rising bass was discovered by him at the age of fifteen in a passage in the C major pianoforte quartet, afterwards developed into bars 27–45 of the first movement of Op. 2, No. 3. No design either of Mozart or Haydn would stand such tension as that of bars 58–92 in the first movement of Op. 2, No. 2.

On the other hand, Parry has compared the opening of Op. 2, No. 1, with that of the finale of Mozart's G minor Symphony, as an illustration of how much closer Beethoven's earliest texture is than that of Mozart's ripest work (*The Evolution of the Art of Music*). Parry himself admits that the comparison is not quite fair. For one thing, it compares a first movement by Beethoven with a finale by Mozart, and moreover a finale which, though in sonata form, has a Rondo-like theme. Had such a comparison been made between Mozart's lightest first movements and Beethoven's most weighty finales, it might have gone very far in the opposite direction. Indeed, the finale of the Sonata Appassionata could swallow whole sections of Mozart in its empty spaces.

We shall utterly fail to understand great music if we set up this or that general condition of form and texture as abstractly better than some other. Some critics who admire Mozart find it regrettable that his developments are " inadequate." But the draughtsmanship of Mozart's developments is exceedingly powerful. Beethoven finds a Mozartean type of development as useful as any other, and he by no means despises an episodic one. (It should be pointed out in passing that many current notions about Mozart are derived almost entirely from his pianoforte sonatas. This gives as incorrect a view of Mozart as we should get of Beethoven by confining our attention to Op. 2, No. 1, the F major Violin Sonata, Op. 24, the Overture to Prometheus, the Sonata Pathétique, and the First Symphony.)

The study of Haydn's quartets and symphonies reveals a

conception of form widely differing from Mozart's. Development, even during exposition, is Haydn's main interest, and recapitulation is replaced by perorations from which Beethoven drew inspiration for his largest codas. We are sometimes told that " with Haydn we see form in the making "—meaning that his forms have not achieved the ripe Mozartean symmetry. This is æsthetically and historically quite untrue. Haydn's forms become less and less symmetrical as his style ripens, and they attain their full freedom in works manifestly influenced by Mozart and written after Mozart's death. The mere addition of Haydn's methods to Mozart's would go far to help Beethoven to transcend both masters. But from the outset his cogent rising and falling basses and his rhythms that can expand to 32 bars and contract to eighths of a bar gave him a power of dramatic tension far greater than that of the Haydn-Mozart comedy of manners.

In this twentieth century we have learnt to take Haydn and Mozart seriously; and readers may be inclined to resent the implication that Haydn and Mozart are comedians while Beethoven is the most tragic of composers. But the question is one of language, not of ultimate values. We may outgrow the crude estimation of the " seriousness " of a work of art by the dictionary meaning of its subject, without forgetting the permanent difference between the language of Moliére and the language of Æschylus. Beethoven has the immense advantage of being in a Shakespearean position that enables him to see tragedy in humour and humour in tragedy. His humour has often been called " gruff and grim," but it is never sardonic. He loves to shock the sentimental listener, but this is primarily because he resents the fundamental callousness and selfishness of sentimentality. His tragic power seemed and still seems violent to conventional-minded people. Strange to say, the only works in which his methods do actually resort to violence are the early ones, where he sometimes takes a short cut with a gesture that disclaims any intention to carry out his purpose with Olympian breadth. Thus, in the finale of Op. 7, bar 161 is a violent way out of the consequences of a most beautiful and legitimate adventure; thus the finale of Op. 10, No. 1, is the very embodiment of nervous irritation; and thus the first movement of Op. 31, No. 1, states mockingly as provocative paradoxes the propositions in tonality which are the Olympian harmonic rules of the Waldstein Sonata.

Of disruptive influences in Beethoven's forms there is only one slight and ephemeral symptom, in the unbarred cadenzas in the codas of the first movements of Op. 2, No. 3, the Violoncello Sonata in F, Op. 5, No. 1, and, at the entry of the recapitulation, in the finale of the Septet. The great passages of recitative have been discussed in their place, both as to quality and quantity. They are no more disruptive of form than a quotation of two lines of poetry or Scripture is destructive of the plot of a novel. The detailed analysis of the last sonatas shows that in Beethoven's later works we have on the one hand to deal often with very small units of structure, but that on the other hand no music has ever been built on bolder and straighter lines. If form springs from the nature of the matter instead of being imposed from without, nothing can be more false than the notion that Beethoven's later works are disruptive of form. As to the " conventional sonata form " which they are supposed to transcend, by far the best representative of that convention is Spohr. He has not the chandelier glitter and heavy diffuseness of Hummel, and he does not take his junior Mendelssohn's numerous short-cuts and liberties. Schumann pointed out, in one of the weightiest sentences in his critical essays, that those people are greatly in error who think that Spohr's forms are easy to imitate. The forms would have remained essentially the same without Spohr's cloying mannerisms; and they remain, whether we like them or not, as an excellent convention in sonata form which Beethoven unquestionably transcended. But were either Beethoven or Spohr aware of its importance ?

A lady once told Sir William Cummings that his adored Purcell was only an imitator of Handel. When Sir William suggested the slight difficulty that Handel was only ten years old when Purcell died, the lady said, " Oh, if you drag in dates you can prove anything ! " Let us therefore refrain from dragging in dates. But we may as well remember that Spohr wrote an Historical Symphony. In this work the first movement represented Bach and Handel ; the second movement represented Mozart; the scherzo represented Beethoven, sufficiently recognizable by the daring innovation of a theme for three drums ; while the finale represented " the very latest period "—viz., Spohr himself. So Beethoven, third period and all, was already of the past, while Spohr was maintaining his own Mozartean forms and showing a surprising capacity to appreciate young Wagner, whose *Fliegender Holländer* and *Tannhäuser* he carefully produced at Cassel. When did sonata forms become classical ?

The fact is that Beethoven's forms—early, middle, and late—have all soared equally far above the heads of people who think of form as a jelly-mould instead of as a vital force. It saves the trouble of individual analysis to call the early works " imitative of Mozart and Haydn "; it even saves us the trouble of studying Mozart and Haydn. It saves many shocks to our self-complacency

to excuse ourselves from learning the drastic messages of the
later works by calling them " formless." But we can so call them
only when we confine ourselves to a low conception of forms
according to which we shall eventually learn to regard Scribe',
libretti as the ultimate consummation of dramatic construction.
From such æsthetic anæsthesia let us pray to the harshest passages
in the Fugue of Op. 106 to deliver us !

BEETHOVEN'S
PIANOFORTE SONATAS

Phrasing, Fingering etc., by

HAROLD CRAXTON

Commentaries by

DONALD FRANCIS TOVEY

Editorial Committee
SIR JOHN B. McEWEN
Principal of the Royal Academy of Music (1924-1936)

SIR HUGH P. ALLEN
Director of the Royal College of Music (1918-1937)

SIR DONALD FRANCIS TOVEY & HAROLD CRAXTON

1	Sonata Op. 2. No. 1. F minor
2	Sonata Op. 2. No. 2. A major
3	Sonata Op. 2. No. 3. C major
4	Sonata Op. 7. E flat major
5	Sonata Op. 10. No. 1. C minor
6	Sonata Op. 10. No. 2. F major
7	Sonata Op. 10. No. 3. D major
8	Sonata Op. 13. C minor
	(*Pathetique*)
9	Sonata Op. 14. No. 1. E major
10	Sonata Op. 14. No. 2. G major
11	Sonata Op. 22. B flat major
12	Sonata Op. 26. A flat major
13	Sonata Op. 27. No. 1. E flat major
	(quasi fantasia)
14	Sonata Op. 27. No. 2. C. sharp minor
	(quasi fantasia) (Moonlight)
15	Sonata Op. 28. D major (*Pastorale*)
16	Sonata Op. 31. No. 1. G major
17	Sonata Op. 31. No. 2. D minor
18	Sonata Op. 31. No. 3. E flat major
19	Sonata Op. 49. No. 1. G minor
20	Sonata Op. 49. No. 2. G major
21	Sonata Op. 53. C major (*Waldstein*)
22	Sonata Op. 54. F major
23	Sonata Op. 57. F minor
	(*Appassionata*)
24	Sonata Op. 78. F sharp major
25	Sonata Op. 79. G major
26	Sonata Op. 81a. E flat major
	(*Les adieux*)
27	Sonata Op. 90. E minor
28	Sonata Op. 101. A major
29	Sonata Op. 106. B flat major
	(*Hammerklavier*)
30	Sonata Op. 109. E major
31	Sonata Op. 110. A flat major
32	Sonata Op. 111. C minor

Separate and in three volumes, paper cover and cloth boards

Published by

The Associated Board of the
ROYAL SCHOOLS OF MUSIC

J. S. BACH
48 PRELUDES AND FUGUES
(Das Wohltemperierte Klavier)
Edited by   Fingered by
DONALD FRANCIS TOVEY   **HAROLD SAMUEL**

In two volumes paper cover and cloth boards

J. S. BACH
18 LITTLE PRELUDES
Revised and edited by
HEDWIG McEWEN and KATHLEEN LONG

J. S. BACH
18 Selected Pieces from
A LITTLE NOTEBOOK
FOR ANNA MAGDALENA BACH
Edited by VIVIAN LANGRISH

HAYDN
8 Selected PIANOFORTE SONATAS
Edited by AUBYN RAYMAR

In one volume, paper cover and cloth boards

Published by
The Associated Board of the
ROYAL SCHOOLS OF MUSIC

MOZART'S
PIANOFORTE   SONATAS
AND MISCELLANEOUS PIECES

Revised and Edited by
YORK BOWEN

Analytical Notes by
AUBYN RAYMAR

Editorial Committee
SIR JOHN B. McEWEN
Principal of the Royal Academy of Music (1924-1936)

SIR HUGH P. ALLEN
Director of the Royal College of Music (1918-1937)

YORK BOWEN & AUBYN RAYMAR

SONATAS

1   Sonata in C (*K.279*)
2   Sonata in F (*K.280*)
3   Sonata in B flat (*K.281*)
4   Sonata in E flat (*K.282*)
5   Sonata in G (*K.283*)
6   Sonata in D (*K.284*)
7   Sonata in C (*K.309*)
8   Sonata in A minor (*K.310*)
9   Sonata in D (*K.311*)
10   Sonata in C (*K.330*)
11   Sonata in A (*K.331*)
12   Sonata in F (*K.332*)
13   Sonata in B flat (*K.333*)
14   Fantasia and Sonata in C minor (*K.475 and 457*)
15   Sonata in C (*K.545*)
16   Sonata in B flat (*K.570*)
17   Sonata in D (*K.576*)
18   Sonata in F (*K.533 and 494*)
19   Sonata in B flat
20   Sonata in F

Separate and in two volumes, paper cover and cloth boards

MISCELLANEOUS PIECES
Minuets, Rondos, Fantasias, Variations etc.

In one volume, paper cover and cloth boards

Published by
The Associated Board of the
ROYAL SCHOOLS OF MUSIC